Understanding Your Financial Calculator

At press time, this edition contains the most complete and accurate information currently available. Owing to the nature of license examinations, however, information may have been added recently to the actual test that does not appear in this edition. Please contact the publisher to verify that you have the most current edition.

This publication is designed to provide accurate and authoritative information in regard to the subject matter covered. It is sold with the understanding that the publisher is not engaged in rendering legal, accounting, or other professional services. If legal advice or other expert assistance is required, the services of a competent professional should be sought.

UNDERSTANDING YOUR FINANCIAL CALCULATOR
5TH EDITION
©2012 Kaplan, Inc. All rights reserved.

Published in June 2012 by Kaplan Schweser.

Printed in the United States of America.

ISBN: 978-1-4277-4189-9 / 1-4277-4189-1

PPN: 3200-2813

Table of Contents

PART TWO: STUDENT WORKBOOK

PART THREE: STUDENT WORKBOOK SOLUTIONS

PART FOUR: EXAM-FOCUSED MULTIPLE-CHOICE QUESTIONS

PART FIVE: EXAM-FOCUSED MULTIPLE-CHOICE SOLUTIONS

Introduction

Financial planning is the process of planning for financial independence. This process necessitates projections and calculations, thus requiring a good understanding of the use of a financial calculator. Many professionals in the areas of financial planning, finance, accounting, and investments use a financial calculator regularly. Many financial professionals use sophisticated computer software developed to solve many of the same problems that can be solved using a financial calculator. However, those who develop and test these software products often rely on hand-held financial calculators to confirm the answers for these types of problems.

Concepts vs. Calculator

Students preparing for professional exams, such as the CFP® Certification Examination, must be intimately familiar with the basics and intricacies of the financial calculator, as well as the underlying concepts that are the foundation for these calculations. The concepts and calculations contained within this text are vital to succeeding on these types of exams. It is also important that professionals who rely on computer software have the ability to interpret and test the output for accuracy, as well as be able to explain computer-generated calculations to clients.

This book illustrates the keystrokes for four of the more popular financial calculators:

- Hewlett Packard: HP 17bII/HP 17bII+ (keystrokes are the same for the HP 17bII and HP 17bII+)
- Hewlett Packard: HP 12C
- Hewlett Packard: HP 10BII and HP 10BII+ (keystrokes are the same for the HP 10BII and the HP 10BII+)
- Texas Instruments: TI BA II Plus

The purpose of this book is to provide the framework and background for students to master the financial calculator and to gain an even greater understanding of the underlying financial planning concepts. This text is designed to guide you from the basics through the more advanced calculations by providing the exact keystrokes for solving problems. Keystrokes are provided for the more popular financial calculators indicated above. In addition to keystrokes, a shortcut method is provided as a general method for solving the specific problems. As you begin to master your financial calculator, you will tend to rely more heavily on the shortcut method and less on the detailed keystrokes. Therefore, all of the solutions for the student workbook section have been provided with the shortcut method only. Any difficulties you experience in the student workbook sections can be resolved by looking back at the detailed problems in the first part of the text.

Using any of the above calculators requires an understanding of a few basic operations. It is strongly recommended that you review your user manual to go over these operations.

Concepts And Calculations

Initial Calculator Settings

I.   SETTING THE NUMBER OF DECIMALS

Set your calculator to four (4) decimal places.

HP 17bII/HP 17bII+		HP 12C		HP 10BII/HP 10BII+	
Keystrokes	*Display*	*Keystrokes*	*Display*	*Keystrokes*	*Display*
[DSP]	SELECT DISPLAY FORMAT	[f] 4	0.0000	*[■][DISP] 4	0.0000
[FIX]	TYPE # DIGITS (0-11);				
4 [INPUT]	0.0000				

TI BA II Plus	
Keystrokes	*Display*
[2nd][Format]	DEC= 0.____
4 [ENTER]	DEC= 4.0000
[CE/C]	4.0000

NOTE: These initial settings must be entered into your financial calculator. Certain assumptions regarding the required keystrokes and the display of each operation are dependent on these initial settings. You should check to make sure that each time you use your calculator it is set accordingly.

*For HP 10BII/HP 10BII+ users, the "Gold" Shift key will be represented by a [■] symbol.

II.   SETTING COMPOUNDING PERIODS PER YEAR TO 1 AND SETTING YOUR CALCULATOR TO END MODE

HP 17bII/HP 17bII+		HP 12C		HP 10BII/HP 10BII+	
Keystrokes	*Display*	*Keystrokes*	*Display*	*Keystrokes*	*Display*
[FIN]	SELECT A MENU	[g][END]	0.0000	1 [■][P/YR]	1.0000
[TVM]	1 P/YR END MODE	Note: The HP 12C is		[■][BEG/END]	1.0000
[OTHER]	1 P/YR END MODE	automatically set to		{Press only if "BEGIN"	
1 [P/YR]	1 P/YR END MODE	1 period per year		is in the lower mid-	
[EXIT]	1 P/YR END MODE			dle of the display}	

TI BA II Plus	
Keystrokes	*Display*
[2nd][P/Y][1][ENTER]	P/Y = 1.0000
[↓]	C/Y = 1.0000
[2nd][QUIT]	0.0000
[2nd][BGN]	BGN SET BEGIN
[2nd][SET]	END SET
[CE/C]	0.0000
{Press only if "BGN" is in the upper right corner of the display}	

NOTE: These initial settings must be entered into your financial calculator. Certain assumptions regarding the required keystrokes and the display of each operation are dependent on these initial settings.

III. CLEARING THE MEMORY

Prior to addressing a new problem, the following keystrokes should be entered to ensure the information from the previous problem is cleared out of the calculator's memory.

HP 17bII/HP 17bII+		HP 12C		HP 10BII/HP 10BII+	
Keystrokes	*Display*	*Keystrokes*	*Display*	*Keystrokes*	*Display*
[■][CLR DATA]	0.0000	[f][REG]	0.0000	[■][C ALL]	0.0000
[EXIT] {Press until the display at right is shown}	0.0000 FIN BUS SUM TIME SOLVE CURRX				

TI BA II Plus	
Keystrokes	*Display*
[2nd][CLR TVM]	0.0000
[2nd][CLR Work]	0.0000

NOTE: When working through practice problems, getting an incorrect answer may be an indication that the calculator memory must be cleared.

IV.   USING THE STO/RCL FUNCTIONS WITH CASH FLOWS

Each of the calculators discussed in this text provides a feature to recall amounts stored in the memory registers. These amounts can be viewed to ensure accuracy in the input of the numbers and the amounts can be changed by using the store feature. The recall and store features are particularly helpful when using the uneven cash flow keys. In this context, the user can determine whether the correct cash flows were entered and then change any necessary cash flows without re-entering all of the cash flows for the problem.

A.   EXAMPLE

Assume the following cash flows: Period 0: $0; Period 1: $100; Period 2: $200; Period 3: $300.

HP 17bII/HP 17bII+		HP 12C		HP 10BII/HP 10BII+	
Keystrokes	*Display*	*Keystrokes*	*Display*	*Keystrokes*	*Display*
Step 1: Storing cash flows					
[FIN]	SELECT A MENU	[F][REG]	0.0000	[■][C ALL]	0.0000
[CFLO]	FLOW (0) = ? *	0[g][CFo]	0.0000	0[CFj]	0.0000
[■][CLR DATA]	CLEAR THE LIST?	100[g][CFj]	100.0000	100[CFj]	100.0000
[YES]	FLOW (0) = ?	200[g][CFj]	200.0000	200[CFj]	200.0000
0[INPUT]	FLOW (1) = ?	300[g][CFj]	300.0000	300[CFj]	300.0000
	0.0000	*Step 2: Recalling cash flows*			
100[INPUT]	# TIMES (1) = 1	[RCL]0	0.0000	[RCL][CFj]0	0.0000
	1.0000	[RCL]1	100.0000	[RCL][CFj]1	100.0000
[INPUT]	FLOW (2) = ?	[RCL]2	200.0000	[RCL][CFj]2	200.0000
	1.0000	[RCL]3	300.0000	[RCL][CFj]3	300.0000
200[INPUT]	# TIMES (2) = 1	*Step 3: Change cash flow for recalculation*			
	1.0000	*(change flow #2 to $400)*			
[INPUT]	FLOW (3) = ?	400[STO]2	400.0000	400[■][STO][CFj]2	400.0000
	1.0000				
300[INPUT]	# TIMES (3) = 1				
	1.0000				
[INPUT]	FLOW (4) = ?				
	1.0000				

Step 2: Recalling cash flows

To recall the cash flows use the [▲] or [▼] buttons. These buttons are located below the input key on the left-hand side of the calculator. You will be able to scroll through both the cash flows as well as frequency of cash flows.

Step 3: Recall and change cash flow for recalculation (change flow #2 to $400)

Press [▲] four times and the display will read (FLOW (2) = 200.0000). Type 400.0000 and [INPUT]. You have just changed the second cash flow to 400.0000.
Displays last cash flow sequence.

TI BA II Plus

Keystrokes	*Display*
Step 1: Storing cash flows	
[CF]	$CF_0 = 0.0000$
[2nd][CLR Work]	$CF_0 = 0.0000$
[↓]	$C01 = 0.0000$
100[ENTER]	$C01 = 100.0000$
[↓][↓]	$C02 = 0.0000$
200[ENTER]	$C02 = 200.0000$
[↓][↓]	$C03 = 0.0000$
300[ENTER]	$C03 = 300.0000$

Step 2: Recalling cash flows

To recall the cash flows, use the [↓] or [↑] keys after pressing the [CF] button. With this feature you are able to view both cash flows and frequency.

Step 3: Recall and change cash flow for recalculation (change flow #2 to $400)

Press [↓] or [↑] until the display reads (CO2 = 200.0000). Type 400.0000 and [ENTER]. You have just changed the second cash flow to 400.0000.

Once the cash flow for period two is changed from $200 to $400, this change can be verified by recalling the cash flows for period two or for all of the periods.

Basic Functions

I. SIMPLE ARITHMETIC CALCULATIONS

Any simple arithmetic calculation involves two numbers and an operation such as addition, subtraction, multiplication, or division.

A. ADDITION

Calculate 31.1 + 53.8

HP 17bII/HP 17bII+		HP 12C		HP 10BII/HP 10BII+	
Keystrokes	*Display*	*Keystrokes*	*Display*	*Keystrokes*	*Display*
31.1 [+]	31.1000 +	31.1 [ENTER]	31.1000	31.1 [+]	31.1000
53.8 [=]	**84.9000**	53.8 [+]	**84.9000**	53.8 [=]	**84.9000**

NOTE: *Once a calculation has been completed, pressing another digit key starts a new calculation. To continue a calculation, simply press an operator key. To clear the number, press [■] [CLR DATA].*	**NOTE:** *Once a calculation has been completed, the number remains in the display so you can perform another calculation using this number. To clear the number, press [f] [REG].*	**NOTE:** *Once a calculation has been completed, pressing another digit key starts a new calculation. To continue a calculation, simply press an operator key. To clear the number, press [C].*

TI BA II Plus	
Keystrokes	*Display*
31.1 [+]	31.1000
53.8 [=]	**84.9000**

NOTE: *Once a calculation has been completed, the number remains in the display so you can perform another calculation using this number. To clear the number, press [CE/C].*

B. SUBTRACTION

Calculate 89.65 – 42.33

HP 17bII/HP 17bII+	
Keystrokes	*Display*
89.65 [–]	89.6500–
42.33 [=]	**47.3200**

NOTE: *Once a calculation has been completed, pressing another digit key starts a new calculation. To continue a calculation, simply press an operator key. To clear the number, press [■] [CLR DATA].*

HP 12C	
Keystrokes	*Display*
89.65 [ENTER]	89.6500
42.33 [–]	**47.3200**

NOTE: *Once a calculation has been completed, the number remains in the display so you can perform another calculation using this number. To clear the number and memory, press [f] [REG].*

HP 10BII/HP 10BII+	
Keystrokes	*Display*
89.65 [–]	89.6500
42.33 [=]	**47.3200**

NOTE: *Once a calculation has been completed, pressing another digit key starts a new calculation. To continue a calculation, simply press an operator key. To clear the number, press [C].*

TI BA II Plus	
Keystrokes	*Display*
89.65 [–]	89.6500
42.33 [=]	**47.3200**

NOTE: *Once a calculation has been completed, the number remains in the display so you can perform another calculation using this number. To clear the number, press [CE/C].*

C. MULTIPLICATION

Calculate 5 × 6

HP 17bII/HP 17bII+	
Keystrokes	*Display*
5 [x]	5.0000x
6 [=]	**30.0000**

NOTE: *Once a calculation has been completed, pressing another digit key starts a new calculation. To continue a calculation, simply press an operator key. To clear the number, press* [■] [CLR DATA].

HP 12C	
Keystrokes	*Display*
5 [ENTER]	5.0000
6 [x]	**30.0000**

NOTE: *Once a calculation has been completed, the number remains in the display so you can perform another calculation using this number. To clear the number and memory, press* [f] [REG].

HP 10BII/HP 10BII+	
Keystrokes	*Display*
5 [x]	5.0000
6 [=]	**30.0000**

NOTE: *Once a calculation has been completed, pressing another digit key starts a new calculation. To continue a calculation, simply press an operator key. To clear the number, press* [C].

TI BA II Plus	
Keystrokes	*Display*
5 [x]	5.0000
6 [=]	**30.0000**

NOTE: *Once a calculation has been completed, the number remains in the display so you can perform another calculation using this number. To clear the number, press* [CE/C].

D. DIVISION

Calculate 42 ÷ 14

HP 17bII/HP 17bII+

Keystrokes	Display
42 [÷]	42.0000÷
14 [=]	**3.0000**

NOTE: *Once a calculation has been completed, pressing another digit key starts a new calculation. To continue a calculation, simply press an operator key. To clear the number, press [■] [CLR DATA].*

HP 12C

Keystrokes	Display
42 [ENTER]	42.0000
14 [÷]	**3.0000**

NOTE: *Once a calculation has been completed, the number remains in the display so you can perform another calculation using this number. To clear the number and memory, press [f] [REG].*

HP 10BII/HP 10BII+

Keystrokes	Display
42 [÷]	42.0000
14 [=]	**3.0000**

NOTE: *Once a calculation has been completed, pressing another digit key starts a new calculation. To continue a calculation, simply press an operator key. To clear the number, press [C].*

TI BA II Plus

Keystrokes	Display
42 [÷]	42.0000
14 [=]	**3.0000**

NOTE: *Once a calculation has been completed, the number remains in the display so you can perform another calculation using this number. To clear the number, press [CE/C].*

II.   CHAIN CALCULATIONS

A.   INTRODUCTION

Any chain calculation involves more than one operation or a series of operations.

HP 17bII/HP 17bII+	HP 12C	HP 10BII/HP 10BII+
Chain calculations are interpreted in the order in which they are entered. To do a chain calculation, you do not need to press [=] after each operation, only after the last number is entered.	Chain calculations are interpreted in the order in which they are entered. Whenever an answer has just been calculated and is, therefore, in the display, you can perform another operation with this number by simply keying in the second number and then pressing the operation key, you do NOT need to press [ENTER].	Chain calculations are interpreted in the order in which they are entered. To do a chain calculation, you do not need to press [=] after each operation, only after the last number is entered.

TI BA II Plus
You can select either the chain calculation method (chn) or the AOS calculation method. Chain calculations are interpreted in the order in which they are entered, when the calculation method is set to chain [chn]. The chain method is the default. When the calculation method is set to AOS, the calculator solves problems according to the standard rules of algebraic hierarchy (multiplication and division before addition and subtraction).   The [2nd] [format] [↓][↓][↓][↓] key sequence to change methods.

B.   EXAMPLE

Calculate $[(300 - 82) \div 8.5] \times (60 \div 2.7)$

This calculation can be written as: $(300 - 82) \div 8.5 \times 60 \div 2.7$

HP 17bII/HP 17bII+		HP 12C		HP 10BII/HP 10BII+	
Keystrokes	*Display*	*Keystrokes*	*Display*	*Keystrokes*	*Display*
300 [–]	300.0000–	300 [ENTER]	300.0000	300 [–]	300.0000
82 [÷]	218.0000÷	82 [–]	218.0000	82 [÷]	218.0000
8.5 [x]	25.6471x	8.5 [÷]	25.6471	8.5 [x]	25.6471
60 [÷]	1,538.8235÷	60 [x]	1,538.8235	60 [÷]	1,538.8235
2.7 [=]	**569.9346**	2.7 [÷]	**569.9346**	2.7 [=]	**569.9346**

TI BA II Plus	
Keystrokes	*Display*
300 [–]	300.0000
82 [÷]	218.0000
8.5 [x]	25.6471
60 [÷]	1,538.8235
2.7 [=]	**569.9346**

III.   POWERS

Powers are a short way to determine multiple-multiplications. For example: Five raised to the sixth power is written as 5^6 which equals $5 \times 5 \times 5 \times 5 \times 5 \times 5$ which equals 15,625. We write y multiplied by itself x times as: y^x

Calculate 5^6

HP 17bII/HP 17bII+		HP 12C		HP 10BII/HP 10BII+	
Keystrokes	*Display*	*Keystrokes*	*Display*	*Keystrokes*	*Display*
5 [■][y^x]	5.0000^	5 [ENTER]	5.0000	5 [■][y^x]	5.0000
6 [=]	**15,625.0000**	6 [y^x]	**15,625.0000**	6 [=]	**15,625.0000**

TI BA II Plus	
Keystrokes	*Display*
5 [y^x]	5.0000
6 [=]	**15,625.0000**

IV.   ROOTS

A.   SQUARE ROOTS

The square root is the method of determining which number, when multiplied by itself, will result in the correct number. For example, what number when multiplied by itself will yield 81?

Calculate $\sqrt{81}$.

HP 17bII/HP 17bII+		HP 12C		HP 10BII/HP 10BII+	
Keystrokes	*Display*	*Keystrokes*	*Display*	*Keystrokes*	*Display*
81[■][$\sqrt{x}$]	**9.0000**	81[ENTER]	81.0000	81 [■][$\sqrt{x}$]	**9.0000**
		[g][$\sqrt{x}$]	**9.0000**		

TI BA II Plus	
Keystrokes	*Display*
81[$\sqrt{x}$]	**9.0000**

NOTE: As a matter of practice, you should always use the y^x key for solving all root problems so that you develop a consistent method for solving those questions. (See the next page.)

B.   ROOTS GREATER THAN 2 (N^TH ROOT OF X)

Finding the Nth root of a number (x) is the method of determining which number, when multiplied by itself N times, will result in the number x. For example, what number, when multiplied by itself 3 times will result in 125?

It is important to know that your financial calculator cannot determine N^{th} roots. However, the following mathematical equality will allow us to solve our problem.

$$\sqrt[N]{x} = x^{1/N}$$

Calculate $\sqrt[3]{125}$ = $125^{1/3}$.

HP 17bII/HP 17bII+		HP 12C		HP 10BII/HP 10BII+	
Keystrokes	*Display*	*Keystrokes*	*Display*	*Keystrokes*	*Display*
125 [■][y^x]	125.0000^	125 [ENTER]	125.0000	125 [■][y^x]	125.0000
3 [■] [$^1/x$]	125.0000^0.3333	3 [$^1/x$]	0.3333	3 [■] [$^1/x$]	0.3333
[=]	**5.0000**	[y^x]	**5.0000**	[=]	**5.0000**

TI BA II Plus	
Keystrokes	*Display*
125 [y^x]	125.0000
3 [$^1/x$]	0.3333
[=]	**5.0000**

NOTE: This type of calculation is common in determining the geometric average return (an investment concept).

V.   RECIPROCAL

The reciprocal is often used in determining the Nth root of a number and is written as:

$^1/x$

Calculate the reciprocal of 6.

HP 17bII/HP 17bII+		HP 12C		HP 10BII/HP 10BII+	
Keystrokes	*Display*	*Keystrokes*	*Display*	*Keystrokes*	*Display*
6 [■] [$^1/x$]	0.1667	6 [$^1/x$]	0.1667	6 [■] [$^1/x$]	0.1667

TI BA II Plus	
Keystrokes	*Display*
6 [$^1/x$]	0.1667

NOTE: The calculators discussed in this book do not display fractions. The decimal equivalent is displayed.

Basic Time Value of Money Calculations

I. INTRODUCTION TO BASIC TIME VALUE OF MONEY

Money received today is worth more than the same amount of money received at a future date. This concept is commonly known as the time value of money. For example, $100 received today is worth more than $100 received a year from now, because the $100 received today can be invested and will be worth more in one year. Another way to look at this concept is through the concept of utility. The $100 received today will allow you to purchase $100 of utility today. Alternatively, the $100 received one year from today will delay your gratification for one year; and thus, you will require additional gratification for your cost of delay (opportunity cost).

Comparisons in terms of dollars at the same point in time are necessary to solve many problems and to make sound decisions, especially in the area of financial planning. Therefore, dollars held today must be accumulated, or future dollars must be discounted to today's value before time comparisons are valid. Thus, time value of money calculations are fundamental to financial planning. These calculations are the tools that allow us to properly plan for our client's goals and objectives.

A. EVEN VERSUS UNEVEN CASH FLOWS

The two broad categories for time value of money include even cash flows (such as annuities or bonds) and uneven cash flows. Calculations with even cash flows are solved using the following five keys:

[PV]   Present Value

[N]   Number of periods

[I/YR]   Interest or earning per period

[PMT]   Periodic payment made each period

[FV]   Future Value

NOTE: For the even cash flows, it is always helpful to write down all five variables and fill in the known information. This will allow you to focus on the unknown factor or information.

Uneven cash flows do not quite fit into the above five keys. This is because the periodic payments do not remain constant over the evaluation period. Calculations with uneven cash flows are usually solved using the following keys:

[CF_0]   Initial cash flow. [Think of this as your initial investment that would occur on the first day of the first year. If there is not an initial investment, you still need to input 0 for this value in order for your calculator to calculate the correct solution.]

[CF_j]   Cash flow key for all cash flows after the initial cash flow.

[N_j]   Total number of identical cash flows [this key is not used in all uneven cash flow calculations].

[NPV]   Net Present Value [this key is not used in all uneven cash flow calculations]. When solving for NPV, you must enter a rate of return or an earnings rate. This will be entered into i.

[IRR]   Internal Rate of Return [this key is not used in all uneven cash flow calculations].

NOTES:

1. For uneven cash flows, it helps to write down all of the steps before entering the keystrokes.

2. The problems demonstrated in this section are examples of both even and uneven cash flow calculations.

B. DEVELOPING A CASH FLOW TIME HORIZON

Before attempting any time value of money problem, it is always useful to visualize the cash flows on a timeline. Many academics teach time value of money analysis this way and suggest that you will not be able to solve the problem correctly if you cannot visualize and draw a picture of the problem. In keeping with this concept, we will generally provide a picture of the cash flows for each problem in this section on a timeline. The cash flows depicted on the timeline will follow the following general format:

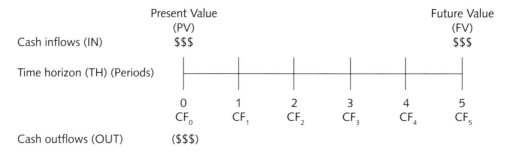

NOTES:

1. The above format is used with all of the timelines in this book. Space limitations prevent the use of titles or other text to describe the various positions on the timeline. You should familiarize yourself with the format of the timelines and understand the concept prior to continuing.

2. The number of periods is problem dependent and may represent months, quarters, years, or any other term (time horizon TH).

3. Cash outflows (OUT) can occur at any time, as can cash inflows (IN).

4. For some problems with a large number of time periods, a break (…) is used to indicate a continuing set of periods, and where applicable, a continuing set of cash flows.

II.   PRESENT VALUE (PV) OF A SUM CERTAIN

A.   APPLICATIONS

This calculation is used to determine what a sum of money to be received in a future year is worth in today's dollars based on a specific discount rate. The formula for finding the PV of a future sum is:

$$PV = \frac{FV}{(1+i)^N}$$

There are a wide variety of problems that require this type of calculation. For example, if you have just won a prize and you have the option of receiving "x" today or "y" some time in the future, which option should you select? Once you determine the appropriate discount rate (usually your opportunity cost rate for similar risk), you can use the calculation to properly compare your options.

B.   ANNUAL INTEREST

Calculate the present value of $1,000 to be received in 5 years assuming an annual interest rate of 6%.

HP 17bII/HP 17bII+		HP 12C		HP 10BII/HP 10BII+	
Keystrokes	*Display*	*Keystrokes*	*Display*	*Keystrokes*	*Display*
[FIN]	SELECT A MENU	1000 [FV]	1,000.0000	1000 [FV]	1,000.0000
[TVM]	1 P/YR END MODE	6 [i]	6.0000	0 [PMT]	0.0000
1000 [FV]	FV=1,000.0000	5 [n]	5.0000	6 [I/YR]	6.0000
0 [PMT]	PMT=0.0000	[PV]	**−747.2582**	5 [N]	5.0000
6 [I%YR]	I%YR=6.0000			[PV]	**−747.2582**
5 [N]	N=5.0000				
[PV]	PV= **−747.2582**				

TI BA II Plus		SHORTCUT	
Keystrokes	*Display*		
1000 [FV]	FV=1,000.0000	*n*	5.0000
0 [PMT]	PMT=0.0000	*i*	6.0000
6 [I/Y]	I/Y=6.0000	PMT	0.0000
5 [N]	N=5.0000	FV	1,000.0000
[CPT][PV]	PV= **−747.2582**	PV	**−747.2582**

NOTE: All of the calculations above produce a negative answer because the calculators assume a cash inflow/outflow concept. Money received is a positive number (e.g., proceeds from a loan) and money paid out is a negative number (e.g., loan payments). In the above example, the PV is negative because it is assumed to be a cash outflow into an investment such as a savings account, and the FV is positive because it is an amount to be received from the savings account at the end of the term.

C. MONTHLY INTEREST

Calculate the present value of $1,000 to be received in 5 years assuming an annual interest rate of 6%, compounded monthly.

$1,000.0000

0	12	24	36	48	60

($741.3722)

HP 17bII/HP 17bII+		HP 12C		HP 10BII/HP 10BII+	
Keystrokes	*Display*	*Keystrokes*	*Display*	*Keystrokes*	*Display*
[FIN]	SELECT A MENU	1000 [FV]	1,000.0000	1000 [FV]	1,000.0000
[TVM]	1 P/YR END MODE	0 [PMT]	0.0000	0 [PMT]	0.0000
1000 [FV]	FV=1,000.0000	6 [ENTER]	12.0000	6 [÷]	6.0000
0 [PMT]	PMT=0.0000	12 [÷][i]	0.5000	12 [=][I/YR]	0.5000
6 [÷]	6.0000÷	5 [ENTER]	5.0000	5 [x]	5.0000
12 [=][I%YR]	I%YR=0.5000	12 [x][n]	60.0000	12 [=][N]	60.0000
5 [x]	5.0000x	[PV]	−741.3722	[PV]	−741.3722
12 [=][N]	N=60.0000				
[PV]	PV= −741.3722				

TI BA II Plus		SHORTCUT	
Keystrokes	*Display*		
1000 [FV]	FV=1,000.0000	*n*	60.0000 (5 × 12)
0 [PMT]	PMT=0.0000	*i*	0.5000 (6 ÷ 12)
6 [÷]	6.0000	PMT	0.0000
12 [=][I/Y]	I/Y=0.5000	FV	1,000.0000
5 [x]	5.0000	PV	**−741.3722**
12 [=][N]	N=60.0000		
[CPT][PV]	PV= −741.3722		

NOTE: Monthly compounding produces a different result from annual compounding. In general, the more frequent the compounding, the smaller the present value or the larger the future value.

NOTE: The HP 17bII/HP 17bII+, HP 10BII/HP 10BII+, and TI BA II Plus are capable of converting the annual interest rate to a daily, monthly, quarterly, or semiannual rate by setting the calculator to the appropriate number of compounding periods per year (e.g., 365, 12, 4, or 2).

The HP 12C is capable of converting the annual interest rate to a monthly rate using the [g] [12÷] keystroke combination. The HP 12C is also capable of converting the number of yearly periods to monthly periods by using the [g] [12x] keystroke combination.

The decision has been made to not use these shortcut features in the demonstrated calculations to maintain consistency among the calculators and to avoid possible calculation mistakes by forgetting to reset the calculator to a different number of periods per year. If you would like more information about these features, please refer to the owner's manual for your calculator.

We have found that it is much easier to simply use single period compounding and adjust interest rates, periods, and payments as necessary.

Any calculations that require compounding more frequently than annually will be done by adjusting the [N], [i], and [PMT] keys. The number of periods is adjusted by multiplying the number of years by the number of compounding periods (i.e., monthly compounding: 5 years x 12 months = 60 periods).

The interest factor and payment amount are adjusted by dividing the number of periods (i.e., monthly compounding: 6% per year ÷ 12 months = 0.5000% per month).

Keep in mind that when solving for any of the [N], [I/YR], and [PMT] keys, you will generally have to adjust the answer from a period basis to an annual basis.

III. FUTURE VALUE (FV) OF A SUM CERTAIN

A. APPLICATIONS

This calculation is used to determine how much a sum invested today at a specific earnings rate will be worth at the end of a certain number of periods. The formula for finding the future value of a sum is:

$$FV = PV \, (1 + i)^N$$

This is a classic example of an everyday problem of "if I invest 'x' today how much will I have at a future date." This is the analysis that motivates many people to save, as opposed to consume. In a sense, you are saying, "if I forego consumption today, how much will I be able to consume later." Alternatively, "if I forego consumption today, how much will it cost me later."

To solve the problem, you must know, or estimate, the earnings rate or interest rate. This calculation can be used:

1. To project future dollar amounts in situations where no additional funds are added to the original balance.

2. To project future dollar amounts in situations where additional funds are added to the original balance in uneven or different amounts. For example, this type of calculation can be used with any investment (e.g., savings account, zero coupon bond, non-dividend paying stock).

3. To estimate a future cost where the present cost is known. For example, future cost of education, home purchases, medical costs, nursing home care, or any other lump sum expenditure. The appropriate interest rate for these cost problems is probably some form of the general price index (CPI) or some specific cost driver index, where appropriate (such as a long term trend line). For example, the projected rate of increase for the cost of education is well above the projected CPI, as are medical costs. Selecting the appropriate interest rate in these types of problems is critical and requires some understanding of basic economics.

B. ANNUAL INTEREST

Calculate the future value of $1,000 invested for 5 years assuming an annual interest rate of 6%.

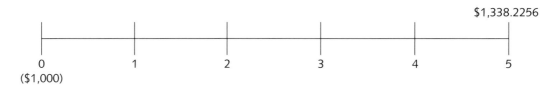

$1,338.2256

HP 17bII/HP 17bII+	
Keystrokes	*Display*
[FIN]	SELECT A MENU
[TVM]	1 P/YR END MODE
1000 [+/–][PV]	PV=–1,000.0000
0 [PMT]	PMT=0.0000
6 [I%YR]	I%YR=6.0000
5 [N]	N=5.0000
[FV]	FV= **1,338.2256**

HP 12C	
Keystrokes	*Display*
1000 [PV][CHS]	–1,000.0000
0 [PMT]	0.0000
6 [i]	6.0000
5 [n]	5.0000
[FV]	**1,338.2256**

HP 10BII/HP 10BII+	
Keystrokes	*Display*
1000 [+/–][PV]	–1,000.0000
0 [PMT]	0.0000
6 [I/YR]	6.0000
5 [N]	5.0000
[FV]	**1,338.2256**

TI BA II Plus	
Keystrokes	*Display*
1000 [+/–]	–1,000
[PV]	PV=–1,000.0000
0 [PMT]	PMT=0.0000
6 [I/Y]	I/Y=6.0000
5[N]	N=5.0000
[CPT][FV]	FV= **1,338.2256**

SHORTCUT	
PV	–1,000.0000
n	5.0000
i	6.0000
PMT	0.0000
FV	**1,338.2256**

C. MONTHLY INTEREST

Calculate the future value of $1,000 invested for 5 years assuming an annual interest rate of 6%, compounded monthly.

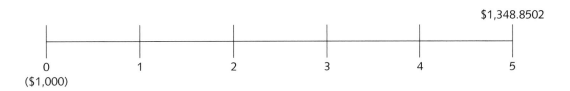

HP 17bII/HP 17bII+		HP 12C		HP 10BII/HP 10BII+	
Keystrokes	*Display*	*Keystrokes*	*Display*	*Keystrokes*	*Display*
[FIN]	SELECT A MENU	1000 [PV][CHS]	−1,000.0000	1000 [+/−][PV]	−1,000.0000
[TVM]	1 P/YR END MODE	0 [PMT]	0.0000	0 [PMT]	0.0000
1000 [+/−][PV]	PV=−1,000.0000	6[ENTER]	6.0000	6 [÷]	6.0000
0 [PMT]	PMT=0.0000	12 [÷][i]	0.5000	12 [=][I/YR]	0.5000
6 [÷]	6.0000÷	5 [ENTER]	5.0000	5 [x]	5.0000
12 [=][I%YR]	I%YR=0.5000	12 [x][n]	60.0000	12 [=][N]	60.0000
5 [x]	5.0000x	[FV]	**1,348.8502**	[FV]	**1,348.8502**
12 [=][N]	N=60.0000				
[FV]	FV= **1,348.8502**				

TI BA II Plus		SHORTCUT	
Keystrokes	*Display*		
1000 [+/−]	−1,000	PV	−1,000.0000
[PV]	PV=−1,000.0000	*n*	60.0000 (5 × 12)
0 [PMT]	PMT=0.0000	*i*	0.5000 (6 ÷12)
6 [÷]	6.0000	PMT	0.0000
12 [=][I/Y]	I/Y=0.5000	FV	**1,348.8502**
5 [x]	5.0000		
12 [=][N]	N=60.0000		
[CPT][FV]	FV= **1,348.8502**		

IV.   PRESENT VALUE (PV) OF AN ORDINARY ANNUITY

A.   APPLICATIONS

An annuity is a series of equal payments that continue for a finite period of time. Ordinary annuities begin one period from the investment. With an annuity due, payments begin on the same day or period of the initial investment (i.e., immediately). Your financial calculator will have a feature (generally a [BEGIN] or [END] key) that allows you to switch between an ordinary annuity and an annuity due. The formula for finding the present value of an annuity is:

$$PV = PMT \left[\frac{1 - \dfrac{1}{(1+i)^N}}{i} \right]$$

This analysis assists financial planners in evaluating:

1. Commercial annuities.

2. Life insurance settlement options where one of the options is an annuity.

3. Settlement options from retirement plans where one of the options is an annuity.

4. The capital needed at retirement for a particular individual (this analysis may also be performed using an annuity due concept, but if done on a monthly basis the ordinary annuity is probably acceptable).

5. The present value of expected Social Security benefits.

6. The present value of remaining debt payments that are scheduled or anticipated.

7. The present value of a series of payments representing a settlement from a lawsuit assuming that it is paid as an ordinary annuity.

8. Calculating the payments for a mortgage loan or any other annuity payment where the payments are equal and in a series.

Calculate the present value of an ordinary annuity of $2,000 received annually for 12 years assuming a discount rate of 6%. Make certain your calculator is in "end mode" for all ordinary annuity calculations.

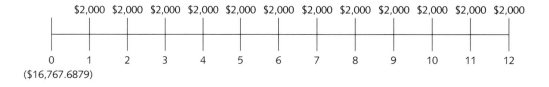

HP 17bII/HP 17bII+		HP 12C		HP 10BII/HP 10BII+	
Keystrokes	*Display*	*Keystrokes*	*Display*	*Keystrokes*	*Display*
[FIN]	SELECT A MENU	12[n]	12.0000	12[N]	12.0000
[TVM]	1 P/YR END MODE	6[i]	6.0000	6[I/YR]	6.0000
12[N]	N=12.0000	2000 [PMT]	2,000.0000	2000 [PMT]	2,000.0000
6[I%YR]	I%YR=6.0000	0[FV]	0.0000	0[FV]	0.0000
2000 [PMT]	PMT=2,000.0000	[PV]	–16,767.6879	[PV]	–16,767.6879
0 [FV]	FV=0.0000				
[PV]	PV= –16,767.6879				

TI BA II Plus		SHORTCUT	
Keystrokes	*Display*		
12[N]	N=12.0000	n	12.0000
6[I/Y]	I/Y=6.0000	i	6.0000
2000 [PMT]	PMT=2,000.0000	PMT_{OA}	2,000.0000
0[FV]	FV=0.0000	FV	0.0000
[CPT][PV]	PV= –16,767.6879	PV	–16,767.6879

NOTE: If you calculated your answer to be –$17,773.7492, it is because your calculator was in "begin mode." Make sure your calculator is in "end mode" for ordinary annuity calculations.

V.   PRESENT VALUE (PV) OF AN ANNUITY DUE

A.   APPLICATIONS

The applications for an annuity due calculation are exactly the same as the ordinary annuity, except that the first payment for the annuity due is made <u>immediately</u>. This is opposite to the ordinary annuity, where the first payment is made at the <u>end</u> of the first term (could be month, quarter, or year). An ordinary annuity payment does not have to be made at the end of the period, just delayed one period.

The usual applications requiring an annuity due analysis include:

1. Capital needs analysis

2. Education needs analysis

Refer back to the present value of an ordinary annuity and notice that any of those applications can be done on an annuity due basis.

The following chart demonstrates the different methods for calculating an annuity due (AD) problem versus an ordinary annuity (OA) problem:

OA	**0**	2,000	2,000	2,000	2,000	2,000	**2,000**
	( )						
	↓	↓	↓	↓	↓	↓	↓
AD	**2,000**	2,000	2,000	2,000	2,000	2,000	**0**
	↓	↓	↓	↓	↓	↓	↓
	( )						

Calculate the present value of an annuity of $2,000 received annually that begins today and continues for 12 years, assuming a discount rate of 6%.

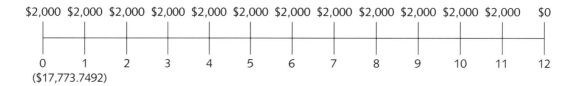

$2,000 $2,000 $2,000 $2,000 $2,000 $2,000 $2,000 $2,000 $2,000 $2,000 $2,000 $2,000 $0

0   1   2   3   4   5   6   7   8   9   10   11   12
($17,773.7492)

HP 17bII/HP 17bII+		HP 12C		HP 10BII/HP 10BII+	
Keystrokes	*Display*	*Keystrokes*	*Display*	*Keystrokes*	*Display*
[FIN]	SELECT A MENU	[g][BEG]	0.0000_{BEGIN}	[■][BEG/END]	0.0000_{BEGIN}
[TVM]	1 P/YR END MODE	12[n]	12.0000	12[N]	12.0000
[OTHER]	1 P/YR END MODE	6[i]	6.0000	6[I/YR]	6.0000
[BEG]	1 P/YR BEGIN MODE	2000 [PMT]	2,000.0000	2000 [PMT]	2,000.0000
[EXIT]	1 P/YR BEGIN MODE	0[FV]	0.0000	0[FV]	0.0000
12[N]	N=12.0000	[PV]	–17,773.7492	[PV]	–17,773.7492
6[I%YR]	I%YR=6.0000				
2000 [PMT]	PMT=2,000.0000				
0 [FV]	FV=0.0000				
[PV]	PV= **–17,773.7492**				

NOTE: If you calculated your answer to be –$16,767.6879, your calculator was in "end mode." Make sure your calculator is in "begin mode" when calculating the present value of an annuity due.

TI BA II Plus		SHORTCUT	
Keystrokes	*Display*		
[2ⁿᵈ][BGN]	END	Begin Mode	
[2ⁿᵈ][SET]	BGN	n	12.0000
[CE/C]	0.0000	i	6.0000
12[N]	N=12.0000	PMT_{AD}	2,000.0000
6[I/Y]	I/Y=6.0000	FV	0.0000
2000 [PMT]	PMT=2,000.0000	PV	**–17,773.7492**
0[FV]	FV=0.0000		
[CPT][PV]	PV=**–17,773.7492**		

NOTE: The PV of an ordinary annuity is related to the PV of an annuity due by one period's earnings. For example, –$17,773.7492 divided by 1.06 equals –$16,767.6879 (the solution to the previous calculation).

You can multiply the PV of an ordinary annuity by (1 + interest rate) to determine the PV of an annuity due or alternatively, divide the PV or an annuity due by (1 + interest rate) to determine PV of an ordinary annuity.

Don't forget to set your calculator to END MODE.

VI.   FUTURE VALUE (FV) OF AN ORDINARY ANNUITY

A.   APPLICATIONS

The formula for finding the future value of an annuity is:

$$FV = PMT \left[\frac{(1+i)^N - 1}{i} \right]$$

This is usually an investment application answering the question of "how much will I have in future dollars from a series of equal cash investments made over the selected term?" Other applications include the accumulation of money for education, retirement, or any other purpose where the deposits take the form of an ordinary annuity.

Calculate the future value of an ordinary annuity of $2,000 invested for 12 years, assuming an earnings rate of 6%. Make certain your calculator is in "end mode" for all ordinary annuity calculations.

	$33,739.8824

0   1   2   3   4   5   6   7   8   9   10   11   12
−$2,000 −$2,000 −$2,000 −$2,000 −$2,000 −$2,000 −$2,000 −$2,000 −$2,000 −$2,000 −$2,000 −$2,000

HP 17bII/HP 17bII+

Keystrokes	Display
[FIN]	SELECT A MENU
[TVM]	1 P/YR END MODE
0 [PV]	PV=0.0000
12[N]	N=12.0000
6[I%YR]	I%YR=6.0000
2000 [+/−][PMT]	PMT=−2,000.0000
[FV]	FV= **33,739.8824**

HP 12C

Keystrokes	Display
0[PV]	0.0000
12[n]	12.0000
6[i]	6.0000
2000 [CHS][PMT]	−2,000.0000
[FV]	**33,739.8824**

HP 10BII/HP 10BII+

Keystrokes	Display
0[PV]	0.0000
12[N]	12.0000
6[I/YR]	6.0000
2000 [+/−][PMT]	−2,000.0000
[FV]	**33,739.8824**

TI BA II Plus

Keystrokes	Display
0[PV]	PV=0.0000
12[N]	N=12.0000
6[I/Y]	I/Y=6.0000
2000 [+/−]	−2,000
[PMT]	PMT=−1,000.0000
[CPT][FV]	FV=**33,739.8824**

SHORTCUT

PV	0.0000
n	12.0000
i	6.0000
PMT_{OA}	−2,000.0000
FV	**33,739.8824**

VII. FUTURE VALUE (FV) OF AN ANNUITY DUE

A. APPLICATIONS

The applications once again are the same as the future value of an ordinary annuity, however, the deposits take the form of an annuity due.

Calculate the future value of an annual annuity of $2,000 beginning today and continuing for 12 years, assuming an earnings rate of 6%. Make certain your calculator is in "begin mode" for all annuity due calculations.

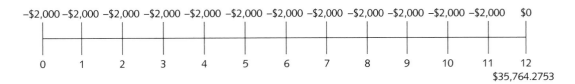

HP 17bII/HP 17bII+		HP 12C		HP 10BII/HP 10BII+	
Keystrokes	*Display*	*Keystrokes*	*Display*	*Keystrokes*	*Display*
[FIN]	SELECT A MENU	[g][BEG]	0.0000$_{BEGIN}$	[■][BEG/END]	0.0000$_{BEGIN}$
[TVM]	1 P/YR END MODE	0[PV]	0.0000	0[PV]	0.0000
[OTHER]	1 P/YR END MODE	12[n]	12.0000	12[N]	12.0000
[BEG]	1 P/YR BEGIN MODE	6[i]	6.0000	6[I/YR]	6.0000
[EXIT]	1 P/YR BEGIN MODE	2000 [CHS][PMT]	−2,000.0000	2000 [+/−][PMT]	−2,000.0000
0 [PV]	PV=0.0000	[FV]	**35,764.2753**	[FV]	**35,764.2753**
12[N]	N=12.0000				
6[I%YR]	I%YR=6.0000				
2000 [+/−][PMT]	PMT=2,000.0000				
[FV]	FV= **35,764.2753**				

TI BA II Plus		SHORTCUT	
Keystrokes	*Display*		
[2ⁿᵈ][BGN]	END	Begin Mode	
[2ⁿᵈ][SET]	BGN	PV	0.0000
[CE/C]	0.0000	n	12.0000
0[PV]	PV=0.0000	i	6.0000
12[N]	N=12.0000	PMT_{AD}	−2,000.0000
6[I/Y]	I/Y=6.0000	FV	**35,764.2753**
2000 [+/−]	−2,000		
[PMT]	PMT=−2,000.0000		
[CPT][FV]	FV= **35,764.2753**		

NOTE: Similar to the relationship between the present value of an ordinary annuity and annuity due, the future value of an ordinary annuity and annuity due are also closely related. For example, $35,764.2753 divided by 1.06 equals $33,739.8824 (the solution to the previous calculation).

VIII. CALCULATING AN ORDINARY ANNUITY (PMT)

A. APPLICATIONS

The usual applications requiring an ordinary annuity payment calculation include:

1. All mortgage payments.

2. All debt repayments that are equal.

3. All installment payments on installment notes.

Also, the applications listed under present value of an ordinary annuity:

4. Commercial annuities.

5. Life insurance settlement options where one option is an annuity.

6. Settlement options from retirement plans where one option is an annuity.

7. The capital needed at retirement for a particular individual (this analysis may also be performed using an annuity due concept but if done on a monthly basis the ordinary annuity is probably acceptable).

8. The present value of your expected Social Security benefits.

9. The present value of remaining debt payments that are scheduled or anticipated.

10. The present value of a series of payments representing a settlement from a law suit assuming that it is paid as an ordinary annuity.

11. Calculating the payments for a mortgage loan or any other annuity payment where the payments are equal and in a series.

Calculate the monthly payment received over 10 years from a single payment investment of $100,000.00 earning 9%, compounded monthly. Make certain your calculator is in "end mode" for all ordinary annuity calculations.

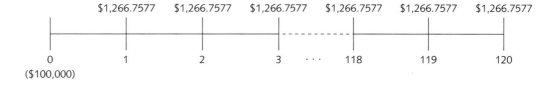

HP 17bII/HP 17bII+	
Keystrokes	*Display*
[FIN]	SELECT A MENU
[TVM]	1 P/YR END MODE
100000 [+/−][PV]	PV=−100,000.0000
0 [FV]	FV=0.0000
9 [÷]	9.0000÷
12 [=][I%YR]	I%YR=0.7500
10 [x]	10.0000x
12[=][N]	N=120.0000
[PMT]	PMT= **1,266.7577**

HP 12C	
Keystrokes	*Display*
100000 [CHS][PV]	−100,000.0000
0 [FV]	0.0000
9 [ENTER]	9.0000
12 [÷][i]	0.7500
10 [ENTER]	10.0000
12 [x][n]	120.0000
[PMT]	**1,266.7577**

HP 10BII/HP 10BII+	
Keystrokes	*Display*
100000 [+/−][PV]	−100,000.0000
0 [FV]	0.0000
9 [÷]	9.0000
12 [=][I/YR]	0.7500
10 [x]	10.0000
12[=][N]	120.0000
[PMT]	**1,266.7577**

TI BA II Plus	
Keystrokes	*Display*
100000 [+/−]	−100,000
[PV]	PV=−100,000.0000
0 [FV]	FV=0.0000
9 [÷]	9.0000
12 [=] [I/Y]	I/Y=0.7500
10 [x]	10.0000
12[=][N]	N=120.0000
[CPT][PMT]	PMT= **1,266.7577**

SHORTCUT	
PV	−100,000.0000
FV	0.0000
i	.7500 (9 ÷ 12)
n	120.0000 (10 ×12)
PMT_{OA}	**1,266.7577**

IX.   CALCULATING AN ANNUITY DUE (PMT)

A.   APPLICATIONS

The applications are the same as ordinary annuity payments, except that they are in the form of an annuity due (e.g., rent).

Calculate the payment received at the beginning of each month for 10 years from an investment of $100,000.00 earning 9%, compounded monthly. Make sure your calculator is in "begin mode" for all annuity due calculations.

HP 17bII/HP 17bII+		HP 12C		HP 10BII/HP 10BII+	
Keystrokes	*Display*	*Keystrokes*	*Display*	*Keystrokes*	*Display*
[FIN]	SELECT A MENU	[g][BEG]	0.0000 BEGIN	[■][BEG/END]	0.0000 BEGIN
[TVM]	1 P/YR END MODE	100000 [CHS][PV]	−100,000.0000	100000 [+/−][PV]	−100,000.0000
[OTHER]	1 P/YR END MODE	0[FV]	0.0000	0 [FV]	0.0000
[BEG]	1 P/YR BEGIN MODE	9 [ENTER]	9.0000	9 [÷]	9.0000
[EXIT]	1 P/YR BEGIN MODE	12 [÷][i]	0.7500	12 [=][I/YR]	0.7500
100000 [+/−][PV]	PV=−100,000.0000	10 [ENTER]	10.0000	10 [x]	10.0000
0[FV]	FV=0.0000	12 [x][n]	120.0000	12[=][N]	120.0000
9 [÷]	9.0000÷	[PMT]	**1,257.3278**	[PMT]	**1,257.3278**
12 [=][I%YR]	I%YR=0.7500	[CLX]	0.0000 BEGIN	[■][C]	0.0000 BEGIN
10 [x]	10.0000x	[g][END]	0.0000	[■][BEG/END]	0.0000
12[=][N]	N=120.0000				
[PMT]	PMT= **1,257.3278**				
[CLR]	0.0000				
[OTHER]	1 P/YR BEGIN MODE				
[END]	1 P/YR END MODE				
[EXIT][EXIT]	1 P/YR END MODE				

TI BA II Plus		SHORTCUT	
Keystrokes	*Display*		
[2ⁿᵈ][BGN]	END	Begin Mode	
[2ⁿᵈ][SET]	BGN	PV	–100,0000.0000
[CE/C]	0.0000	n	120.0000 (10 × 12)
100000 [+/–]	–100,000	i	0.7500 (9 ÷ 12)
[PV]	PV=–100,000.0000	FV	0.0000
0 [FV]	FV=0.0000	PMT_{AD}	**1,257.3278**
9 [÷]	9.0000		
12 [=] [I/Y]	I/Y=0.7500		
10 [x]	10.0000		
12[=][N]	N=120.0000		
[CPT] [PMT]	PMT= **1,257.3278**		
[CE/C]	0.0000		
[2ⁿᵈ][BGN]	BGN		
[2ⁿᵈ][SET]	END		
[CE/C]	0.0000		

NOTE: Be sure to reset your calculator to END MODE after calculating an ANNUITY DUE problem.

X.   AMORTIZATION

A.   APPLICATIONS

Amortization calculations are especially useful in:

1. Debt management.

2. Mortgage analysis and debt analysis, where the planner wants to determine the balance of the indebtedness, the amount of interest paid during a particular term, or the amount of principal reduction for a particular payment or for a term. An amortization table is also useful to recalculate the number of payments, assuming there is some change in the original payment schedule, such as in refinancing a home or rescheduling debt payments.

3. Determining the impact of a change in payment on the term of repayment, such as where a client adds $100 to each monthly mortgage payment.

Calculate the monthly payment for a home loan of $90,000 at 5% annual interest for 30 years. Because mortgage payments are made after monthly interest is charged, they would be considered ordinary annuities. Make sure your calculator is in "end mode" with all ordinary annuity calculations.

HP 17bII/HP 17bII+		HP 12C		HP 10BII/HP 10BII+	
Keystrokes	*Display*	*Keystrokes*	*Display*	*Keystrokes*	*Display*
[FIN]	SELECT A MENU	90000 [PV]	90,000.0000	90000 [PV]	90,000.0000
[TVM]	1 P/YR END MODE	0 [FV]	0.0000	0 [FV]	0.0000
90000 [PV]	PV=90,000.0000	5 [ENTER]	5.0000	5 [÷]	5.0000
0 [FV]	FV=0.0000	12 [÷][i]	0.4167	12 [=][I/YR]	0.4167
5 [÷]	5.0000÷	12 [ENTER]	12.0000	30 [x]	30.0000
12 [=][I%YR]	I%YR=0.4167	30 [x][n]	360.0000	12[=][N]	360.0000
30 [x]	30.0000x	[PMT]	**−483.1395**	[PMT]	**−483.1395**
12[=][N]	N=360.0000				
[PMT]	PMT= **−483.1395**				

TI BA II Plus		SHORTCUT	
Keystrokes	*Display*		
90000 [PV]	PV=90,000.0000	PV	90,000.0000
0 [FV]	FV=0.0000	*n*	360.0000 (12 × 30)
5 [÷]	5.0000	*i*	.4167 (5 ÷ 12)
12 [=][I/Y]	I/Y=0.4167	FV	0.0000
30 [x]	30.0000	PMT	**−483.1395**
12[=][N]	N=360.0000		
[CPT][PMT]	PMT= **−483.1395**		

XI.   NET PRESENT VALUE OF A SERIES OF CASH FLOWS (NPV) – EVEN OR UNEVEN

A.   APPLICATIONS

Net present value (NPV) analysis is a common technique employed by businesses and investors to evaluate capital projects and capital expenditures. The concept is common to the capital budgeting area. The model itself is deterministic, that is, it assumes that the information is known about the future (cash flows, life, etc.). The NPV model assumes that all reinvestments in non-like life assets are made at the weighted average cost of capital of the firm. This is a more conservative assumption than the internal rate of return (IRR) method, which assumes the reinvestment rate is the IRR calculated. Therefore, the NPV is considered a superior model to IRR, when comparing investment projects of unequal lives. This analysis helps to answer the question of whether you should buy this equipment or make this investment. The result of the analysis is in dollars.

NPV is the difference between the initial cash outflow (investment) and the present value of discounted cash inflows. For example, if the present value of a series of cash flows is $200 and the initial outflow is $150, then the NPV is $50 ($200 – $150). A NPV, which is greater than zero, implies that the IRR of the cash flows is greater than the discount rate used to discount the future cash flows. A NPV of zero implies that the discount rate used is equal to the IRR for the cash flows. A NPV that is negative implies that the discount rate used is greater than the true IRR of the cash flows. As a general rule, you should look for investments that have a positive NPV.

Calculate the NPV of a machine which is purchased for $3,000.00, sold at the end of year 5 for $2,000.00, and produces the following net after-tax cash flows: year 1) +$500; year 2) +$500; year 3) +$400; year 4) +$400; year 5) +$200. Assume the cost of capital is 5% (discount rate).

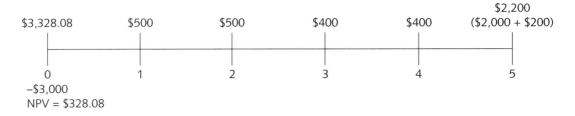

$3,328.08 $500 $500 $400 $400 $2,200 ($2,000 + $200)

0   1   2   3   4   5

–$3,000
NPV = $328.08

HP 17bII/HP 17bII+		HP 12C		HP 10BII/HP 10BII+	
Keystrokes	*Display*	*Keystrokes*	*Display*	*Keystrokes*	*Display*
[FIN]	SELECT A MENU	3000[CHS]	–3,000.	3000[+/–]	–3,000
[CFLO]	FLOW(0)=?	[g][CF$_0$]	–3,000.0000	[CFj]	–3,000.0000
[■][CLR DATA]	CLEAR THE LIST?	500[g][CFj]	500.0000	500[CFj]	500.0000
[YES]	FLOW(0)=?	2[g][Nj]	2.0000	2[■][Nj]	2.0000
3000 [+/–] [INPUT]	FLOW(1)=?	400[g][CFj]	400.0000	400[CFj]	400.0000
	–3,000.0000	2[g][Nj]	2.0000	2[■][Nj]	2.0000
500[INPUT]	#TIMES(1)=1	200[ENTER]	200.0000	200 [+]	200.0000
	1.0000	2000[+]	2,200.0000	2000[=]	2,200.0000
2[INPUT]	FLOW(2)=?	[g][CFj]	2,200.0000	[CFj]	2,200.0000
	2.0000	5[i]	5.0000	5[I/YR]	5.0000
400[INPUT]	#TIMES(2)=1	[f][NPV]	**328.0788**	[■][NPV]	**328.0788**
	1.0000				
2[INPUT]	FLOW(3)=?				
	2.0000				
200[+]	FLOW(3)=?				
	200.0000+				
2000[=]	FLOW(3)=?				
	2,200.0000				
[INPUT]	#TIMES(3)=1				
	1.0000				
[INPUT]	FLOW(4)=?				
	1.0000				
[EXIT]	FLOW(4)=?				
[CALC]	NPV, NUS, NFV NEED I%				
5[I%]	I%=5.0000				
[NPV]	NPV=**328.0788**				

TI BA II Plus		SHORTCUT	
Keystrokes	*Display*		
[CF][2ⁿᵈ][CLR Work]	CF_0=0.0000	CF_0	−3,000.0000
[CF]3000[+/−]	CF_0=−3,000	CF_1	500.0000
[ENTER]	CF_0=−3,000.0000	CF_2	500.0000
[↓]500[ENTER]	C01=500.0000	CF_3	400.0000
[↓]2[ENTER]	F01=2.0000	CF_4	400.0000
[↓]400[ENTER]	C02=400.0000	CF_5	2,200.0000
[↓]2[ENTER]	F02=2.0000	*i*	5.0000
[↓]200[+]	C03=200.0000	NPV	**328.0788**
2000[=][ENTER]	C03=2,200.0000		
[NPV]5[ENTER]	I=5.0000		
[↓][CPT]	NPV=**328.0788**		

Another way to solve this problem would be to find the PV of the cash flows discounted at 5%, which is $3,328.08, and then subtract from it the initial cost of $3,000. This results in a difference or NPV of $328.08. Another way to say the same thing is that you would be paying $3,000 for a stream of income that you would value at $3,328.08.

XII.   INTERNAL RATE OF RETURN – IRR (I)

As discussed in the previous section, the IRR is the discounted rate that makes the PV of the cash inflows equal to initial cash outflows such that the NPV is equal to zero. An important assumption of the IRR model is that all cash flows that occur during the measurement period can be and are reinvested at the IRR.

Calculate the IRR of a project that requires an initial cash outflow of $5,000.00, and will be sold at the end of year 5 for $3,000.00. The project produces the following cash flows: year 1) +$500; year 2) +$800; year 3) +$1,000; year 4) +$1,000; year 5) +$200.

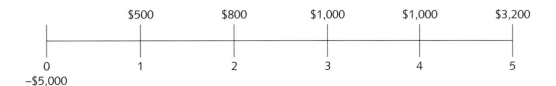

HP 17bII/HP 17bII+		HP 12C		HP 10BII/HP 10BII+	
Keystrokes	*Display*	*Keystrokes*	*Display*	*Keystrokes*	*Display*
[FIN]	SELECT A MENU	5000[CHS]	–5,000.	5000[+/–]	–5,000
[CFLO]	FLOW(0)=?	[g][CF₀]	–5,000.0000	[CFj]	–5,000.0000
[■][CLR DATA]	CLEAR THE LIST?	500[g][CFj]	500.0000	500[CFj]	500.0000
[YES]	FLOW(0)=?	800[g][CFj]	800.0000	800[CFj]	800.0000
5,000 [+/–][INPUT]	FLOW(1)=?	1000[g][CFj]	1,000.0000	1000[CFj]	1,000.0000
	–5,000.0000	2[g][Nj]	2.0000	2[■][Nj]	2.0000
500[INPUT]	#TIMES(1)=1	200[ENTER]	200.0000	200 [+]	200.0000
	1.0000	3000[+]	3,200.0000	3000[=]	3,200.0000
[INPUT]	FLOW(2)=?	[g][CFj]	3,200.0000	[CFj]	3,200.0000
	1.0000	[f][IRR]	**7.1533**	[■][IRR/YR]	**7.1533**
800[INPUT]	#TIMES(2)=1				
	1.0000				
[INPUT]	FLOW(3)=?				
	1.0000				
1000[INPUT]	#TIMES(3)=1				
	1.0000				
2[INPUT]	FLOW(4)=?				
	2.0000				
200[+]	FLOW(4)=?				
	200.0000				
3000[=]	FLOW(4)=?				
	3,200.0000				
[INPUT]	#TIMES(4)=1				
	1.0000				
[INPUT]	FLOW(5)=?				
	1.0000				
[EXIT]	FLOW(5)=?				
[CALC]	NPV, NUS, NFV NEED I%				
[IRR%]	IRR=**7.1533**				

TI BA II Plus		SHORTCUT	
Keystrokes	*Display*		
[CF][2nd][CLR Work]	CF_0=0.0000	CF_0	−5,000.0000
[CF]5000[+/−]	CF_0=−5,000	CF_1	500.0000
[ENTER]	CF_0=−5,000.0000	CF_2	800.0000
[↓]500[ENTER]	C01=500.0000	CF_3	1,000.0000
[↓]	F01=1.0000	CF_4	1,000.0000
[↓]800[ENTER]	C02=800.0000	CF_5	3,200.0000
[↓]	F02=1.0000	IRR	**7.1533**
[↓]1000[ENTER]	C03=1,000.0000		
[↓]2[ENTER]	F03=2.0000		
[↓]200[+]	C04=200.0000		
3000[=][ENTER]	C04=3,200.0000		
[IRR][CPT]	**IRR=7.1533**		

Proof of IRR

Period	Cash Flow (CF)	Divisor (x)	Factor (1/x)	Present Value (CF * 1/x)
1	500	$1 \div (1.071533)^1$	.933242	466.621
2	800	$1 \div (1.071533)^2$	.870941	696.753
3	1,000	$1 \div (1.071533)^3$	.812799	812.799
4	1,000	$1 \div (1.071533)^4$	.758539	758.539
5	3,200	$1 \div (1.071533)^5$	.707901	2,265.282
				4,999.994

XIII.   SOLVING FOR TERM OR PERIODS (N)

A.   APPLICATIONS

This kind of analysis answers the question of how long (in months, quarters, or years) to save or pay to accomplish some goal, if you save or pay at a given rate. This analysis is particularly useful in debt management, such as determining the:

■   Term to pay off student loans;

■   Term to pay off mortgage;

■   Term to save for college education;

■   Term to save for a special purchase (car, home, vacation).

Calculate the number of years it will take $5,000 to grow to $20,000 assuming an annual rate of return of 7%.

HP 17bII/HP 17bII+		HP 12C		HP 10BII/HP 10BII+	
Keystrokes	*Display*	*Keystrokes*	*Display*	*Keystrokes*	*Display*
[FIN]	SELECT A MENU	5000 [CHS]	−5,000.	5000[+/−]	−5,000
[TVM]	1 P/YR END MODE	[PV]	−5,000.0000	[PV]	−5,000.0000
5000[+/−][PV]	PV=−5,000.0000	20000[FV]	20,000.0000	20000[FV]	20,000.0000
20000[FV]	FV=20,000.0000	0[PMT]	0.0000	0 [PMT]	0.0000
0[PMT]	PMT=0.0000	15[i]	7.0000	7[I/YR]	7.0000
7[I%YR]	I%YR=7.0000	[n]	**21.0000**	[N]	**20.4895**
[N]	N=**20.4895**				

TI BA II Plus		SHORTCUT	
Keystrokes	*Display*		
5000[+/−]	−5,000	PV	−5,000.000
[PV]	PV=−5,000.0000	i	7.0000
20000[FV]	FV=20,000.0000	PMT	0.0000
0[PMT]	PMT=0.0000	FV	20,000.0000
7[I/Y]	I/Y=7.0000	n	**20.4895**
[CPT][N]	N=**20.4895**		

NOTE: When solving for [n] on the HP 12C, only integers (whole numbers) are displayed as a solution. This calculator cannot solve for non-integers (numbers with decimals). Therefore, your initial answer may be incorrect and will not match the answers of other calculators (See above). To get the correct term, you will have to substitute numbers for the term until you get the correct future value or present value. If the future value or present value does not match, you must adjust the term up or down and recalculate. This process must be done until the term you substitute equals the future value or present value. The first place to begin is the term which is calculated initially.

Time Value of Money & Fundamentals Problems

I. FUTURE VALUE

A. FUTURE VALUE—COMPOUNDED ANNUALLY

Today Tom Smith purchased an investment grade gold coin for $150,000. He expects it to increase in value at a rate of 7% compounded annually for the next 5 years. How much will the coin be worth at the end of the fifth year if his expectations are correct?

HP 17bII/HP 17bII+		HP 12C		HP 10BII/HP 10BII+	
Keystrokes	*Display*	*Keystrokes*	*Display*	*Keystrokes*	*Display*
[FIN]	SELECT A MENU	5 [n]	5.0000	5 [N]	5.0000
[TVM]	1 P/YR END MODE	7 [i]	7.0000	7 [I/YR]	7.0000
5 [N]	N=5.0000	150000 [CHS][PV]	−150,000.0000	150000 [+/−][PV]	−150,000.0000
7 [I%YR]	I%YR=7.0000	0 [PMT]	0.0000	0 [PMT]	0.0000
150000 [+/−][PV]	PV=−150,000.0000	[FV]	210,382.7596	[FV]	210,382.7596
0 [PMT]	PMT=0.0000				
[FV]	FV=210,382.7596				

TI BA II Plus		SHORTCUT	
Keystrokes	*Display*		
5 [N]	N=5.0000	PV	−150,000.0000
7 [I/Y]	I/Y=7.0000	n	5.0000
150000 [+/−]	−150,000	i	7.0000
[PV]	PV=−150,000.0000	PMT	0.0000
0 [PMT]	PMT=0.0000	FV	210,382.7596
[CPT][FV]	FV=210,382.7596		

B.   FUTURE VALUE—COMPOUNDED MONTHLY

A client invested $20,000 in an interest-bearing promissory note earning a 9% annual rate of interest compounded monthly. How much will the note be worth at the end of 8 years assuming all interest is reinvested at the 9% rate?

HP 17bII/HP 17bII+		HP 12C		HP 10BII/HP 10BII+	
Keystrokes	*Display*	*Keystrokes*	*Display*	*Keystrokes*	*Display*
[FIN]	SELECT A MENU	8 [ENTER]	8.0000	8 [x]	8.0000
[TVM]	1 P/YR END MODE	12 [x][n]	96.0000	12 [=][N]	96.0000
8 [x]	8.0000x	9 [ENTER]	9.0000	9 [÷]	9.0000
12 [=][N]	N=96.0000	12 [÷][i]	0.7500	12 [=][I/YR]	0.7500
9 [÷]	9.0000÷	20000 [CHS][PV]	−20,000.0000	20000 [+/−][PV]	−20,000.0000
12 [=][I%YR]	I%YR=0.7500	0 [PMT]	0.0000	0 [PMT]	0.0000
20000 [+/−][PV]	PV=−20,000.0000	[FV]	**40,978.4246**	[FV]	**40,978.4246**
0 [PMT]	PMT=0.0000				
[FV]	FV=**40,978.4246**				

TI BA II Plus		SHORTCUT	
Keystrokes	*Display*		
8 [x]	8.0000	PV	−20,000.0000
12 [=][N]	N=96.0000	n	96.0000 (8 × 12)
9 [÷]	9.0000	i	.7500 (9 ÷ 12)
12 [=][I/Y]	I/Y=0.7500	PMT	0.0000
20000 [+/−]	−20,000	FV	**40,978.4246**
[PV]	PV=−20,000.0000		
0 [PMT]	PMT=0.0000		
[CPT][FV]	FV=**40,978.4246**		

II.   PRESENT VALUE

A.   PRESENT VALUE—COMPOUNDED ANNUALLY

Mary Hoffman wants to give her daughter $35,000 to start her own business in 10 years. How much should she invest today at an annual growth rate of 9% compounded annually to have $35,000 in 10 years?

$35,000

0   1   2   3   4   5   6   7   8   9   10

−$14,784.38

HP 17bII/HP 17bII+		HP 12C		HP 10BII/HP 10BII+	
Keystrokes	*Display*	*Keystrokes*	*Display*	*Keystrokes*	*Display*
[FIN]	SELECT A MENU	10 [n]	10.0000	10 [N]	10.0000
[TVM]	1 P/YR END MODE	9 [i]	9.0000	9 [I/YR]	9.0000
10 [N]	N=10.0000	0 [PMT]	0.0000	0 [PMT]	0.0000
9 [I%YR]	I%YR=9.0000	35000 [FV]	35,000.0000	35000 [FV]	35,000.0000
0 [PMT]	PMT=0.0000	[PV]	**−14,784.3782**	[PV]	**−14,784.3782**
35000 [FV]	FV=35,000.0000				
[PV]	PV=**−14,784.3782**				

TI BA II Plus		SHORTCUT	
Keystrokes	*Display*		
10 [N]	N=10.0000	FV	35,000.0000
9 [I/Y]	I/Y=9.0000	*n*	10.0000
0 [PMT]	PMT=0.0000	*i*	9.0000
35000 [FV]	FV=35,000.0000	PMT	0.0000
[CPT][PV]	FV=**−14,784.3782**	PV	**−14,784.3782**

B.   PRESENT VALUE—COMPOUNDED SEMIANNUALLY

Cohen expects to receive $95,000 from a trust fund in 7 years. What is the present value of this fund if it is discounted at 8% compounded semiannually?

HP 17bII/HP 17bII+		HP 12C		HP 10BII/HP 10BII+	
Keystrokes	Display	Keystrokes	Display	Keystrokes	Display
[FIN]	SELECT A MENU	7 [ENTER]	7.0000	7 [x]	7.0000
[TVM]	1 P/YR END MODE	2 [x][n]	14.0000	2 [=][N]	14.0000
7 [x]	7.0000x	8 [ENTER]	8.0000	8 [÷]	8.0000
2 [=][N]	N=14.0000	2 [÷][i]	4.0000	2 [=][I/YR]	4.0000
8 [÷]	8.0000÷	0 [PMT]	0.0000	0 [PMT]	0.0000
2 [=][I%YR]	I%YR=4.0000	95000 [FV]	95,000.0000	95000 [FV]	95,000.0000
0 [PMT]	PMT=0.0000	[PV]	–54,860.1329	[PV]	–54,860.1329
95000 [FV]	FV=95,000.0000				
[PV]	PV=–54,860.1329				

TI BA II Plus		SHORTCUT	
Keystrokes	Display		
7 [x]	7.0000	FV	95,000.0000
2 [=][N]	N=14.0000	n	14.0000 (7 × 2)
8 [÷]	8.0000	i	4.0000 (8 ÷ 2)
2 [=][I/Y]	I/Y=4.0000	PMT	0.0000
0 [PMT]	PMT=0.0000	PV	–54,860.1329
95000 [FV]	FV=95,000.0000		
[CPT][PV]	PV=–54,860.1329		

C.   PRESENT VALUE—COMPOUNDED MONTHLY

Billy Mack expects to receive $105,000 in 9 years. His opportunity cost is 8% compounded monthly. What is this sum worth to Billy today?

HP 17bII/HP 17bII+	
Keystrokes	*Display*
[FIN]	SELECT A MENU
[TVM]	1 P/YR END MODE
9 [x]	9.0000x
12 [=][N]	N=108.0000
8 [÷]	8.0000÷
12 [=][I%YR]	I%YR=0.6667
0 [PMT]	PMT=0.0000
105000 [FV]	FV=105,000.0000
[PV]	PV=**−51,231.2520**

HP 12C	
Keystrokes	*Display*
9 [ENTER]	9.0000
12 [x][n]	108.0000
8 [ENTER]	8.0000
12 [÷][i]	0.6667
0 [PMT]	0.0000
105000 [FV]	105,000.0000
[PV]	**−51,231.2520**

HP 10BII/HP 10BII+	
Keystrokes	*Display*
9 [x]	9.0000
12 [=][N]	108.0000
8 [÷]	8.0000
12 [=][I/YR]	0.6667
0 [PMT]	0.0000
105000 [FV]	105,000.0000
[PV]	**−51,231.2520**

TI BA II Plus	
Keystrokes	*Display*
9 [x]	9.0000
12 [=][N]	N=108.0000
8 [÷]	8.0000
12 [=][I/Y]	I/Y=0.6667
0 [PMT]	PMT=0.0000
105000 [FV]	FV=105,000.0000
[CPT][PV]	PV=**−51,231.2520**

SHORTCUT	
FV	105,000.0000
n	108.0000 (9 × 12)
i	.6667 (8 ÷ 12)
PMT	0.0000
PV	**−51,231.2520**

D. PRESENT VALUE—COMPOUNDED QUARTERLY

Mary wants to accumulate $75,000 in 11.5 years to purchase a boat. She expects an annual rate of return of 6% compounded quarterly. How much does Mary need to invest today to meet her goal?

HP 17bII/HP 17bII+		HP 12C		HP 10BII/HP 10BII+	
Keystrokes	*Display*	*Keystrokes*	*Display*	*Keystrokes*	*Display*
[FIN]	SELECT A MENU	11.5 [ENTER]	11.5000	11.5 [x]	11.5000
[TVM]	1 P/YR END MODE	4 [x][n]	46.0000	4 [=][N]	46.0000
11.5 [x]	11.5000x	6 [ENTER]	6.0000	6 [÷]	6.0000
4 [=][N]	N=46.0000	4 [÷][i]	1.5000	4 [=][I/YR]	1.5000
6 [÷]	6.0000÷	0 [PMT]	0.0000	0 [PMT]	0.0000
4 [=][I%YR]	I%YR=1.5000	75000 [FV]	75,000.0000	75000 [FV]	75,000.0000
0 [PMT]	PMT=0.0000	[PV]	**–37,811.4489**	[PV]	**–37,811.4489**
75000 [FV]	FV=75,000.0000				
[PV]	PV=**–37,811.4489**				

TI BA II Plus		SHORTCUT	
Keystrokes	*Display*		
11.5 [x]	11.5000	FV	75,000.0000
4 [=][N]	N=46.0000	*n*	46.0000 (11.5 × 4)
6 [÷]	6.0000	*i*	1.5000 (6 ÷ 4)
4 [=][I/Y]	I/Y=1.5000	PMT	0.0000
0 [PMT]	PMT=0.0000	PV	**–37.811.4489**
75000 [FV]	FV=75,000.0000		
[CPT][PV]	PV=**–37,811.4489**		

III.   INTERNAL RATE OF RETURN (IRR)

A.   EXAMPLE 1

Jeff purchased 100 shares of an aggressive growth mutual fund for $82 per share 12 years ago. Today he sold all 100 shares for $24,000. What was his average annual compound rate of return on this investment before tax?

HP 17bII/HP 17bII+		HP 12C		HP 10BII/HP 10BII+	
Keystrokes	*Display*	*Keystrokes*	*Display*	*Keystrokes*	*Display*
[FIN]	SELECT A MENU	12 [n]	12.0000	12 [N]	12.0000
[TVM]	1 P/YR END MODE	0 [PMT]	0.0000	0 [PMT]	0.0000
12 [N]	N=12.0000	82[CHS][ENTER]	–82.0000	82 [+/–][x]	–82.0000
0 [PMT]	PMT=0.0000	100 [x][PV]	–8,200.0000	100 [=][PV]	–8,200.0000
82 [+/–][x]	–82.0000x	24000 [FV]	24,000.0000	24000 [FV]	24,000.0000
100 [=][PV]	PV=–8,200.0000	[i]	**9.3620**	[I/YR]	**9.3620**
24000 [FV]	FV=24,000.0000				
[I%YR]	I%YR=**9.3620**				

TI BA II Plus		SHORTCUT	
Keystrokes	*Display*		
12 [N]	N=12.0000	*n*	12.0000
0 [PMT]	PMT=0.0000	PV	–8,200.0000
82 [+/–][x]	–82.0000	PMT	0.0000
100 [=][PV]	PV=–8,200.0000	FV	24,000.0000
24000 [FV]	FV=24,000.0000	*i*	**9.3620**
[CPT][I/Y]	I/Y=**9.3620**		

B.   EXAMPLE 2

James borrowed $1,800 from his father to purchase a mountain bike. James paid back $2,600 to his father at the end of 4 years. What was the average annual compound rate of interest on James' loan from his father?

HP 17bII/HP 17bII+		HP 12C		HP 10BII/HP 10BII+	
Keystrokes	*Display*	*Keystrokes*	*Display*	*Keystrokes*	*Display*
[FIN]	SELECT A MENU	4 [n]	4.0000	4 [N]	4.0000
[TVM]	1 P/YR END MODE	0 [PMT]	0.0000	0 [PMT]	0.0000
4 [N]	N=4.0000	1800 [PV]	1,800.0000	1800 [PV]	1,800.0000
0 [PMT]	PMT=0.0000	2600[CHS][FV]	−2,600.0000	2600 [+/−][FV]	−2,600.0000
1800 [PV]	PV=1,800.0000	[i]	**9.6289**	[I/YR]	**9.6289**
2600 [+/−][FV]	FV=−2,600.0000				
[I%YR]	I%YR=**9.6289**				

TI BA II Plus		SHORTCUT	
Keystrokes	*Display*		
4 [N]	N=4.0000	*n*	4.0000
0 [PMT]	PMT=0.0000	PV	1,800.0000
1800 [PV]	PV=1,800.0000	PMT	0.0000
2600 [+/−][FV]	FV=−2,600.0000	FV	−2,600.0000
[CPT][I/Y]	I/Y=**9.6289**	*i*	**9.6289**

C. **EXAMPLE 3**

Susan Smith purchased a zero-coupon bond 9.5 years ago for $700.00. If the bond matures today and the face value is $1,000, what is the average annual compound rate of return that Susan realized on her investment?

HP 17bII/HP 17bII+		HP 12C		HP 10BII/HP 10BII+	
Keystrokes	*Display*	*Keystrokes*	*Display*	*Keystrokes*	*Display*
[FIN]	SELECT A MENU	9.5 [n]	9.5000	9.5 [N]	9.5000
[TVM]	1 P/YR END MODE	0 [PMT]	0.0000	0 [PMT]	0.0000
9.5 [N]	N=9.5000	700.00 [CHS][PV]	−700.00	700.00[+/−][PV]	−700.00
0 [PMT]	PMT=0.0000	1000 [FV]	1,000.0000	1000 [FV]	1,000.0000
700.00 [+/−][PV]	PV=−700.0000	[i]	**3.8239**	[I/YR]	**3.8258**
1000 [FV]	FV=1,000.0000				
[I%YR]	I%YR=**3.8258**				

TI BA II Plus		SHORTCUT	
Keystrokes	*Display*		
9.5 [N]	N=9.5000	*n*	9.5000
0 [PMT]	PMT=0.0000	PV	−700.00
700.00 [+/−][PV]	PV=−700.00	PMT	0.0000
1000 [FV]	FV=1,000.0000	FV	1,000.0000
[CPT][I/Y]	I/Y=**3.8258**	*i*	**3.8258**

Which answer is correct 3.8258% or 3.8239%? The correct answer is 3.8258%. The HP 12C does not calculate this correctly as illustrated below.

Proof of Internal Rate of Return with Non-Integer Compounding

By adding the internal rate of return to one and raising the sum to the power of 9.5 and multiplying the result by $700.00, you should end up with $1,000.00.

HP 17bII, HP 10BII, TI BA II Plus	HP 12C
$(1.038258)^{9.5} \times \$700.00 = \$1,000.00$	$(1.038239)^{9.5} \times 700.00 = \$999.8222$

NOTE: The HP 12C does not handle non-integer terms very well. Thus, the HP 12C does not calculate the correct answer; however, it is reasonably close.

IV.   TERM CALCULATIONS

A.   TERM CALCULATION—COMPOUNDED ANNUALLY

Fred purchased an Oriental rug for $28,000. Today, he sold the rug for $49,345.57. Fred estimated his average annual opportunity cost on the rug was 8%. Approximately how many years did Fred own the rug? (rounded to the nearest .000)

HP 17bII/HP 17bII+		HP 12C		HP 10BII/HP 10BII+	
Keystrokes	*Display*	*Keystrokes*	*Display*	*Keystrokes*	*Display*
[FIN]	SELECT A MENU	8[i]	8.0000	8[I/YR]	8.0000
[TVM]	1 P/YR END MODE	0[PMT]	0.0000	0[PMT]	0.0000
8[I%YR]	I%YR=8.0000	28000[CHS][PV]	−28,000.0000	28000[+/−][PV]	−28,000.0000
0[PMT]	PMT=0.0000	49345.57[FV]	49,345.5700	49345.57 [FV]	49,345.5700
28000[+/−][PV]	PV=−28,000.0000	[n]	**8.0000**	[N]	**7.3627**
49345.57[FV]	FV=49,345.5700				
[N]	N=**7.3627**				

TI BA II Plus		SHORTCUT	
Keystrokes	*Display*		
8[I/Y]	I/Y=8.0000	*i*	8.0000
0[PMT]	PMT=0.0000	PV	−28,000.0000
28000[+/−][PV]	PV=−28,000.0000	PMT	0.0000
49345.57 [FV]	FV=49,345.5700	FV	49,345.5700
[CPT][N]	N=**7.3627**	*n*	**7.3627**

NOTE: When solving for [n] on the HP 12C, only integers (whole numbers) are displayed as a solution. The HP 12C calculator cannot solve for non-integers (numbers with decimals). Therefore, your answer may be incorrect and will not match the answers of other calculators. For example, the HP 12C will give a result of n = 8.0000 for the above problem. This result will not happen with the other four calculators.

B. TERM CALCULATION—COMPOUNDED MONTHLY

Today, Willis put all of his cash into an account earning an annual interest rate of 5% compounded monthly. Assuming he makes no withdrawals from or additions to this account, approximately how many years must Willis wait to double his money? (rounded to the nearest .00) (Suggestion: Use $1 as the amount to be invested.)

HP 17bII/HP 17bII+		HP 12C		HP 10BII/HP 10BII+	
Keystrokes	*Display*	*Keystrokes*	*Display*	*Keystrokes*	*Display*
[FIN]	SELECT A MENU	5 [ENTER]	5.0000	5 [÷]	5.0000
[TVM]	1 P/YR END MODE	12 [÷][i]	0.4167	12 [=][I/YR]	0.4167
5 [÷]	5.0000÷	0 [PMT]	0.0000	0 [PMT]	0.0000
12 [=][I%YR]	I%YR=0.4167	1 [CHS][PV]	–1.0000	1 [+/–][PV]	–1.0000
0 [PMT]	PMT=0.0000	2 [FV]	2.0000	2 [FV]	2.0000
1 [+/–][PV]	PV=–1.0000	[n]	167.0000	[N]	166.7017
2 [FV]	FV=2.0000	[ENTER]	167.0000	[÷] 12 [=]	**13.8918**
[N]	N=166.7017	12 [÷]	**13.9167**		
[÷] 12 [=]	**13.8918**				

TI BA II Plus		SHORTCUT	
Keystrokes	*Display*		
5 [÷]	5.0000	*i*	.4167 (5 ÷ 12)
12 [=][I/Y]	I/Y=0.4167	PV	–1.0000
0 [PMT]	PMT=0.0000	PMT	0.0000
1 [+/–][PV]	PV=–1.0000	FV	2.0000
2 [FV]	FV=2.0000	*n*	166.7017
[CPT][N]	N=166.7017	÷ 12	**13.8918**
[÷] 12 [=]	**13.8918**		

NOTE: As previously stated, when solving for [n] on the HP 12C, only integers (whole numbers) are displayed as a solution. The HP 12C calculator cannot solve for non-integers (numbers with decimals). In this particular problem, the solution returned by the HP 12C is not the correct answer, however it is close.

Using the solution of 13.9167 for [n] returned by the HP 12C, when calculating the FV, you do not get 2.00 as the future value as you would expect. Instead, the FV is calculated as 2.0025, because the [n] is rounded. This can be verified by adding the following keystrokes to the end of the problem: 167[n], [FV] and the calculator will display 2.0025.

RULE OF 72: The Rule of 72 states that by dividing 72 by the interest rate, you will get a reasonable approximation of the number of years it will take for your money to double. For example: 72 divided by 10 equals 7.2 years. From the above calculation, the exact answer is 6.9603 years.

V. ANNUITIES

A. FUTURE VALUE OF AN ORDINARY ANNUITY (END MODE)—COMPOUNDED ANNUALLY

Hector Cushman has been investing $2,000 at the end of each year for the past 18 years in an equity mutual fund. How much is the fund worth now assuming he has earned 8.5% compounded annually on his investment?

HP 17bII/HP 17bII+		HP 12C		HP 10BII/HP 10BII+	
Keystrokes	*Display*	*Keystrokes*	*Display*	*Keystrokes*	*Display*
[FIN]	SELECT A MENU	18 [n]	18.0000	18 [N]	18.0000
[TVM]	1 P/YR END MODE	8.5 [i]	8.5000	8.5 [I/YR]	8.5000
18 [N]	N=18.0000	0 [PV]	0.0000	0 [PV]	0.0000
8.5 [I%YR]	I%YR=8.5000	2000 [CHS][PMT]	−2,000.0000	2000[+/−][PMT]	−2,000.0000
0 [PV]	PV=0.0000	[FV]	**78,645.9908**	[FV]	**78,645.9908**
2000 [+/−][PMT]	PMT=−2,000.0000				
[FV]	FV=**78,645.9908**				

TI BA II Plus		SHORTCUT	
Keystrokes	*Display*		
18 [N]	N=18.0000	n	18.0000
8.5 [I/Y]	I/Y=8.5000	i	8.5000
0 [PV]	PV=0.0000	PV	0.0000
2000 [+/−][PMT]	PMT=−2,000.0000	PMT_{OA}	−2,000.0000
[CPT][FV]	FV=**78,645.9908**	FV	**78,645.9908**

NOTE: The description PMT_{OA} indicates the payment of an ordinary annuity. An annuity due would be denoted as PMT_{AD}.

B. FUTURE VALUE OF AN ANNUITY DUE (BEGIN MODE)—COMPOUNDED ANNUALLY

Russell has been investing $5,000 at the beginning of each year for the past 23 years. How much has he accumulated assuming he has earned 6% compounded annually on his investment?

HP 17bII/HP 17bII+		HP 12C		HP 10BII/HP 10BII+	
Keystrokes	*Display*	*Keystrokes*	*Display*	*Keystrokes*	*Display*
[FIN]	SELECT A MENU	[g][BEG]	0.0000 BEGIN	[■][BEG/END]	0.0000 BEGIN
[TVM]	1 P/YR END MODE	23 [n]	23.0000	23 [N]	23.0000
[OTHER]	1 P/YR END MODE	6 [i]	6.0000	6 [I/YR]	6.0000
[BEG]	1 P/YR BEGIN MODE	0 [PV]	0.0000	0 [PV]	0.0000
[EXIT]	1 P/YR BEGIN MODE	5000 [CHS][PMT]	–5,000.0000	5000 [+/–][PMT]	–5,000.0000
23 [N]	N=23.0000	[FV]	**249,077.8868**	[FV]	**249,077.8868**
6 [I%YR]	I%YR=6.0000	[g][END][CLX]	0.0000	[■][BEG/END][C]	0.0000
0[PV]	PV=0.0000				
5000 [+/–][PMT]	PMT=–5,000.0000				
[FV]	FV=**249,077.8868**				
[OTHER]	1 P/YR BEGIN MODE				
[END]	1 P/YR END MODE				
[EXIT][EXIT]					
[EXIT][CLR]	0.0000				

TI BA II Plus		SHORTCUT	
Keystrokes	*Display*		
[2nd][BGN]	END	Begin Mode	
[2nd][SET]	BGN	n	23.0000
[CE/C]	0.0000	i	6.0000
23 [N]	N=23.0000	PV	0.0000
6 [I/Y]	I/Y=6.0000	PMT_{AD}	–5,000.0000
0 [PV]	PV=0.0000	FV	**249,077.8868**
5000 [+/–][PMT]	PMT=–5,000.0000		
[CPT][FV]	FV=**249,077.8868**		
[CE/C]	0.0000		
[2nd][BGN]	BGN		
[2nd][SET]	END		
[CE/C]	0.0000		

NOTE: The description PMT_{AD} indicates the payment of an annuity due. Make sure your calculator is in "begin mode" when calculating any type of annuity due calculation.

C.   PRESENT VALUE OF AN ORDINARY ANNUITY (END MODE)—COMPOUNDED ANNUALLY

Stewart expects to receive $9,000 at the end of each of the next 4 years from a trust fund. His opportunity cost is 7% compounded annually. What are these payments worth today?

HP 17bII/HP 17bII+		HP 12C		HP 10BII/HP 10BII+	
Keystrokes	*Display*	*Keystrokes*	*Display*	*Keystrokes*	*Display*
[FIN]	SELECT A MENU	4 [n]	4.0000	4 [N]	4.0000
[TVM]	1 P/YR END MODE	7 [i]	7.0000	7 [I/YR]	7.0000
4 [N]	N=4.0000	0 [FV]	0.0000	0 [FV]	0.0000
7 [I%YR]	I%YR=7.0000	9000 [PMT]	9,000.0000	9000 [PMT]	9,000.0000
0 [FV]	FV=0.0000	[PV]	−30,484.9013	[PV]	−30,484.9013
9000 [PMT]	PMT=9,000.0000				
[PV]	PV=−30,484.9013				

TI BA II Plus		SHORTCUT	
Keystrokes	*Display*		
4 [N]	N=4.0000	n	4.0000
7 [I/Y]	I/Y=7.0000	i	7.0000
0 [FV]	FV=0.0000	FV	0.0000
9000 [PMT]	PMT=9,000.0000	PMT_{OA}	9,000.0000
[CPT][PV]	PV=−30,484.9013	PV	−30,484.9013

D. PRESENT VALUE OF AN ORDINARY ANNUITY (END MODE)— COMPOUNDED SEMIANNUALLY

Jim, who was injured in an automobile accident, won a judgment that provides him $3,500 at the end of each 6-month period for the next 6 years. If the escrow account that holds Jim's settlement award earns an average annual rate of 5% compounded semiannually, how much was the defendant initially required to deposit so that Jim would be compensated for his injuries?

HP 17bII/HP 17bII+		HP 12C		HP 10BII/HP 10BII+	
Keystrokes	*Display*	*Keystrokes*	*Display*	*Keystrokes*	*Display*
[FIN]	SELECT A MENU	6 [ENTER]	6.0000	6 [x]	6.0000
[TVM]	1 P/YR END MODE	2 [x][n]	12.0000	2 [=][N]	12.0000
6 [x]	6.0000x	5 [ENTER]	5.0000	5 [÷]	5.0000
2 [=][N]	N=12.0000	2 [÷][i]	2.5000	2 [=][I/YR]	2.5000
5 [÷]	5.0000÷	3500 [PMT]	3,500.0000	3500 [PMT]	3,500.0000
2 [=][I%YR]	I%YR=2.5000	0 [FV]	0.0000	0 [FV]	0.0000
3500 [PMT]	PMT=3,500.0000	[PV]	–35,902.1761	[PV]	–35,902.1761
0 [FV]	FV=0.0000				
[PV]	PV=–35,902.1761				

TI BA II Plus		SHORTCUT	
Keystrokes	*Display*		
6 [x]	6.0000	*n*	12.0000 (6 × 2)
2 [=][N]	N=12.0000	*i*	2.5000 (5 ÷ 2)
5 [÷]	5.0000	PMT	3,500.0000
2 [=][I/Y]	I/Y=2.5000	FV	0.0000
3500 [PMT]	PMT=3,500.0000	PV	–35,902.1761
0 [FV]	FV=0.0000		
[CPT][PV]	PV=–35,902.1761		

E. PRESENT VALUE OF AN ANNUITY DUE (BEGIN MODE)—COMPOUNDED ANNUALLY

Joan wants to withdraw $10,000 at the beginning of each year for the next 9 years. She wants to have $50,000 left at the end of the 9 years. She expects to earn 4% compounded annually on her investment. What lump sum should Joan deposit today?

HP 17bII/HP 17bII+		HP 12C		HP 10BII/HP 10BII+	
Keystrokes	*Display*	*Keystrokes*	*Display*	*Keystrokes*	*Display*
[FIN]	SELECT A MENU	[g][BEG]	0.0000 BEGIN	[■][BEG/END]	0.0000 BEGIN
[TVM]	1 P/YR END MODE	9 [n]	9.0000	9 [N]	9.0000
[OTHER]	1 P/YR END MODE	4 [i]	4.0000	4 [I/YR]	4.0000
[BEG]	1 P/YR BEGIN MODE	10000[PMT]	10,000.0000	10000 [PMT]	10,000.0000
[EXIT]	1 P/YR BEGIN MODE	50000[FV]	50,000.0000	50000 [FV]	50,000.0000
9 [N]	N=9.0000	[PV]	−112,456.7855	[PV]	−112,456.7855
4 [I%YR]	I%YR=4.0000	[g][END][CLX]	0.0000	[■][C ALL]	0.0000 BEGIN
10000 [PMT]	PMT=10,000.0000			[■][BEG/END]	0.0000
50000 [FV]	FV=50,000.0000				
[PV]	PV=−112,456.7855				
[OTHER]	1 P/YR BEGIN MODE				
[END]	1 P/YR END MODE				
[EXIT][EXIT]					
[EXIT][CLR]	0.0000				

TI BA II Plus		SHORTCUT	
Keystrokes	*Display*		
[2nd][BGN]	END	Begin Mode	
[2nd][SET]	BGN	*n*	9.0000
[CE/C]	0.0000	*i*	4.0000
9 [N]	N=9.0000	PMT	10,000.0000
4 [I/Y]	I/Y=4.0000	FV	50,000.0000
10000 [PMT]	PMT=10,000.0000	PV_{AD}	−112,456.7855
50000 [FV]	FV=50,000.0000		
[CPT][PV]	PV=−112,456.7855		
[CE/C]	0.0000		
[2nd][BGN]	BGN		
[2nd][SET]	END		
[CE/C]	0.0000		

NOTE: The description PV_{AD} indicates the present value of an annuity due. Make sure your calculator is in "begin mode" when calculating annuity due problems.

F. PRESENT VALUE OF AN ANNUITY DUE (BEGIN MODE)—COMPOUNDED MONTHLY

Michelle wants to withdraw $4,200 at the beginning of each month for the next 5 years. She expects to earn 6% compounded monthly on her investments. What lump sum should she deposit today?

HP 17bII/HP 17bII+		HP 12C		HP 10BII/HP 10BII+	
Keystrokes	*Display*	*Keystrokes*	*Display*	*Keystrokes*	*Display*
[FIN]	SELECT A MENU	[g][BEG]	0.0000$_{BEGIN}$	[■][BEG/END]	0.0000$_{BEGIN}$
[TVM]	1 P/YR END MODE	5 [ENTER]	5.0000	5 [x]	5.0000
[OTHER]	1 P/YR END MODE	12 [x][n]	60.0000	12 [=][N]	60.0000
[BEG]	1 P/YR BEGIN MODE	6 [ENTER]	6.0000	6 [÷]	6.0000
[EXIT]	1 P/YR BEGIN MODE	12 [÷][i]	0.5000	12 [=][I/YR]	0.5000
5 [x]	5.0000x	4200 [PMT]	4,200.0000	4200 [PMT]	4,200.0000
12 [=][N]	N=60.0000	0 [FV]	0.0000	0 [FV]	0.0000
6 [÷]	6.0000÷	[PV]	–218,333.5919	[PV]	–218,333.5919
12 [=][I%YR]	I%YR=0.5000	[g][END][CLX]	0.0000	[■] [C ALL]	0.0000$_{BEGIN}$
4200 [PMT]	PMT=4,200.0000			[■][BEG/END]	0.0000
0 [FV]	FV=0.0000				
[PV]	PV=**–218,333.5919**				
[OTHER]	1 P/YR BEGIN MODE				
[END]	1 P/YR END MODE				
[EXIT][EXIT]					
[EXIT][CLR]	0.0000				

TI BA II Plus		SHORTCUT	
Keystrokes	*Display*		
[2nd][BGN]	END	Begin Mode	
[2nd][SET]	BGN	n	60.0000 (5 × 12)
[CE/C]	0.0000	i	0.5000 (6 ÷ 12)
5 [x]	5.0000	PMT	4,200.0000
12 [=][N]	N=60.0000	FV	0.0000
6 [÷]	6.0000	PV$_{AD}$	**–218,333.5919**
12 [=][I/Y]	I/Y=0.5000		
4200 [PMT]	PMT=4,200.0000		
0 [FV]	FV=0.0000		
[CPT][PV]	PV=**–218,333.5919**		
[CE/C]	0.0000		
[2nd][BGN]	BGN		
[2nd][SET]	END		
[CE/C]	0.0000		

G.   ANNUITY DUE (BEGIN MODE) WITH LUMP SUM DEPOSIT—COMPOUNDED MONTHLY

Alex received an inheritance of $500,000. He wants to withdraw equal periodic payments at the beginning of each month for the next 15 years. He expects to earn 7% compounded monthly on his investments. How much can he receive each month?

HP 17bII/HP 17bII+		HP 12C		HP 10BII/HP 10BII+	
Keystrokes	*Display*	*Keystrokes*	*Display*	*Keystrokes*	*Display*
[FIN]	SELECT A MENU	[g][BEG]	0.0000$_{BEGIN}$	[■][BEG/END]	0.0000$_{BEGIN}$
[TVM]	1 P/YR END MODE	15 [ENTER]	15.0000	15 [x]	15.0000
[OTHER]	1 P/YR END MODE	12 [x][n]	180.0000	12 [=][N]	180.0000
[BEG]	1 P/YR BEGIN MODE	7 [ENTER]	7.0000	7 [÷]	7.0000
[EXIT]	1 P/YR BEGIN MODE	12 [÷][i]	0.5833	12 [=][I/YR]	0.5833
15 [x]	15.0000x	500000 [CHS][PV]	−500,000.0000	500000 [+/−][PV]	−500,000.0000
12 [=][N]	N=180.0000	0 [FV]	0.0000	0 [FV]	0.0000
7 [÷]	7.0000÷	[PMT]	**4,468.0776**	[PMT]	**4,468.0776**
12 [=][I%YR]	I%YR=0.5833	[g][END][CLX]	0.0000	[■][C ALL]	0.0000$_{BEGIN}$
500000 [+/−][PV]	PV=−500,000.0000			[■][BEG/END]	0.0000
0 [FV]	FV=0.0000				
[PMT]	PMT=**4,468.0776**				
[OTHER]	1 P/YR BEGIN MODE				
[END]	1 P/YR END MODE				
[EXIT][EXIT]					
[EXIT][CLR]	0.0000				

TI BA II Plus		SHORTCUT	
Keystrokes	*Display*		
[2nd][BGN]	END	Begin Mode	
[2nd][SET]	BGN	n	180.0000 (15 × 12)
[CE/C]	0.0000	i	0.5833 (7 ÷ 12)
15 [x]	15.0000	PV	−500,000.0000
12 [=][N]	N=180.0000	FV	0.0000
7 [÷]	7.0000	PMT$_{AD}$	**4,468.0776**
12 [=][I/Y]	I/Y=0.5833		
500000 [+/−]	−500,000		
[PV]	PV=−500,000.0000		
0 [FV]	FV=0.0000		
[CPT][PMT]	PMT=**4,468.0776**		
[CE/C]	0.0000		
[2nd][BGN]	BGN		
[2nd][SET]	END		
[CE/C]	0.0000		

H. PRESENT VALUE OF INFLATION-ADJUSTED RETIREMENT NEEDS OF AN ANNUITY DUE (BEGIN MODE)

Billy and Marlene are ready to retire. They want to receive the equivalent of $25,000 in today's dollars at the beginning of each year for the next 20 years. They assume inflation will average 2% over the long run, and they can earn 8% compounded annually on investments. (The inflation-adjusted formula is $\{[(1 + r) \div (1 + i)] - 1\} \times 100$, where r is the nominal rate of return and i is the annual rate of inflation.) What lump sum do they need to invest today to attain their goal?

HP 17bII/HP 17bII+		HP 12C		HP 10BII/HP 10BII+	
Keystrokes	*Display*	*Keystrokes*	*Display*	*Keystrokes*	*Display*
[FIN]	SELECT A MENU	[g][BEG]	0.0000 BEGIN	[■][BEG/END]	0.0000 BEGIN
[TVM]	1 P/YR END MODE	20 [n]	20.0000	20 [N]	20.0000
[OTHER]	1 P/YR END MODE	1.08 [ENTER]	1.0800	1.08 [÷]	1.0800
[BEG]	1 P/YR BEGIN MODE	1.02 [÷]	1.0588	1.02 [–]	1.0588
[EXIT]	1 P/YR BEGIN MODE	1 [–]	0.0588	1 [x]	0.0588
20 [N]	N=20.0000	100 [x][i]	5.8824	100 [=][I/YR]	5.8824
1.08 [÷]	1.0800÷	25000 [PMT]	25,000.0000	25000 [PMT]	25,000.0000
1.02 [–]	1.0588–	0 [FV]	0.0000	0 [FV]	0.0000
1 [x]	0.0588x	[PV]	–306,536.6925	[PV]	–306,536.6925
100 [=][I%YR]	I%YR=5.8824	[g][END][CLX]	0.0000	[■] [C ALL]	0.0000 BEGIN
25000 [PMT]	PMT=25,000.0000			[■][BEG/END]	0.0000
0 [FV]	FV=0.0000				
[PV]	PV=–306,536.6925				
[OTHER]	1 P/YR BEGIN MODE				
[END]	1 P/YR END MODE				
[EXIT][EXIT]					
[EXIT][CLR]	0.0000				

TI BA II Plus		SHORTCUT	
Keystrokes	*Display*		
[2nd][BGN]	END	Begin Mode	
[2nd][SET]	BGN	n	20.0000
[CE/C]	0.0000	PMT	25,000.0000
20 [N]	N=20.0000	i	5.8824
1.08 [÷]	1.0800		$[(1.08 \div 1.02) - 1] \times 100$
1.02 [–]	1.0588	FV	0.0000
1 [x]	0.0588	PV_{AD}	**–306,536.6925**
100 [=][I/Y]	I/Y=5.8824		
25000 [PMT]	PMT=25,000.0000		
0 [FV]	FV=0.0000		
[CPT][PV]	PV=–306,536.6925		
[CE/C]	0.0000		
[2nd][BGN]	BGN		
[2nd][SET]	END		
[CE/C]	0.0000		

I.   PRESENT VALUE OF INFLATION-ADJUSTED ANNUITY DUE (BEGIN MODE)—COMPOUNDED ANNUALLY

James needs an income stream equivalent to $60,000 in today's dollars at the beginning of each year for the next 15 years to maintain his standard of living. He assumes inflation will average 3% over the long run, and he can earn 8.5% compounded annually on investments. What lump sum does James need to invest today to fund his needs?

HP 17bII/HP 17bII+		HP 12C		HP 10BII/HP 10BII+	
Keystrokes	*Display*	*Keystrokes*	*Display*	*Keystrokes*	*Display*
[FIN]	SELECT A MENU	[g][BEG]	0.0000 BEGIN	[■][BEG/END]	0.0000 BEGIN
[TVM]	1 P/YR END MODE	15 [n]	15.0000	15 [N]	15.0000
[OTHER]	1 P/YR END MODE	1.085 [ENTER]	1.0850	1.085 [÷]	1.0850
[BEG]	1 P/YR BEGIN MODE	1.03 [÷]	1.0534	1.03 [–]	1.0534
[EXIT]	1 P/YR BEGIN MODE	1 [–]	0.0534	1 [x]	0.0534
15 [N]	N=15.0000	100 [x][i]	5.3398	100 [=][I/YR]	5.3398
1.085 [÷]	1.0850÷	60000 [PMT]	60,000.0000	60000 [PMT]	60,000.0000
1.03 [–]	1.0534–	0 [FV]	0.0000	0 [FV]	0.0000
1 [x]	0.0534x	[PV]	**–641,222.7302**	[PV]	**–641,222.7302**
100 [=][I%YR]	I%YR=5.3398	[g][END][CLX]	0.0000	[■] [C ALL]	0.0000 BEGIN
60000 [PMT]	PMT=60,000.0000			[■][BEG/END]	0.0000
0 [FV]	FV=0.0000				
[PV]	PV=**–641,222.7302**				
[OTHER]	1 P/YR BEGIN MODE				
[END]	1 P/YR END MODE				
[EXIT][EXIT]					
[EXIT][CLR]	0.0000				

TI BA II Plus		SHORTCUT	
Keystrokes	*Display*		
[2ⁿᵈ][BGN]	END	Begin Mode	
[2ⁿᵈ][SET]	BGN	n	15.0000
[CE/C]	0.0000	PMT	60,0000.0000
15 [N]	N=15.0000	i	5.3398
1.085 [÷]	1.0850		$[(1.085 \div 1.03)-1] \times 100$
1.03 [–]	1.0534	FV	0.0000
1 [x]	0.0534	PV_{AD}	**–641,222.7302**
100 [=][I/Y]	I/Y=5.3398		
60000 [PMT]	PMT=60,000.0000		
0 [FV]	FV=0.0000		
[CPT][PV]	PV=**–641,222.7302**		
[CE/C]	0.0000		
[2ⁿᵈ][BGN]	BGN		
[2ⁿᵈ][SET]	END		
[CE/C]	0.0000		

VI.   SERIAL PAYMENTS

A.   INTRODUCTION

A serial payment is a term of art. A term of art means that the words have a particular and specific meaning within the profession, such that professionals understand it. It is a payment that increases at some constant rate (usually the inflation rate) on an annual (ordinarily) basis. There are many situations where it is more affordable or comfortable to increase payments on an annual basis since the payor expects to have increases in cash flows or earnings to make those increasing payments (e.g., life insurance, education needs, retirement needs).

Serial payments differ from fixed annuity payments (both ordinary and annuity due payments) in that serial payments are not a fixed amount per year. The result is that the initial serial payment is less than its respective annuity due or ordinary annuity payment. The last serial payment will obviously be greater than the last respective fixed annuity payment, but will have the same purchasing power as the first serial payment.

B.   EXAMPLE 1: SERIAL PAYMENTS TO ACHIEVE A FUTURE SUM— COMPOUNDED ANNUALLY

John wants to start his own business in 6 years. He needs to accumulate $200,000 (today's dollars) in 6 years to sufficiently finance his business. He assumes inflation will average 2.5%, and he can earn a 7.5% compound annual after-tax return on investments. What serial payment should John invest at the end of the first year to attain his goal?

HP 17bII/HP 17bII+		HP 12C		HP 10BII/HP 10BII+	
Keystrokes	*Display*	*Keystrokes*	*Display*	*Keystrokes*	*Display*
[FIN]	SELECT A MENU	200000[FV]	200,000.0000	200000[FV]	200,000.0000
[TVM]	1 P/YR END MODE	6 [n]	6.0000	6 [N]	6.0000
200000[FV]	FV=200,000.0000	0 [PV]	0.0000	0 [PV]	0.0000
6 [N]	N=6.0000	1.075 [ENTER]	1.0750	1.075 [÷]	1.0750
0 [PV]	PV=0.0000	1.025 [÷]	1.0488	1.025 [−]	1.0488
1.075 [÷]	1.0750÷	1 [−]	0.0488	1 [x]	0.0488
1.025 [−]	1.0488−	100 [x][i]	4.8780	100 [=][I/YR]	4.8780
1 [x]	0.0488x	[PMT]	−29,493.8556	[PMT]	−29,493.8556
100 [=][I%YR]	I%YR=4.8780	1.025 [x]	**−30,231.2020**	[x] 1.025 [=]	**−30,231.2020**
[PMT]	−29,493.8556				
[x] 1.025 [=]	**−30,231.2020**				

(Continued on next page)

TI BA II Plus		SHORTCUT	
Keystrokes	*Display*		
200000 [FV]	FV=200,000.0000	FV	200,000.0000
6 [N]	N=6.0000	n	6.0000
0 [PV]	PV=0.0000	i	4.8780
1.075 [÷]	1.0750		[(1.075 ÷ 1.025)−1]x100
1.025 [−]	1.0488	PV	0.0000
1 [x]	0.0488	PMT	−29,493.8556
100 [=][I/Y]	I/Y=4.8780	x 1.025	**−30,231.2020**
[CPT][PMT]	−29,493.8556		
[x] 1.025 [=]	**−30,231.2020**		

C. EXAMPLE 2: SERIAL PAYMENTS TO ACHIEVE A FUTURE SUM— COMPOUNDED ANNUALLY

Sarah wants to start her own business in 6 years. She needs to accumulate $200,000 (today's dollars) in 6 years to sufficiently finance her business. She assumes inflation will average 2.5%, and she can earn a 7.5% compound annual after-tax return on investments. What will be Sarah's payment at the end of the second year?

HP 17bII/HP 17bII+		HP 12C		HP 10BII/HP 10BII+	
Keystrokes	*Display*	*Keystrokes*	*Display*	*Keystrokes*	*Display*
[FIN]	SELECT A MENU	200,000[FV]	200,000.0000	200000[FV]	200,000.0000
[TVM]	1 P/YR END MODE	6 [n]	6.0000	6 [N]	6.0000
200000[FV]	FV=200,000.0000	0 [PV]	0.0000	0 [PV]	0.0000
6 [N]	N=6.0000	1.075 [ENTER]	1.075	1.075 [÷]	1.075
0 [PV]	PV=0.0000	1.025 [÷]	1.0488	1.025 [–]	1.0488
1.075 [÷]	1.0750÷	1 [–]	0.0488	1 [x]	0.0488
1.025 [–]	1.0488–	100 [x][i]	4.8780	100 [=][I/YR]	4.8780
1 [x]	0.0488x	[PMT]	–29,493.8556	[PMT]	–29,493.8556
100 [=][I%YR]	I%YR=4.8780	[ENTER]	–29,493.8556	[x] 1.025 [=]	**–30,231.2020**
[PMT]	–29,493.8556	1.025 [x]	**–30,231.2020**	[x] 1.025 [=]	**–30,986.9820**
[x] 1.025 [=]	**–30,231.2020**	1.025 [x]	**–30,986.9820**		
[x] 1.025 [=]	**–30,986.9820**				

TI BA II Plus		SHORTCUT		
Keystrokes	*Display*			
200000 [FV]	FV=200,000.0000	FV	200,000.0000	
6 [N]	N=6.0000	*n*	6.0000	
0 [PV]	PV=0.0000	*i*	4.8780	
1.075 [÷]	1.0750		[(1.075÷1.025)–1]×100	
1.025 [–]	1.0488	PV	0.0000	
1 [x]	0.0488	PMT	–29,493.8556	
100 [=][I/Y]	I/Y=4.8780	x 1.025	**–30,231.2020**	
[CPT][PMT]	–29,493.8556	x 1.025	**–30,986.9820**	
[x] 1.025 [=]	**–30,231.2020**			
[x] 1.025 [=]	**–30,986.9820**			

VII.   MORTGAGES

A.   MORTGAGES—MONTHLY PAYMENT

David Cray recently purchased a house for $350,000. He made a down payment of 20% and financed the balance over 30 years at 5%. How much will David's monthly mortgage payment be?

HP 17bII/HP 17bII+	
Keystrokes	*Display*
[FIN]	SELECT A MENU
[TVM]	1 P/YR END MODE
30 [x]	30.0000x
12 [=][N]	N=360.0000
5 [÷]	5.0000÷
12 [=][I/YR]	I%YR=0.4167
0 [FV]	FV=0.0000
350000 [x]	350,000.0000x
.8 [=][PV]	PV=280,000.0000
[PMT]	PMT=−1,503.1005

HP 12C	
Keystrokes	*Display*
30 [ENTER]	30.0000
12 [x][n]	360.0000
5 [ENTER]	5.0000
12 [÷][i]	0.4167
0 [FV]	0.0000
350000[ENTER]	350,000.0000
.8 [x][PV]	280,000.0000
[PMT]	**−1,503.1005**

HP 10BII/HP 10BII+	
Keystrokes	*Display*
30 [x]	30.0000
12 [=][N]	360.0000
5 [÷]	5.0000
12 [=][I/YR]	0.4167
0 [FV]	0.0000
350000 [x]	350,000.0000
.8 [=][PV]	280,000.0000
[PMT]	**−1,503.1005**

TI BA II Plus	
Keystrokes	*Display*
30 [x]	30.0000
12 [=][N]	N=360.0000
5 [÷]	5.0000
12 [=][I/Y]	I/Y=0.4167
0 [FV]	FV=0.0000
350000 [x]	350,000.0000
.8 [=][PV]	PV=280,000.0000
[CPT][PMT]	PMT=−1,503.1005

SHORTCUT	
PV	280,000.0000
	(350,000 × .8)
n	360.0000
i	.4167 (5 ÷ 12)
FV	0.0000
PMT	**−1,503.1005**

B.   EXAMPLE 1: MORTGAGES—INTEREST

David Cray recently purchased his house for $350,000. He made a down payment of 20% and financed the balance over 30 years at 5%. If David's first payment is due on July 1st of the current year, how much interest can he deduct in the current year? How much interest can David deduct next year? Do not clear your calculator after each step. This is a progressive calculation.

First Method:

HP 17bII/HP 17bII+		HP 12C		HP 10BII/HP 10BII+	
Keystrokes	*Display*	*Keystrokes*	*Display*	*Keystrokes*	*Display*
Step 1: Calculate the monthly payment.					
[■][CLR DATA]	0.0000	[f][REG]	0.0000	[■][C ALL]	0.0000
[FIN]	SELECT A MENU	350000 [ENTER]	350,000.0000	350000 [x]	350,000.0000
[TVM]	1 P/YR END MODE	.8 [x][PV]	280,000.0000	.8 [=][PV]	280,000.0000
350000 [x]	350,000.0000x	0 [FV]	0.0000	0 [FV]	0.0000
.8 [=][PV]	PV=280,000.0000	30 [ENTER]	30.0000	30 [x]	30.0000
0 [FV]	FV=0.0000	12 [x][n]	360.0000	12 [=][N]	360.0000
30 [x]	30.0000x	5 [ENTER]	5.0000	5 [÷]	5.0000
12 [=][N]	N=360.0000	12 [÷][i]	0.4167	12 [=][I/YR]	0.4167
5 [÷]	5.0000÷	[PMT]	**–1,503.1005**	[PMT]	**–1,503.1005**
12 [=][I%YR]	I%YR=0.4167				
[PMT]	PMT=**–1,503.1005**				
Step 2: Calculate the PV of the mortgage at the end of the current year. (6 payments paid)					
360[–]	360.0000–	360 [ENTER]	360.0000	360 [–]	360.0000
6 [=][N]	N=354.0000	6 [–][n]	354.0000	6 [=][N]	354.0000
[PV]	PV=**277,960.2524**	[PV]	**277,960.2524**	[PV]	**277,960.2524**
Step 3: Calculate the amount of deductible interest at the end of the current year.					
280000 [–]	280,000.0000–	280000 [ENTER]	280,000.0000	280000 [–]	280,000.0000
277960.2524 [=]	**2,039.7476**	277960.2524[–]	**2,039.7476**	277960.2524 [=]	**2,039.7476**
1,503.1005 [x]	1,503.1005x	1503.1005 [ENTER]	1,503.1005	1,503.1005 [x]	1,503.1005
6 [=][–]	9,018.6030–	6[x]	9,018.6030	6 [=][–]	9,018.6030
2039.7476 [=]	**6,978.8554**	2039.7476[–]	**6,978.8554**	2039.7476 [=]	**6,978.8554**
Step 4: Calculate the PV of the mortgage at the end of next year. (18 payments paid)					
360 [–]	360.0000–	360[ENTER]	360.0000	360 [–]	360.0000
18 [=][N]	N=342.0000	18[–][n]	342.0000	18 [=][N]	342.0000
[PV]	PV=**273,724.8721**	[PV]	**273,724.8721**	[PV]	**273,724.8721**
Step 5: Calculate the amount of deductible interest at the end of next year.					
277960.2524 [–]	277,960.2524–	277960.2524	277,960.2524	277960.2524 [–]	277,960.2524
273724.8721 [=]	**4,235.3803**	[ENTER]		273724.8721 [=]	**4,235.3803**
1503.1005[x]	1,503.1005x	273724.8721 [–]	**4,235.3803**	1503.1005 [x]	1,503.1005
12[=][–]	18,037.2060–	1503.1005[ENTER]	1,503.1005	12 [=][–]	18,037.2060
4235.1279[=]	**13,802.0781**	12[x]	18,037.2060	4235.1279 [=]	**13,802.0781**
		4235.1279[–]	**13,802.0781**		

TI BA II Plus		SHORTCUT	
Keystrokes	*Display*		
Step 1: Calculate the monthly payment.			
[2ⁿᵈ][CLR Work]	0.0000	PV	280,000.0000
350000 [x]	350,000.0000		(350,000 × .8)
.8 [=][PV]	PV=280,000.0000	*n*	360.0000
0 [FV]	FV=0.0000	*i*	.4167 (5 ÷ 12)
30 [x]	30.0000	FV	0.0000
12 [=][N]	N=360.0000	PMT	**–1,503.1005**
5 [÷]	5.0000		
12 [=][I/Y]	I/Y=0.4167		
[CPT][PMT]	PMT=**–1,503.1005**		
Step 2: Calculate the PV of the mortgage at the end of the current year. (6 payments paid)			
360 [–]	360.0000	360 [–]	360.0000
6 [=][N]	N=354.0000	6 [=] *n*	354.0000
[CPT][PV]	**PV=277,960.2524**	PV	**277,960.2524**
Step 3: Calculate the amount of deductible interest at the end of the current year.			
280000 [–]	280,000.0000	280,000[–]	280,000.0000
277960.2524 [=]	**2,039.7476**	277,960.2524 [=]	2,039.7476
1503.1005 [x]	1,503.1005	1,503.1005 [x]	1,503.1005
6 [=][–]	9,018.6030	6 [=][–]	9,018.6030
2039.7476 [=]	**6,978.8554**	2,039.7476 [=]	**6,978.8554**
Step 4: Calculate the PV of the mortgage at the end of next year. (18 payments paid)			
360 [–]	360.0000	360 [–]	360.0000
18 [=][N]	N=342.0000	18 [=] *n*	342.0000
[CPT][PV]	**PV=273,724.8721**	PV	**273,724.8721**
Step 5: Calculate the amount of deductible interest at the end of next year.			
277960.2524 [–]	277,960.2524	277,960.2524 [–]	277,960.2524
273724.8721 [=]	**4,235.3803**	273,724.8721 [=]	4,235.3803
1503.1005 [x]	1,503.1005	1,503.1005 [x]	1,503.1005
12 [=][–]	18,037.2060	12 [=][–]	18,037.2060
4235.1279 [=]	**13,802.0781**	4,235.1279 [=]	**13,802.0781**

Second Method:

HP 17bII/HP 17bII+		HP 12C		HP 10BII/HP 10BII+	
Keystrokes	*Display*	*Keystrokes*	*Display*	*Keystrokes*	*Display*
Step 1: Calculate the monthly payment.					
[■][CLR DATA]	0.0000	[f][REG]	0.0000	[■][C ALL]	0.0000
[FIN]	SELECT A MENU	350000 [ENTER]	350,000.0000	350000 [x]	350,000.0000
[TVM]	1 P/YR END MODE	.8 [x][PV]	280,000.0000	.8 [=][PV]	280,000.0000
350000 [x]	350,000.0000x	0 [FV]	0.0000	0 [FV]	0.0000
.8 [=][PV]	PV=280,000.0000	30 [ENTER]	30.0000	30 [x]	30.0000
0 [FV]	FV=0.0000	12 [x][n]	360.0000	12 [=][N]	360.0000
30 [x]	30.0000x	5 [ENTER]	5.0000	5 [÷]	5.0000
12 [=][N]	N=360.0000	12 [÷][i]	0.4167	12 [=][I/YR]	0.4167
5 [÷]	5.0000÷	[PMT]	**−1,503.1005**	[PMT]	**−1,503.1005**
12 [=][I%YR]	I%YR=0.4167				
[PMT]	PMT=−1,503.1005				
Step 2: Calculate the amount of deductible interest at the end of the current year (1ˢᵗ 6 months).					
[OTHER][AMRT] 6[#P][INT]	−6,978.8558	6[f] [AMORT]	−6,978.8558	1[INPUT] 6	6
				[■][AMORT]	1–6
				[=]	−2,039.7476
				[=]	−6,978.8558
Step 3: Calculate the amount of deductible interest at the end of next year (Payments 7 – 18).					
12[#P][INT]	−13,801.8262	12[f] [AMORT]	−13,801.8262	7[INPUT] 18	
				[■][AMORT]	7–18
				[=]	−4,235.3798
				[=]	−13,801.8262

TI BA II Plus		SHORTCUT	
Keystrokes	*Display*		
Step 1: Calculate the monthly payment.			
[2ⁿᵈ][CLR Work]	0.0000	PV	280,000.0000
350000 [x]	350,000.0000		(350,000 × .8)
.8 [=][PV]	PV=280,000.0000	*n*	360.0000
0 [FV]	FV=0.0000	*i*	.4167 (5 ÷ 12)
30 [x]	30.0000	FV	0.0000
12 [=][N]	N=360.0000	PMT	**–1,503.1005**
5 [÷]	5.0000		
12 [=][I/Y]	I/Y=0.4167		
[CPT][PMT]	PMT=–1,503.1005		
Step 2: Calculate the amount of deductible interest at the end of the current year (1ˢᵗ 6 months).			
[2ⁿᵈ][Amort]	P1=1.0000	N/A	
[2ⁿᵈ][CLR Work]	P1=1.0000		
1[ENTER][↓]	P2=1.0000		
6[ENTER][↓]	BAL=277,960.2528		
[↓]	PRN=–2,039.7472		
[↓]	INT=**–6,978.8558**		
Step 3: Calculate the amount of deductible interest at the end of next year (Payments 7 – 18).			
[2ⁿᵈ][Amort]	P1=1.0000	N/A	
[2ⁿᵈ][CLR Work]	P1=1.0000		
7[ENTER][↓]	P2=1.0000		
18[ENTER][↓]	BAL=273,724.8730		
[↓]	PRN=–4,235.3798		
[↓]	INT=**–13,801.8262**		

C. EXAMPLE 2: MORTGAGES—INTEREST

David Cray recently purchased his house for $350,000. He put down 20% and financed the balance over 30 years at 5%. How much interest will he pay over the life of the loan if he pays it as agreed?

HP 17bII/HP 17bII+		HP 12C		HP 10BII/HP 10BII+	
Keystrokes	*Display*	*Keystrokes*	*Display*	*Keystrokes*	*Display*
		Step 1: Calculate payment.			
[FIN]	SELECT A MENU	30 [ENTER]	30.0000	30 [x]	30.0000
[TVM]	1 P/YR END MODE	12 [x][n]	360.0000	12 [=][N]	360.0000
30 [x]	30.0000x	5 [ENTER]	5.0000	5 [÷]	5.0000
12 [=][N]	N=360.000	12 [÷][i]	0.4167	12 [=][I/YR]	0.4167
5 [÷]	5.0000÷	0 [FV]	0.0000	0 [FV]	0.0000
12 [=][I%YR]	I%YR=0.4167	350000[ENTER]	350,000.0000	350000 [x]	350,000.0000
0 [FV]	FV=0.0000	.8 [x][PV]	280,000.0000	.8 [=][PV]	280,000.0000
350000 [x]	350,000.0000x	[PMT]	**–1,503.1005**	[PMT]	**–1,503.1005**
.8 [=][PV]	PV=280,000.000				
[PMT]	PMT=**–1,503.1005**				
		Step 2: Calculate total payments and subtract principal.			
[+/–][x]	1,503.1005x	[CHS][ENTER]	1,503.1005	[+/–][x]	1,503.1005
360 [–]	541,116.1960–	360 [x]	541,116.1960	360[–]	541,116.1960
280000 [=]	**261,116.1960**	280000 [–]	**261,116.1960**	280000[=]	**261,116.1960**

TI BA II Plus		SHORTCUT	
Keystrokes	*Display*		
	Step 1: Calculate payment.		
30 [x]	30.0000	PV	280,000.0000 (350,000 × .8)
12 [=][N]	N=360.000	*n*	360.0000
5 [÷]	5.0000	*i*	.4167 (5 ÷ 12)
12 [=][I/Y]	I/Y=0.4167	FV	0.0000
0 [FV]	FV=0.0000	PMT	**1,503.1005**
350000 [x]	350,000.0000		
.8 [=][PV]	PV=280,000.0000		
[CPT][PMT]	PMT=**–1,503.1005**		
	Step 2: Calculate total payments and subtract principal.		
[+/–][x]	1,503.1005	360 x	541,116.1960
360 [–]	541,116.1960	280,000 –	**261,116.1960**
280000 [=]	**261,116.1960**		

VIII.   EDUCATION CALCULATIONS

A.   INTRODUCTION

There are numerous ways to calculate the required funding for a child's college education. Three possible methods for solving this problem are:

1.   The traditional method. (Section VIII – C)

2.   The uneven cash flow method. (Section VIII – D)

3.   The account balance method. (Section VIII – E)

Each of the methods relies on the inflation-adjusted discount rate to minimize the number of calculations. In most cases, the client's goal is to establish a savings schedule for the child's education. The following information is usually provided in these types of questions:

1.   The age of the child.

2.   The age the child will attend college (generally at age 18).

3.   The parents' after-tax earnings rate.

4.   The current cost of tuition, at the projected institution or category of schools, and the rate of increase. The rate of increase will be the rate of inflation used when calculating the inflation-adjusted discount rate. The rate is probably the long-term trend line for education cost.

5.   The CPI inflation rate. (Generally, this figure should not be used, because it does not represent an accurate rate of increase in the cost of college tuition.)

The education calculation problem will usually ask for an amount of money that must be saved each period to meet projected tuition costs. It is important to note that these types of problems could ask for the payments to be made over any time period, such as:

1.   Payments will begin today (i.e., an annuity due) and the last payment will be made when the child begins school.

2.   Same as "1" except payments begin 1 year from today (i.e., an ordinary annuity).

3.   Same as "1" except the last payment will be made at the beginning of the last year of college.

4.   Same as "3" except payments will begin 1 year from today (i.e., an ordinary annuity).

5.   Payments will be made over the next 10 years at the end of each year (or any other term).

These are five possible variations on how the payments might be made, however, there are certainly other possibilities.

The education calculation problem becomes even more complex when a second child of a different age is introduced into the calculation. When the calculation concerns multiple children, the uneven cash flow method is generally the easiest method for students to use.

B. EXAMPLE

Billy would like to plan for his son's college education. He would like his son, who was born today, to attend a private university for 4 years beginning at age 18. Tuition is currently $20,000 a year and has increased at an annual rate of 5%, while inflation has only increased at 2% per year. Billy can earn an after-tax rate of return of 8%. How much must Billy save at the end of each year if he would like to make his last payment at the beginning of his son's first year of college?

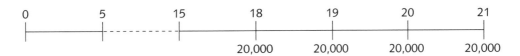

C. THE TRADITIONAL METHOD (NOTE: THIS CALCULATION IS COMPLETED IN 3 STEPS):

■ *Step 1 determines the present value of the 4 years of tuition at the end of year 17, using an inflation-adjusted interest rate.* (**NOTE:** *You must use this tuition amount in step 2.*)

■ *Step 2 determines the present value of the amount calculated in step 1 using an inflation-adjusted interest rate.*

■ *Step 3 determines the annual payments needed to fund college tuition costs. This step uses the actual after-tax return earned on the investments.* (**NOTE:** *This step is identical to the calculation of the payment for a mortgage.*)

HP 17bII/HP 17bII+		HP 12C		HP 10BII/HP 10BII+	
Keystrokes	*Display*	*Keystrokes*	*Display*	*Keystrokes*	*Display*
Step 1: Determine the present value of the 4 years of tuition at age 17.					
[FIN]	SELECT A MENU	20000 [PMT]	20,000.0000	20000 [PMT]	20,000.0000
[TVM]	1 P/YR END MODE	4 [n]	4.0000	4 [N]	4.0000
20000 [PMT]	PMT=20,000.000	0 [FV]	0.0000	0 [FV]	0.0000
4 [N]	N=4.0000	1.08[ENTER]	1.0800	1.08 [÷]	1.0800
0 [FV]	FV=0.0000	1.05 [÷]	1.0286	1.05 [–]	1.0286
1.08 [÷]	1.0800÷	1 [–]	0.0286	1 [x]	0.0286
1.05 [–]	1.0286	100[x][i]	2.8571	100 [=][I/YR]	2.8571
1 [x]	0.0286	[PV]	**–74,596.6340**	[PV]	**–74,596.6340**
100 [=][I%YR]	I%YR=2.8571				
[PV]	PV=**–74,596.6340**				
Step 2: Determine the present value of the lump sum calculated in step 1 assuming that the 4 years of the tuition is the future value.					
[+/–][FV]	FV=74,596.6340	[CHS][FV]	74,596.6340	[+/–][FV]	74,596.6340
17 [N]	N=17.0000	17[n]	17.0000	17 [N]	17.0000
0 [PMT]	PMT=0.0000	0 [PMT]	0.0000	0 [PMT]	0.0000
[PV]	PV=**–46,209.7344**	[PV]	**–46,209.7344**	[PV]	**–46,209.7344**
Step 3: Determine the annual payments needed to fund college tuition costs.					
[+/–][PV]	PV=46,209.7344	[CHS] [PV]	46,209.7344	[+/–][PV]	46,209.7344
18 [N]	N=18.0000	18 [n]	18.0000	18 [N]	18.0000
8 [I%YR]	I%YR=8.0000	8 [i]	8.0000	8 [I/YR]	8.0000
0 [FV]	FV=0.0000	0 [FV]	0.0000	0 [FV]	0.0000
[PMT]	PMT=**–4,930.6755**	[PMT]	**–4,930.6755**	[PMT]	**–4,930.6755**

TI BA II Plus		SHORTCUT	
Keystrokes	*Display*		
Step 1: Determine the present value of the 4 years of tuition at age 17.			
20000 [PMT]	PMT=20,000.000	PMT	20,000.0000
4 [N]	N=4.0000	n	4.0000
0 [FV]	FV=0.0000	i	2.8571
1.08 [÷]	1.0800		$[(1.08 \div 1.05)-1] \times 100$
1.05 [–]	1.0286	$PV_{OA@17}$	**–74,596.6340**
1 [x]	0.0286		
100 [=][I/Y]	I/Y=2.8571		
[CPT][PV]	PV=**–74,596.6340**		
Step 2: Determine the present value of the lump sum calculated in step 1 assuming that the 4 years of the tuition is the future value.			
[+/–][FV]	FV=74,596.6340	FV	74,596.6340
17 [N]	N=17.0000	n	17.0000
0 [PMT]	PMT=0.0000	PMT	0.0000
[CPT][PV]	PV=**–46,209.7344**	PV_0	**–46,209.7344**
Step 3: Determine the annual payments needed to fund college tuition costs.			
[+/–][PV]	PV=46,209.7344	PV_0	46,209.7344
18 [N]	N=18.0000	n	18.0000
8 [I/Y]	I/Y=8.0000	i	8.0000
0 [FV]	FV=0.0000	PMT_{OA}	**–4,930.6755**
[CPT][PMT]	PMT=**–4,930.6755**		

D. THE UNEVEN CASH FLOW METHOD

This method makes use of the uneven cash flow keys on your calculator. As you look at the timeline for this calculation, you should notice that there are two series of cash flows (a cash flow of $0 for periods 0 through 17 and a cash flow of $20,000 for periods 18 through 21). The first step of this approach determines the present value of the four years of tuition as of period zero. The first step accomplishes the same result as the first two steps in the Traditional Method. The second step of this method is identical to the third step of the Traditional Method.

HP 17bII/HP 17bII+		HP 12C		HP 10BII/HP 10BII+	
Keystrokes	*Display*	*Keystrokes*	*Display*	*Keystrokes*	*Display*
Step 1: Determine the cost of college tuition for the four year period, in today's dollars.					
[FIN]	SELECT A MENU	[f][CLX]	0.0000	[■][C ALL]	0.0000
[CFLO]	FLOW(0)=?	0[g][CF₀]	0.0000	0 [CFⱼ]	0.0000
[■] [CLR DATA]	CLEAR THE LIST?	18[g][Nⱼ]	18.0000	0 [CFⱼ]	0.0000
[YES]	FLOW(0)=?	20000[g][CFⱼ]	20,0000.0000	17[■][Nⱼ]	17.0000
0[INPUT]	FLOW(1)=?	4[g][Nⱼ]	4.0000	20000[CFⱼ]	20,0000.0000
	0.0000	1.08[ENTER]	1.0800	4[■][Nⱼ]	4.0000
0[INPUT]	#TIMES(1)=1	1.05[÷]	1.0286	1.08[÷]1.05[=]	1.0286
	1.0000	1[–]	0.0286	[–]1[x]100[I/YR]	2.8571
17[INPUT]	FLOW(2)=?	100[x][i]	2.8571	[■][NPV]	**46,209.7344**
	17.0000	[f][NPV]	**46,209.7344**		
20000[INPUT]	#TIMES(2)=1				
	1.0000				
4[INPUT]	FLOW(3)=?				
	4.0000				
[EXIT][CALC]	NPV, NUS, NFV NEED I%				
1.08[÷]1.05[–]	1.0286–				
1[=]	0.0286				
[x]100[=][I%]	I%=2.8571				
[NPV]	NPV=**46,209.7344**				
Step 2: Determine the annual payments needed to fund college tuition costs.					
[EXIT][EXIT]	46,209.7344	[PV]	46,209.7344	[PV]	46,209.7344
[TVM]	1 P/YR END MODE	18 [n]	18.0000	18 [N]	18.0000
46209.7344[PV]	PV=46,209.7344	8 [i]	8.0000	8 [I/YR]	8.0000
18 [N]	N=18.0000	0 [FV]	0.0000	0 [FV]	0.0000
8 [I%YR]	I%YR=8.0000	[PMT]	**–4,930.6755**	[PMT]	**–4,930.6755**
0 [FV]	FV=0.0000				
[PMT]	PMT=**–4,930.6755**				

TI BA II Plus		SHORTCUT	
Keystrokes	*Display*		
Step 1: Determine the future cost of college tuition for the four-year period, in today's dollars.			
[CF]	CF_0=(Old work)	$CF_{0 \text{ to } 17}$	0.0000
[2nd][CLR Work]	CF_0=0.0000	$CF_{18 \text{ to } 21}$	20,000.000
0[ENTER]	CF_0=0.0000	i	2.8571
[↓] 0 [ENTER]	C01=0.0000	NPV	**46,209.7344**
[↓] 17 [ENTER]	F01=17.0000		
[↓]20000[ENTER]	C02=20,000.0000		
[↓] 4 [ENTER]	F02=4.0000		
[NPV]	I=0.0000		
1.08[÷]1.05[–]	I=1.0286		
1[x]100[=][ENTER]	I=2.8571		
[↓] [CPT]	NPV=**46,209.7344**		
Step 2: Determine the annual payments needed to fund college tuition costs.			
[2nd][QUIT]		PV	46,209.7344
46209.7344[PV]	PV=46,209.7344	n	18.0000
18 [N]	N=18.0000	i	8.0000
8 [I/Y]	I/Y=8.0000	PMT_{OA}	**–4,930.6755**
0 [FV]	FV=0.0000		
[CPT][PMT]	PMT=**–4,930.6755**		

E.   THE ACCOUNT BALANCE METHOD

This approach requires three steps. The first step is to inflate the current cost of tuition by the tuition inflation rate for the number of years until the child begins college. The second step is to calculate the present value of an annuity due (BEGIN mode) for the number of years the child will attend college. You will use the inflation-adjusted discount rate for this second step. The amount which is calculated in step two is the amount which must be accumulated by the time the child goes to school. Step three determines the periodic payment that must be made to reach the account balance from step two.

HP 17bII/HP 17bII+		HP 12C		HP 10BII/HP 10BII+	
Keystrokes	*Display*	*Keystrokes*	*Display*	*Keystrokes*	*Display*
Step 1: Determine the future cost of college tuition for the first year of school.					
[FIN]	SELECT A MENU	[f][CLX]	0.0000	[■][C ALL]	0.0000
[TVM]	1 P/YR END MODE	20000[PV]	20,0000.0000	20000[PV]	20000.0000
20000 [PV]	PV=20,000.0000	18[n]	18.0000	18[N]	18.0000
18 [N]	N=18.0000	5[i]	5.0000	5[I/YR]	5.0000
5 [I%YR]	I%YR=5.0000	0[PMT]	0.0000	0[PMT]	0.0000
0 [PMT]	PMT=0.0000	[FV]	–48,132.3847	[FV]	–48,132.3847
[FV]	FV=**–48,132.3847**				
Step 2: Determine the account balance necessary to fund college education.					
[+/–][PMT]	PMT=48,132.3847	[CHS][PMT]	48,132.3847	[+/–][PMT]	48,132.3847
[OTHER][BEG]	1 P/YR BEGIN MODE	[g][BEG]	48,132.3847	[■][BEG/END]	48,132.3847
[EXIT]	1 P/YR BEGIN MODE	0[FV]	0.0000	0[FV]	0.0000
0[FV]	FV=0.0000	4[n]	4.0000	4[N]	4.0000
4[N]	N=4.0000	1.08[ENTER]	1.0800	1.08[÷]1.05[–]	1.0286
1.08[÷]1.05[–]	1.0286–	1.05[÷]	1.0286	1[x]100[=][I/YR]	2.8571
1[x]100[=][I%YR]	I%YR=2.8571	1[–]100[x][i]	2.8571	[PV]	**–184,654.9997**
[PV]	PV=**–184,654.9997**	[PV]	**–184,654.9997**		
Step 3: Determine the annual payment needed to fund college education.					
[+/–][FV]	FV=–184,654.9997	[g][END]	–184,654.9997	[■][BEG/END]	
[OTHER][END]	1 P/YR END MODE	[CHS][FV]	184,654.9997	[FV]	184,654.9997
[EXIT]	1 P/YR END MODE	18[n]	18.0000	18[N]	18.0000
18[N]	N=18.0000	8[i]	8.0000	8[I/YR]	8.0000
8[I%YR]	I%YR=8.0000	0[PV]	0.0000	0[PV]	0.0000
0[PV]	PV=0.0000	[PMT]	**–4,930.6755**	[PMT]	**–4,930.6755**
[PMT]	PMT=**–4,930.6755**				

TI BA II Plus		SHORTCUT	
Keystrokes	*Display*		
Step 1: Determine the future cost of college tuition for the first year of school.			
[2ⁿᵈ][CLR TVM]	0.0000	PV	20,000.0000
20000[PV]	PV=20,000.0000	n	18.0000
18[N]	N=18.0000	i	5.0000
5[I/Y]	I/Y=5.0000	PMT	0.0000
0[PMT]	PMT=0.0000	FV	**–48,132.3847**
[CPT][FV]	FV=**–48,132.3847**		
Step 2: Determine the account balance necessary to fund college education.			
[+/–][PMT]	PMT=48,132.3847	Begin Mode	
[2ⁿᵈ][BGN]	END	PMT_{AD}	48,132.3847
[2ⁿᵈ][SET]	BGN	n	4.0000
[CE/C]	0.0000	i	2.8571
0[FV]	FV=0.0000		$[((1.08 \div 1.05) - 1) \times 100]$
4[N]	N=4.0000	FV	0.0000
1.08[÷]1.05[–]	1.0286	PV_{AD}	**–184,654.9997**
1[x]100[=][I/Y]	I/Y=2.8571		
[CPT][PV]	PV=**–184,654.9997**		
Step 3: Determine the annual payment needed to fund college education.			
[+/–] [FV]	FV=184,654.9997	End Key	
[2ⁿᵈ][BGN]	BGN	FV	184,654.9997
[2ⁿᵈ][SET]	END	n	18.0000
[CE/C]	0.0000	i	8.0000
18[N]	N=18.0000	PV	0.0000
8[I/Y]	I/Y=8.0000	PMT	**–4,930.6755**
0[PV]	PV=0.0000		
[CPT][PMT]	PMT=**–4,930.6755**		

F. ADVANTAGES AND DISADVANTAGES TO THE THREE METHODS

As the previous examples illustrate, each of the three methods (traditional, uneven cash flow, and account balance) are effective for solving for the annual payment required to fund one child's education. However, when multiple children are introduced into the problem, both the traditional method and the account balance method become problematic due to the additional steps required to calculate the payment.

Another problem arises with the account balance method if the ending date of the annuity to fund the education does not correspond to the date upon which the account balance was determined (generally age 18). Assume the same facts as in the previous example, except assume that the client would like to make his last deposit at the beginning of his son's last year of college. Using the account balance method, we determine the amount that needs to be accumulated at age 18 is $184,654.9997. However, how can we determine an annuity payment if the amount we are comparing to the annuity falls in the middle of the annuity stream instead of at the beginning or the end of the annuity? The answer is that we have to make an adjustment to the account balance so that it becomes the future value at the beginning of the last year of college. Once the $184,654.9997 has been inflated until the last year of college, the annuity payment can be determined. However, this example illustrates that unless the annuity stream ends on the date upon which the account balance was determined, additional steps are required to solve the problem.

The uneven cash flow method is flexible enough to easily overcome both of the issues discussed. It can easily handle multiple children and funding periods that do not correspond to the date the child will go to college. The following example illustrates the flexibility of the uneven cash flow method.

G. EXAMPLE

Paul and Kristi have two children, ages 7 and 4. The couple wants to start saving for their children's education. Each child will spend 5 years at a private college and will begin at age 18. College currently costs $25,000 per year and is expected to increase at 5% per year. Assuming Paul and Kristi can earn an after-tax annual compound return of 8% and inflation is 2%, how much must they deposit at the end of each year to pay for their children's education requirements until the youngest goes to school? Assume that education expenses are withdrawn at the beginning of each year and that the last deposit will be made at the beginning of the first year of the youngest child.

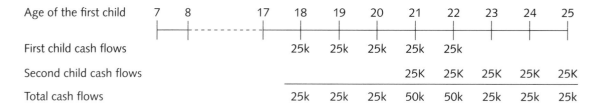

HP 17bII/HP 17bII+		HP 12C		HP 10BII/HP 10BII+	
Keystrokes	*Display*	*Keystrokes*	*Display*	*Keystrokes*	*Display*
Step 1: Determine the present value of the tuition payments as of today.					
[FIN]	SELECT A MENU	[f][CLX]	0.0000	[■][C ALL]	0.0000
[CFLO]	FLOW(0)=?	0[g][CF₀]	0.0000	0 [CFⱼ]	0.0000
[■][CLR DATA]	CLEAR THE LIST?	11[g][Nⱼ]	11.0000	0 [CFⱼ]	0.0000
[YES]	FLOW(0)=?	25000[g][CFⱼ]	25,0000.0000	10[■][Nⱼ]	10.0000
0[INPUT]	FLOW(1)=?	3[g][Nⱼ]	3.0000	25000[CFⱼ]	25,000.0000
	0.0000	50000[g][CFⱼ]	50,000.0000	3 [■][Nⱼ]	3.0000
0[INPUT]	#TIMES(1)=1	2[g][Nⱼ]	2.0000	50000[CFⱼ]	50,000.0000
	1.0000	25000[g][CFⱼ]	25,000.0000	2 [■][Nⱼ]	2.0000
10[INPUT]	FLOW(2)=?	3[g][Nⱼ]	3.0000	25000[CFⱼ]	25,000.0000
	10.0000	1.08[ENTER]	1.0800	3 [■][Nⱼ]	3.0000
25000[INPUT]	#TIMES(2)=1	1.05[÷]	1.0286	1.08[÷]1.05[=]	1.0286
	1.0000	1[−]	0.0286	[−]1[x]100[I/YR]	2.8571
3[INPUT]	FLOW(3)=?	100[x][i]	2.8571	[■][NPV]	**166,445.7110**
	3.0000	[f][NPV]	**166,445.7110**		
50000[INPUT]	#TIMES(3)=1				
	1.0000				
2[INPUT]	FLOW(4)=?				
	2.0000				
25000[INPUT]	#TIMES(4)=1				
	1.0000				
3[INPUT]	FLOW(5)=?				
	3.0000				
[EXIT][CALC]	NPV, NUS, NFV NEED I%				
1.08[÷]1.05[−]	1.0286−				
1[=]	0.0286				
[x]100[=][I%]	I%=2.8571				
[NPV]	NPV=**166,445.7110**				
Step 2: Determine the annual payments needed to fund college tuition costs.					
[EXIT][EXIT]	166,445.7110	[PV]	166,445.7110	[PV]	166,445.7110
[TVM]	1 P/YR END MODE	14 [n]	14.0000	14 [N]	14.0000
166445.7110[PV]	PV=166,445.7110	8 [i]	8.0000	8 [I/YR]	8.0000
14 [N]	N=14.0000	0 [FV]	0.0000	0 [FV]	0.0000
8 [I%YR]	I%YR=8.0000	[PMT]	**−20,189.3409**	[PMT]	**−20,189.3409**
0 [FV]	FV=0.0000				
[PMT]	PMT=**−20,189.3409**				

TI BA II Plus		SHORTCUT	
Keystrokes	*Display*		
Step 1: Determine the present value of the tuition payments as of today.			
[CF]	$CF_0=$	$CF_{7\ to\ 17}$	0.0000
[2ⁿᵈ][CLR Work]	$CF_0=0.0000$	$CF_{18\ to\ 20}$	25,000.0000
0[ENTER]	$CF_0=0.0000$	$CF_{21\ to\ 22}$	50,000.0000
[↓] 0 [ENTER]	C01=0.0000	$CF_{23\ to\ 25}$	25,000.0000
[↓]10 [ENTER]	F01=10.0000	i	2.8571
[↓]25000[ENTER]	C02=25,000.0000	NPV	**166,445.7110**
[↓] 3 [ENTER]	F02=3.0000		
[↓]50000[ENTER]	C03=50,000.0000		
[↓] 2 [ENTER]	F03=2.0000		
[↓]25000[ENTER]	C04=25,000.0000		
[↓] 3 [ENTER]	F04=3.0000		
[NPV]	I=0.0000		
1.08[÷]1.05[–]	I=1.0286		
1[x]100[=][ENTER]	I=2.8571		
[↓] [CPT]	NPV=**166,445.7110**		
Step 2: Determine the annual payments needed to fund college tuition costs.			
[2ⁿᵈ][QUIT]		PV	166,445.7110
166445.7110 [PV]	PV=166,445.7110	n	14.0000
14 [N]	N=14.0000	i	8.0000
8 [I/Y]	I/Y=8.0000	PMT_{OA}	**–20,189.3409**
0 [FV]	FV=0.0000		
[CPT][PMT]	PMT=**–20,189.3409**		

IX.   RETIREMENT NEEDS ANALYSIS

A.   INTRODUCTION

Retirement needs analysis, also known as the capital needs analysis, is performed to determine the amount of money a person will need to fund retirement. Several different assumptions are made to perform the calculation. These assumptions include: retirement age, percentage of current income needed at retirement, future rate of inflation, expected investments after-tax or pre-tax rate of return and the life expectancy (age of expected death) of the person. The calculation and approach used for determining retirement needs will be identical to the account balance method of the education calculation.

B.   EXAMPLE

Linda, a single woman, age 35, has come to you for help in determining her financial needs in retirement. She would like to retire at age 67, and expects to live to age 90. Her current income is $40,000 per year. She estimates that she will need 80% of her current income annually while in retirement. Linda expects that her Social Security benefit will be $14,000 per year (in today's dollars). Inflation is expected to average 2.5%. Linda expects to make an 7% annual return on her investments. How much must Linda save at the end of each year, beginning now, to meet her retirement goals?

This calculation requires four (4) steps.

1. Determine the amount of annual income needed during retirement in today's dollars.

2. Determine the amount of annual income needed in the first period of retirement by inflating the amount calculated in Step 1 by the expected inflation rate.

3. Determine the amount of funds that must be accumulated at retirement. This is done by finding the present value of an annuity (annuity due) of the amount calculated in Step 2 using an inflation-adjusted discount rate. The term of the annuity will be determined by the number of years from retirement to life expectancy.

4. Determine the annual amount of savings required to accumulate the necessary funds for retirement.

HP 17bII/HP 17bII+		HP 12C		HP 10BII/HP 10BII+	
Keystrokes	*Display*	*Keystrokes*	*Display*	*Keystrokes*	*Display*
Step 1: Determine the amount of income needed during retirement in today's dollars.					
[FIN]	SELECT A MENU	40000[ENTER]	40,000.0000	40000 [x]	40,000.0000
[TVM]	1 P/YR END MODE	.8 [x]	32,000.0000	.8 [–]	32,000.0000
40000 [x]	40,000.0000x	14000 [–]	18,000.0000	14000 [=]	18,000.0000
.8 [–]	32,000.0000–				
14000 [=]	18,000.0000				
Step 2: Determine the amount of annual income needed in the first period of retirement by inflating the amount calculated in Step 1 by the expected inflation rate.					
[PV]	PV=18,000.0000	[PV]	18,000.0000	[PV]	18,000.0000
2.5 [I%YR]	I%YR=2.5000	2.5 [i]	2.5000	2.5 [I/YR]	2.5000
32 [N]	N=32.0000	32 [n]	32.0000	32 [N]	32.0000
0 [PMT]	PMT=0.0000	0 [PMT]	0.0000	0 [PMT]	0.0000
[FV]	FV=–39,667.6249	[FV]	–39,667.6249	[FV]	–39,667.6249
Step 3: Determine the amount of funds that must be accumulated by retirement.					
[+/–][PMT]	PMT=39,667.6249	[g][BEG]	–39,667.6249	[■][BEG/END]	–39,667.6249
[OTHER]	1 P/YR END MODE	[CHS][PMT]	39,667.6249	[+/–][PMT]	39,667.6249
[BEG]	1 P/YR BEGIN MODE	1.07[ENTER]	1.0700	1.07 [÷]	1.0700
[EXIT]	1 P/YR BEGIN MODE	1.025 [÷]	1.0439	1.025 [–]	1.0439
1.07 [÷]	1.0700÷	1 [–]	0.0439	1 [x]	0.0439
1.025 [–]	1.0439–	100 [x][i]	4.3902	100 [=][I/YR]	4.3902
1 [x]	0.0439x	23 [n]	23.0000	23 [N]	23.0000
100[=][I%YR]	I%YR=4.3902	0 [FV]	0.0000	0 [FV]	0.0000
23 [N]	N=23.0000	[PV]	–592,109.0613	[PV]	–592,109.0613
0 [FV]	FV=0.0000				
[PV]	PV=–592,109.0613				
Step 4: Determine the annual amount of savings required to accumulate the necessary funds for retirement.					
[+/–][FV]	FV=592,109.0613	[g][END]	–592,109.0613	[■][BEG/END]	–592,109.0613
[OTHER]	1 P/YR BEGIN MODE	[CHS][FV]	592,109.0613	[+/–][FV]	592,109.0613
[END]	1 P/YR END MODE	0 [PV]	0.0000	0 [PV]	0.0000
[EXIT]	1 P/YR END MODE	7 [i]	7.0000	7 [I/YR]	7.0000
0 [PV]	PV=0.0000	32 [n]	32.0000	32 [N]	32.0000
7 [I%YR]	I%YR=7.0000	[PMT]	**–5,372.1555**	[PMT]	**–5,372.1555**
32 [N]	N=32.0000				
[PMT]	PMT=**–5,372.1555**				

TI BA II Plus		SHORTCUT	
Keystrokes	*Display*		
Step 1: Determine the present value of annual income needed in retirement.			
40000 [x]	40,000.0000	40000 [x]	40,000.0000
.8 [–]	32,000.0000	.8 [–]	32,000.0000
14000 [=]	18,000.0000	14000 [=]	18,000.0000
Step 2: Determine the amount of annual income needed in the first period of retirement by inflating the amount calculated in Step 1 by the expected inflation rate.			
[PV]	PV=18,000.0000	PV	18,000
2.5 [I/Y]	I/Y=2.5000	i	2.5
32 [N]	N=32.0000	n	32
0 [PMT]	PMT=0.0000	PMT	0
[CPT][FV]	FV=–39,667.6249	FV	**–39,667.6249**
Step 3: Determine the amount of funds that must be accumulated by retirement.			
[+/–][PMT]	PMT=39,667.6249	BEGIN Mode	
[2ⁿᵈ][BGN]	END	PMT	39,667.6249
[2ⁿᵈ][SET]	BGN	i	4.3902 [(1.07 ÷ 1.025) –1] x 100
[CE/C]	0.0000	n	23
1.07 [÷]	1.0700	FV	0
1.025 [–]	1.0439	PV	–592,109.0613
1 [x]	0.0439		
100 [=][I/Y]	I/Y=4.3902		
23 [N]	N=23.0000		
0 [FV]	FV=0.0000		
[CPT][PV]	PV=**–592,109.0613**		
Step 4: Determine the annual amount of savings required to accumulate the necessary funds for retirement.			
[+/–][FV]	FV=592,109.0613	END Mode	
[2ⁿᵈ][BGN]	BGN	FV	592,109.0613
[2ⁿᵈ][SET]	END	PV	0
[CE/C]	0.0000	i	7
0 [PV]	PV=0.0000	n	32
7 [I/Y]	I/Y=7.0000	PMT	**–5,372.1555**
32 [N]	N=32.0000		
[CPT][PMT]	PMT=**–5,372.1555**		

C.   ADVANCED METHODS

The capital needs analysis used throughout this book is known as the annuity method. The annual annuity of $5,372.1555 will accumulate and grow to the point where the balance will provide the level of retirement income that Linda is requiring, assuming that all assumptions are achieved. Based on this approach, how much will Linda have in her account when she dies at the age of 90? The answer is, based on the assumptions, she will spend her last dollar on the last day she is alive, leaving a balance of zero. The problem with the annuity method of capital needs analysis is that Linda might outlive her plan by living beyond the age of 90. This risk is known as superannuation.

Following are two other approaches to retirement planning that help mitigate against this potential problem of superannuation:

1. The capital preservation method.

2. The purchasing power preservation method.

The *capital preservation method* assumes that when the client dies, the amount of capital (or dollars) in the client's account will be the same as it was at retirement. To make this adjustment in the calculation, an adjustment must be made to Step 3. Once Step 3 is calculated, use the amount calculated in Step 3 as the future value (instead of having a future value of zero). After recalculating Step 3, continue with Step 4 based on the new Step 3 amount.

The *purchasing power preservation model* assumes that the client dies with an account balance equal to the same purchasing power as they would have had at retirement. The adjustment for this method is similar to the adjustment for the capital preservation method. The adjustment is to determine the present value of the amount calculated in Step 3 discounted at an inflation-adjusted discount rate for a period equal to the number of years expected for retirement. This amount ($220,408.2903) should be added to the amount calculated in Step 3.

Investment Planning Concepts & Calculations

I. INTERNAL RATE OF RETURN (IRR)

A. INTRODUCTION

The internal rate of return (IRR) is the earnings rate at which the present value of a series of cash flows will equal its cost or initial outflow. The formula below describes the basic present value model used for discounting cash flows. The formula states that the PV of a series of cash flows is equal to each cash flow divided by one plus the discount rate raised to a power equal to the period in which the cash flow occurs.

$$PV = \frac{CF_1}{(1+y)^1} + \frac{CF_2}{(1+y)^2} + \ldots + \frac{CF_t}{(1+y)^t}$$

where:
PV $\;=\;$ the present value of the security
$CF_t \;=\;$ the future cash flows from the security
y $\quad=\;$ the discount rate per period (IRR)
t $\quad=\;$ the number of cash flows to be evaluated

The internal rate of return (y) is the discount rate that makes the discounted cash flows equal to the initial outflow. The underlying assumption inherent in the above equation is that the cash flows that occur during the investment period will be reinvested at the investment's internal rate of return. This is the same assumption used in calculating the yield to maturity. The IRR is equivalent to the YTM, the compound average rate of return, and the geometric mean. All of these methods have been developed to determine what earnings rate occurs over the life, or period, of the investment.

B. EXAMPLE

Kristen owns 1 share of ABC stock. She purchased this share three years ago for $50.00. The current market value of the stock is $40.00 per share. Since buying the stock, the following dividends have been paid:

Dividend year 1 (end) $4.80 per share

Dividend year 2 (end) $5.90 per share

Dividend year 3 (end) $7.25 per share

What is the IRR that Kristen has earned on her investment?

HP 17bII/HP 17bII+		HP 12C		HP 10BII/HP 10BII+	
Keystrokes	*Display*	*Keystrokes*	*Display*	*Keystrokes*	*Display*
[FIN]	SELECT A MENU	[f] [REG]	0.0000	[■] [C ALL]	0.0000
[CFLO]	FLOW(0)=?	50 [CHS]	–50.	50 [+/–][CF$_j$]	–50.0000
[■][CLR DATA]	CLEAR THE LIST?	[g][CF$_0$]	–50.0000	4.8 [CF$_j$]	4.8000
[YES]	FLOW(0)=?	4.8 [g][CF$_j$]	4.8000	5.9 [CF$_j$]	5.9000
50 [+/–][INPUT]	FLOW(1)=?	5.9 [g][CF$_j$]	5.9000	7.25 [+]	7.2500
	–50.0000	7.25 [ENTER]	7.2500	40 [=][CF$_j$]	47.2500
4.8 [INPUT]	#TIMES(1)=1	40 [+][g][CF$_j$]	47.2500	[■][IRR/YR]	**5.5695**
	1.0000	[f][IRR]	**5.5695**		
[INPUT]	FLOW(2)=?				
	1.0000				
5.9 [INPUT]	#TIMES(2)=1				
	1.0000				
[INPUT]	FLOW(3)=?				
	1.0000				
7.25[+]	FLOW(3)=?				
	7.2500+				
40 [=] [INPUT]	#TIMES(3)=1				
	1.0000				
[INPUT]	FLOW(4)=?				
	1.0000				
[EXIT]	FLOW(4)=?				
[CALC]	NPV, NUS, NFV NEED I%				
[IRR%]	IRR=**5.5695**				

TI BA II Plus		SHORTCUT	
Keystrokes	*Display*		
[CF]	CF$_0$=(Old work)	CF$_0$	–50.0000
[2nd][CLR Work]	CF$_0$=0.0000	CF$_1$	4.8000
50 [+/–][ENTER]	CF$_0$=–50.0000	CF$_2$	5.9000
[↓] 4.8 [ENTER]	C01=4.8000	CF$_3$	47.25 (7.25 + 40.00)
[↓][↓]		IRR	**5.5695**
5.9 [ENTER]	C02=5.9000		
[↓][↓]			
7.25 [+]	C03=7.2500		
40 [=][ENTER]	C03=47.2500		
[IRR][CPT]	IRR=**5.5695**		

Proof of Internal Rate of Return

Period	Cash Flow	Divisor (x)	Factor (1/x)	Present Value (CF*i/x)
1	4.80	$1 \div (1.055695)^1$	.947243	4.547
2	5.90	$1 \div (1.055695)^2$	.897270	5.294
3	47.25	$1 \div (1.055695)^3$	.849933	40.159
				50.000

II.   CURRENT YIELD

A.   INTRODUCTION

The current yield of a bond is the return represented by the amount of interest income paid in relation to the current market value of the bond. Current yield is calculated by dividing the annual interest payment on the bond (as reflected by its coupon rate multiplied by the par value of the bond) by the bond's current market price.

B.   EXAMPLE

Jeff has a bond with a coupon rate of 5% that is currently trading at $955 in the secondary market. What is the current yield of the bond?

Annual interest payment = .05 × $1,000 = $50

Current yield = $50 ÷ $955 = .0524 = 5.24%

You should also note that the current yield of 5.24% is higher than the coupon rate, or nominal yield, of 5% on Jeff's bond. This is because the bond is currently trading at a *discount* in the secondary market.

HP 17bII/HP 17bII+		HP 12C		HP 10BII/HP 10BII+	
Keystrokes	*Display*	*Keystrokes*	*Display*	*Keystrokes*	*Display*
.05 [×]	0.0500×	.05 [ENTER]	0.0500	.05 [×]	0.0500
1000 [=]	50.0000	1000 [×]	50.0000	1000 [=]	50.0000
[÷] 955 [=]	**0.0524**	955[÷]	**0.0524**	[÷] 955 [=]	**0.0524**

TI BA II Plus		SHORTCUT	
Keystrokes	*Display*		
.05 [×]	0.0500	.05 [×]	0.0500
1000 [=]	50.0000	1000 [=]	50.0000
[÷] 955 [=]	**0.0524**	[÷] 955 [=]	**0.0524**

III.   YIELD TO MATURITY (YTM)

A.   INTRODUCTION

Yield to maturity (YTM) is the calculation of that rate of return or IRR that will make the discounted cash flows of the bond equal to the current price of the bond. YTM is generally calculated based on semiannual coupon payments (even with zero-coupon bonds). There are three adjustments that have to be made in order to calculate the YTM for a bond that makes semiannual coupon payments:

1.   N – The number of periods is determined by multiplying the number of years by 2 so as to reflect two coupon payments per year. For example, the N for a 10-year bond would be 20 to reflect 20 coupon payments.

2.   PMT – The coupon is stated as a percent of the face value of the bond. Therefore, a 5% coupon bond will pay a total of $50 each year ($25 twice per year). The adjustment is to divide the $50 by 2 to reflect the two payments of $25 during the year.

3.   YTM – The YTM that will be calculated will be a semiannual YTM rate. Therefore, the calculated YTM should be multiplied by 2 to determine the annual YTM.

B.   EXAMPLE

Terri is considering purchasing a 5-year bond that is selling for $1,162.22. What is the YTM for this bond if it has a 6% coupon, paid semiannually?

HP 17bII/HP 17bII+		HP 12C		HP 10BII/HP 10BII+	
Keystrokes	*Display*	*Keystrokes*	*Display*	*Keystrokes*	*Display*
[FIN]	SELECT A MENU	1162.22 [CHS][PV]	–1,162.2200	1162.22 [+/–][PV]	–1,162.2200
[TVM]	1 P/YR END MODE	5 [ENTER]	5.0000	5 [x]	5.0000
1162.22[+/–]	–1,162.22	2 [x][n]	10.0000	2 [=][N]	10.0000
[PV]	PV = –1,162.2200	60 [ENTER]	60.0000	60 [÷]	60.0000
5 [x]	5.0000x	2 [÷][PMT]	30.0000	2 [=][PMT]	30.0000
2 [=][N]	N=10.0000	1000 [FV]	1,000.0000	1000 [FV]	1,000.0000
60 [÷]	60.0000÷	[i] [ENTER]	1.2630	[I/YR]	1.2630
2 [=][PMT]	PMT=30.0000	2 [x]	**2.5260**	[x] 2 [=]	**2.5260**
1000 [FV]	FV=1,000.0000				
[I%YR]	I%YR=1.2630				
[x] 2 [=]	**2.5260**				

TI BA II Plus		SHORTCUT	
Keystrokes	*Display*		
1162.22[+/–][PV]	PV= –1,162.2200	PV	–1,162.2200
5 [x]	5.0000	*n*	10.0000
2 [=][N]	N=10.0000	PMT	30.0000
60 [÷]	60.0000	FV	1,000.0000
2 [=][PMT]	PMT=30.0000	*i*	1.2630
1000 [FV]	FV=1,000.0000	2 x	**2.5260**
[CPT][I/Y]	I/Y=1.2630		
[x] 2 [=]	**2.5260**		

IV.   YIELD TO CALL

A.   INTRODUCTION

Bonds will often be issued with a call feature permitting the issuer to pay off the debt obligation at a predetermined price and time. This feature is a benefit to the issuer because it allows the issuer to effectively refinance the debt in the event that interest rates decline. Therefore, a call feature causes the required yield for investors to increase because the investment horizon is no longer certain. In addition, if the bond is called, it will generally be called at a premium (an amount in excess of par value, usually $1,000). The yield to call (YTC) is calculated to determine what the yield would be should the bond be called. There are two adjustments that need to be made from calculating a YTM:

1. N – The first available call date.

2. FV – The call value of the bond.

B.   EXAMPLE

Davis Company issues a series of 25-year bonds paying a 5% coupon semiannually and selling at par ($1,000). If Davis Co. has the option to call the bonds in 5 years for 105% of par value, what is the yield to call?

HP 17bII/HP 17bII+		HP 12C		HP 10BII/HP 10BII+	
Keystrokes	*Display*	*Keystrokes*	*Display*	*Keystrokes*	*Display*
[FIN]	SELECT A MENU	1050 [FV]	1,050.0000	1050 [FV]	1,050.0000
[TVM]	1 P/YR END MODE	1000[CHS][PV]	–1,000.0000	1000 [+/–][PV]	–1,000.0000
1050[FV]	FV=1,050.0000	50 [ENTER]	50.0000	50 [÷]	50.0000
1000[+/–][PV]	PV= –1,000.0000	2 [÷] [PMT]	25.0000	2 [=][PMT]	25.0000
50[÷]	50.0000÷	5 [ENTER]	5.0000	5 [x]	5.0000
2 [=][PMT]	PMT=25.0000	2 [x][n]	10.0000	2 [=][N]	10.0000
5 [x]	5.0000x	[i] [ENTER]	2.9374	[I/YR]	2.9374
2 [=][N]	N=10.0000	2 [x]	**5.8748**	[x] 2 [=]	**5.8748**
[I%YR]	I%YR=2.9374				
[x] 2 [=]	**5.8748**				

TI BA II Plus		SHORTCUT	
Keystrokes	*Display*		
1050 [FV]	FV=1,050.0000	FV	1,050.0000
1000 [+/–][PV]	PV= –1,000.0000	PV	–1,000.0000
50 [÷]	50.0000	PMT	25.0000
2 [=][PMT]	PMT=25.0000	*n*	10.0000
5 [x]	5.0000	*i*	2.9374
2 [=][N]	N=10.0000	x 2	**5.8748**
[CPT][I/Y]	2.9374		
[x] 2 [=]	**5.8748**		

V. DURATION

A. INTRODUCTION

The concept of duration, developed by Fredrick Macaulay, provides a time-weighted measure of a security's cash flows in terms of payback and is widely used in managing fixed income portfolios. Duration is used to compare the volatility of fixed income securities or portfolios of fixed income securities, to estimate the price change in a fixed income security, and to immunize fixed income portfolios.

Duration is a measure of the price sensitivity of a bond to changes in yield or interest rates. When interest rates change, bonds with shorter durations are less volatile than bonds with longer durations. When interest rates decline, the value of bonds will increase, and when interest rates increase, the value of bonds will decline. Understanding how coupon rate, maturity, and yield to maturity, which are all used in the calculation of duration, impact the volatility of a bond is important. The following table summarizes these relationships.

Factor	Relationship
Coupon rate	Inverse
Time to maturity	Direct
Yield to maturity	Inverse

The duration of a zero-coupon bond is the bond's maturity. Thus, the duration of a thirty year zero-coupon bond is thirty years. If the coupon rate was increased from zero, then the duration would decline. This is because it takes less time for the investor to be paid back some of his original investment. If the maturity of the bond was reduced from thirty years to twenty years, the duration would also decrease. Finally, when market rates increase, the duration of bonds will decline. However, this factor will not impact the duration of a zero-coupon bond.

Two common methods of calculating duration will be discussed on the following pages.

B. METHOD 1: THE TRADITIONAL METHOD

The formula equation for this method is as follows:

$$D = \frac{\displaystyle\sum_{t=1}^{n} \frac{c_t(t)}{(1+i)^t}}{\displaystyle\sum_{t=1}^{n} \frac{c_t}{(1+i)^t}}$$

where:
D = duration
c = cash flow that occurs in period t
n = number of periods until maturity
i = yield to maturity
t = time period

This method utilizes a table format and the financial calculator to determine the duration for a bond. The five steps for this approach are as follows:

1. List the years.

2. List the cash flows.

3. Determine the present value of the cash flows using the year and the YTM for the bond.

4. Multiply the digit associated with the year by the present value.

5. Sum the last column and divide by the current market price (the sum of column four by the sum of column three).

In this calculation, the market price of the bond is defined as the present value of future cash flows beginning in period 1. The numerator is the sum of each discounted cash flow adjusted for the period in which it occurs.

C. EXAMPLE

Calculate the duration using a five-year bond selling for $1,065.85, paying interest annually, with a face value of $1,000, a coupon rate of 6% and a YTM of 4.5%.

Duration is calculated as follows:

Year	Cash Flow	PV of CF @ YTM	PV x Year
1	$60.00	$57.42	$57.42
2	$60.00	$54.94	$109.88
3	$60.00	$52.58	$157.74
4	$60.00	$50.31	$201.24
5	$1,060.00	$850.60	$4,253.00
		$1,065.85	**$4,779.28**

Duration = $4,779.28 ÷ $1,065.85 = 4.4840

HP 17bII/HP 17bII+		HP 12C		HP 10BII/HP 10BII+	
Keystrokes	*Display*	*Keystrokes*	*Display*	*Keystrokes*	*Display*
Step 1: Calc. PV					
[FIN]	SELECT A MENU	60 [CHS][FV]	–60.0000	60 [+/–][FV]	–60.0000
[TVM]	1 P/YR END MODE	0 [PMT]	0.0000	0 [PMT]	0.0000
60[+/–][FV]	FV = –60.0000	4.5 [i]	4.5000	4.5 [I/YR]	4.5000
0 [PMT]	PMT = 0.0000	1 [n]	1.0000	1 [N]	1.0000
4.5 [I%YR]	I%YR = 4.5000	[PV]	**57.4163**	[PV]	**57.4163**
1[N]	N = 1.0000	2 [n]	2.0000	2 [N]	2.0000
[PV]	**PV = 57.4163**	[PV]	**54.9438**	[PV]	**54.9438**
2 [N]	N = 2.0000	3 [n]	3.0000	3 [N]	3.0000
[PV]	**PV = 54.9438**	[PV]	**52.5778**	[PV]	**52.5778**
3 [N]	N = 3.0000	4 [n]	4.0000	4 [N]	4.0000
[PV]	**PV = 52.5778**	[PV]	**50.3137**	[PV]	**50.3137**
4 [N]	N = 4.0000	1060 [CHS][FV]	–1,060.0000	1060 [+/–][FV]	–1060.0000
[PV]	**PV = 50.3137**	5 [n]	5.0000	5 [N]	5.0000
1060 [+/–][FV]	FV = –1,060.0000	[PV]	**850.5981**	[PV]	**850.5981**
5 [N]	N = 5.0000				
[PV]	**PV = 850.5981**				
Step 2: (PV x yrs)					
57.42 [x]	57.4200 x	57.42 [ENTER]	57.4200	57.42 [x]	57.4200
1 [=]	**57.4200**	1 [x]	**57.4200**	1 [=]	**57.4200**
54.94 [x]	54.9400 x	54.94 [ENTER]	54.9400	54.94 [x]	54.9400
2 [=]	**109.8800**	2 [x]	**109.8800**	2 [=]	**109.8800**
52.58 [x]	52.5800 x	52.58 [ENTER]	52.5800	52.58 [x]	52.5800
3 [=]	**157.7400**	3 [x]	**157.7400**	3 [=]	**157.7400**
50.31 [x]	50.3100 x	50.31 [ENTER]	50.3100	50.31 [x]	50.3100
4 [=]	**201.2400**	4 [x]	**201.2400**	4 [=]	**201.2400**
850.60 [x]	850.6000 x	850.60 [ENTER]	850.6000	850.60 [x]	850.6000
5 [=]	**4,253.0000**	5 [x]	**4,253.0000**	5 [=]	**4,253.0000**
57.42 [+]	57.4200 +	57.42 [ENTER]	57.4200	57.42 [+]	57.4200
109.88 [+]	167.3000 +	109.88 [+]	167.3000	109.88 [+]	167.3000
157.74 [+]	325.0400 +	157.74 [+]	325.0400	157.74 [+]	325.0400
201.24 [+]	526.2800 +	201.24 [+]	526.2800	201.24 [+]	526.2800
4253.00 [=]	**4,779.2800**	4253.00 [+]	**4,779.2800**	4253.00 [=]	**4,779.2800**
Step 3: Calc. Dur					
4779.2800 [÷]	4,779.2800 ÷	4779.2800[ENTER]	4,779.2800	4779.2800 [÷]	4,779.2800
1065.85 [=]	**4.4840**	1065.85 [÷]	**4.4840**	1065.85 [=]	**4.4840**

TI BA II Plus		SHORTCUT	
Keystrokes	*Display*		
Step 1: Calc. PV			
60 [+/–][FV]	FV = –60.0000	FV	–60.0000
0 [PMT]	PMT = 0.0000	PMT	0
4.5 [I/Y]	I/Y = 4.5000	*i*	4.5000
1 [N]	N = 1.0000	*n*	1.0000
[CPT][PV]	**PV = 57.4163**	PV	57.4163
2 [N]	N = 2.0000	*n*	2.0000
[CPT][PV]	**PV = 54.9438**	PV	54.9438
3 [N]	N = 3.0000	*n*	3.0000
[CPT][PV]	**PV = 52.5778**	PV	52.5778
4 [N]	N = 4.0000	*n*	4.0000
[CPT][PV]	**PV = 50.3137**	PV	50.3137
1060 [+/–][FV]	FV = –1,060.0000	FV	1,060.0000
5 [N]	N = 5.0000	*n*	5.0000
[CPT][PV]	**850.5981**	PV	**850.5981**
Step 2: (PV x yrs)			
57.42 [x]	57.4200	57.42 × 1 =	57.4200
1 [=]	**57.4200**	54.94 × 2 =	109.8800
54.94 [x]	54.9400	52.58 × 3 =	157.7400
2 [=]	**109.8800**	50.31 × 4 =	201.2400
52.58 [x]	52.5800	850.60 × 5 =	4,253.0000
3 [=]	**157.7400**		4,779.2800
50.31 [x]	50.3100		
4 [=]	**201.2400**	4,779.2800 ÷ 1,065.8500 =	**4.4840**
850.60 [x]	850.6000		
5 [=]	**4,253.0000**		
57.42 [+]	57.42000		
109.88 [+]	167.3000		
157.74 [+]	325.0400		
201.24 [+]	526.2800		
4253.00 [=]	**4,779.2800**		
Step 3: Calc. Dur.			
4779.28 [÷]	4,779.2800		
1065.8500 [=]	**4.4840**		

D. ADDITIONAL SHORTCUT USING THE NPV KEY FOR METHOD 1

Duration may also be calculated using the financial calculator's NPV keys. The steps are as follows:

1. List the years.

2. List the cash flows.

3. Multiply the digit associated with the year by the Cash Flow.

4. Use the Cash Flow and NPV keys on the financial calculator to determine the NPV.

5. Divide the NPV by the market price of the bond.

This method saves several steps in calculating duration.

E. EXAMPLE

Calculate the duration using a five-year bond selling for $1,065.85, paying interest annually, with a face value of $1,000, a coupon rate of 6% and a YTM of 4.5%.

Duration is calculated as follows:

Year	Cash Flow	CF × Year
1	$60	$60
2	$60	$120
3	$60	$180
4	$60	$240
5	$1,060	$5,300

Cash Flow Inputs

CF_0	0
CF_1	60
CF_2	120
CF_3	180
CF_4	240
CF_5	5300
i	4.5
NPV	4,779.28

Duration = NPV ÷ Price of the Bond

Duration = $4,779.28 ÷ $1,065.85 = 4.4840

HP 17bII/HP 17bII+		HP 12C		HP 10BII/HP 10BII+	
Keystrokes	*Display*	*Keystrokes*	*Display*	*Keystrokes*	*Display*
[FIN]	SELECT A MENU	60[ENTER]1[x] g CFj	60.0000	0 CFj	0.0000
[CFLO]	FLOW (0) = ?	60[ENTER]2[x] g CFj	120.0000	60[x]1[=] CFj	60.0000
[■][CLR DATA]	CLEAR THE LIST?	60[ENTER]3[x] g CFj	180.0000	60[x]2[=] CFj	120.0000
[YES]	FLOW (0) = ?	60[ENTER]4[x] g CFj	240.0000	60[x]3[=] CFj	180.0000
0[INPUT]	FLOW (1) = ?	1060[ENTER]5[x] g CFj	5,300.0000	60[x]4[=] CFj	240.0000
	0.0000	4.5 i	4.5000	1060[x]5[=] CFj	5,300.0000
60[x]1[=][INPUT]	# TIMES (1) = 1	[f]NPV	4,779.2825	4.5 [I/YR]	4.5000
	1.0000	[ENTER] 1065.85 [÷]	4.4840	[■] NPV	4,779.2825
[INPUT]	FLOW (2) = ?			[÷] 1065.85[=]	4.4840
	1.0000				
60[x]2[=][INPUT]	# TIMES (2) = 1				
	1.0000				
1[INPUT]	FLOW (3) = ?				
	1.0000				
60[x]3[=][INPUT]	# TIMES (3) = 1				
	1.0000				
1[INPUT]	FLOW (4) = ?				
	1.0000				
60[x]4[=][INPUT]	# TIMES (4) = 1				
	1.0000				
1[INPUT]	FLOW (5) = ?				
	1.0000				
1060[x]5[=][INPUT]	# TIMES (5) = 1				
	1.0000				
[EXIT]	#TIMES(5)=1				
[CALC]	NPV, NUS, NFV NEED I%				
4.5 [I%]	I% = 4.5000				
NPV	4,779.2825				
[EXIT][EXIT]	4,779.2825				
[÷] 1065.85 [=]	4.4840				

TI BA II Plus		SHORTCUT	
Keystrokes	*Display*		
[CF]	CF_0 = (OLD work)	CF_0	0
[2ND][CLR Work]	CF_0 = 0.0000	CF_1	60 × 1 = 60.0000
0 [ENTER]	CF_0 = 0.0000	CF_2	60 × 2 = 120.0000
[↓]60[x]1[=][ENTER]	C01 = 60.0000	CF_3	60 × 3 = 180.0000
[↓][↓]60[x]2[=][ENTER]	C02 = 120.0000	CF_4	60 × 4 = 240.0000
[↓][↓]60[x]3[=][ENTER]	C03 = 180.0000	CF_5	1060 × 5 = 5,300.0000
[↓][↓]60[x]4[=][ENTER]	C04 = 240.0000		
[↓][↓]1060[x]5[=][ENTER]	C05 = 5,300.0000	i	4.5000
[NPV]	I = 0.0000	NPV	4,779.2825
4.5 [ENTER]	I = 4.5000		
[↓] [CPT]	NPV = 4,779.2825	4,779.2825 ÷ 1,065.85 = 4.4840	
[2ND] [QUIT]	0.0000		
4779.28 [÷]	4,779.2800		
1065.85 [=]	4.4840		

F.   METHOD 2: CLOSED-END FORMULA

Another method of calculating duration is using the following formula:

$$D = \frac{1+y}{y} - \frac{(1+y) + t(c-y)}{c[(1+y)^t - 1] + y}$$

where:
D = duration
c = coupon rate (as a decimal)
y = yield to maturity (as a decimal)
t = time period

G.   EXAMPLE

The formula can be illustrated using the previous example:

$$D = \frac{1 + 0.045}{0.045} - \frac{(1 + 0.045) + 5(0.06 - 0.045)}{0.06[(1 + 0.045)^5 - 1] + 0.045}$$

$$D = 23.2222 - \frac{1.1200}{0.0598}$$

$$D = 23.2222 - 18.7291$$

$$D = 4.4931 \text{ years (there is a small rounding error)}$$

NOTE: Carrying this calculation to eight decimal places results in a more accurate calculation and eliminates the rounding error.

This formula is a more efficient method of calculating duration than the previous method for longer-term bonds. In addition, it can be used easily in a spreadsheet when building economic models involving duration.

HP 17bII/HP 17bII+		HP 12C		HP 10BII/HP 10BII+	
Keystrokes	*Display*	*Keystrokes*	*Display*	*Keystrokes*	*Display*
1 [+]	1.0000 +	1[ENTER]	1.0000	1 [+]	1.0000
0.045 [÷]	1.0450 ÷	0.045 [+]	1.0450	0.045 [=]	1.0450
0.045 [=]	**23.2222**	0.045 [÷]	**23.2222**	[÷] .045 [=]	**23.2222**
0.06 [–]	0.0600 –	1[ENTER]	1.0000	1 [+]	1.0000
0.045 [=]	0.0150	0.045 [+] [ENTER]	1.0450	0.045 [=]	1.0450
[x] 5 [=]	0.0750	.06 [ENTER]	0.0600	0.06 [–]	0.0600
[+] 1 [+]	1.0750 +	0.045 [–]	0.0150	0.045 [=]	0.0150
0.045 [=]	**1.1200**	5 [x]	0.0750	[x] 5 [=]	0.0750
1 [+]	1.0000 +	[+]	**1.1200**	[+] 1.045 [=]	**1.1200**
0.045 [=]	1.0450	1[ENTER]	1.0000	1 [+]	1.0000
[■][y^x] 5 [=]	1.2462	.045 [+]	1.0450	0.045 [=]	1.0450
[–] 1 [=]	0.2462	5 [y^x]	1.2462	[■][y^x] 5 [=]	1.2462
[x] 0.06 [=]	0.0148	1 [–]	0.2462	[–] 1 [=]	0.2462
[+] 0.045 [=]	**0.0598**	0.06 [×]	0.0148	[x] 0.06 [=]	0.0148
23.2222 [–]	23.2222 –	0.045 [+]	**0.0598**	[+] 0.045 [=]	**0.0598**
[(] 1.12 [÷]	23.2222 – (1.1200 ÷	23.2222 [ENTER]	23.2222	1.12 [÷]	1.1200
.0598 [)] [=]	**4.4931**	1.12 [ENTER]	1.1200	0.0598 [=]	18.7291
		0.0598 [÷]	18.7291	23.2222 [–]	23.2222
		[–]	**4.4931**	18.7291 [=]	**4.4931**

TI BA II Plus		SHORTCUT
Keystrokes	*Display*	
1[+]	1.0000	
0.045 [÷]	1.0450	(1 + 0.045) ÷ 0.045 = 23.2222
0.045 [=]	**23.2222**	(1 + 0.045) + 5(0.06 – 0.045) = 1.12
0.06 [–]	0.0600	0.06 [(1 + 0.045)^5 – 1] + 0.045 = 0.0598
0.045 [=]	0.0150	23.2222 – (1.12 ÷ 0.0598) = **4.4931**
[x] 5 [=]	0.0750	
[+] 1 [+]	1.0750	
0.045 [=]	**1.1200**	
1 [+]	1.0000	
0.045 [=]	1.0450	
[y^x] 5 [=]	1.2462	
[–] 1 [x]	0.2462	
0.06 [+]	0.0148	
0.045 [=]	**0.0598**	
23.2222 [–]	23.2222	
[(] 1.12 [÷]	1.1200	
0.0598 [)]	18.7291	
[=]	**4.4931**	

H. MODIFIED DURATION

An important application of duration is its use in estimating the change in price of a bond or bond portfolio based on changes in interest rates. Managers of portfolios of fixed income securities are interested in the exposure of a portfolio to changes in interest rates. Modified duration is a useful tool in determining this exposure.

The percent change in the bond or bond portfolio given a specific change in interest rates can be determined by understanding the relationship between a bond's price and its duration. The same factors that impact duration (coupon rate, maturity, and YTM) also determine the price of a bond. Therefore, duration can assist us in determining the estimated change in the price of a bond based on changes in interest rates.

Modified duration is a "modified" version of Macaulay duration. Modified duration is the linear approximation (first derivative) of the price-yield relationship for a bond. It is a useful tool to approximate the impact that a small change in interest rates has on the value of a non-callable bond and equals Macaulay duration divided by 1 plus the current yield to maturity (y).

$$\text{Modified Duration} = \frac{\text{Macaulay Duration}}{1+y}$$

Modified Duration, as shown in the above formula, provides the estimated change in the price of a bond based on a 1 percent (100 basis points) change in interest rates. By quickly estimating this number, the investor can easily determine by approximately how much a bond or bond portfolio will change for a given change in interest rates.

I. EXAMPLE

Using our previous example, the modified duration equals 4.29 percent:

$$\text{Modified Duration} = \frac{4.4840}{1+0.045} = 4.29\%$$

This number indicates that for a given change in interest rates of 1 percent (100 basis points), the price of the bond should change by approximately 4.29 percent. If interest rates increase by 1 percent, then the price of the bond should decrease by approximately 4.29 percent. If interest rates decrease by 1 percent, then the price of the bond should increase by approximately 4.29 percent.

J.   ESTIMATING BOND PRICES – APPLICATION OF MODIFIED DURATION

Where as the previous formula estimates the change in price of a bond given a change in interest rates of 1%, the formula below estimates the percentage change in price (or value) given any change in interest rates. The percentage change can then be used to calculate the new estimated bond price.

$$\frac{\Delta P}{P} = -D\left[\frac{\Delta y}{1+y}\right]$$

where:
$\Delta P / P$ = percentage change in the price of a bond
D = duration of the bond
y = yield to maturity for the bond
Δy = change in YTM as a decimal

As the formula above describes, the change in the price of a bond equals the duration of a bond divided by one plus the YTM and multiplied by the change in interest rates.

K.   EXAMPLE

Using the previous example of duration, how much will the price of the bond change in value if interest rates decrease by 1 percent or 100 basis points to 3.5 percent?

$$\frac{\Delta P}{P} = -4.4840\left[\frac{(0.035 - 0.045)}{1 + 0.045}\right]$$

$$\frac{\Delta P}{P} = -4.4840 \times -0.01$$

$$\frac{\Delta P}{P} = 0.0429 = 4.29\%$$

HP 17bII/HP 17bII+		HP 12C		HP 10BII/HP 10BII+	
Keystrokes	*Display*	*Keystrokes*	*Display*	*Keystrokes*	*Display*
.035 [–]	0.0350–	.035 [ENTER]	0.0350	.035 [–]	0.0350
.045 [=]	–0.0100	.045 [–]	–0.0100	.045 [=]	–0.0100
[÷][(]1[+]	–0.0100÷(1.0000+	1[ENTER]	1.0000	[÷][■][(]1[+]	1.0000
.045[)][=]	–0.0100÷1.0450	.045[+]	1.0450	.045[■][)][=]	–0.0096
[=]	–0.0096	[÷]	–0.0096	[x]4.4840[+/–][=]	**0.0429**
[x]4.4840[+/–]	–0.0096×–4.4840	4.4840[CHS][x]	**0.0429**		
[=]	**0.0429**				

TI BA II Plus		SHORTCUT
Keystrokes	*Display*	
4.4840 [+/–]	–4.4840	0.035 – 0.045 = –0.0100
[x][(]0.0350[–]	0.0350	–0.0100 ÷ (1 + 0.045) = –0.0096
0.045[)]	–0.0100	–0.0096 x –4.4840 = **0.0429**
[÷][(]1[+]	1.0000	
0.045[)]	1.0450	
[=]	**0.0429**	

Based on the above formula, the price of the bond should increase by approximately 4.29 percent. Based on this estimate, we would expect the new price of the bond to equal $1,111.58 ($1,065.85 × 1.0429). This estimate can be evaluated by calculating the price of the bond using time value of money concepts.

FV $= \$1,000$

n $= 5$

i $= 3.5\%$ (instead of 4.5%)

PMT $= \$60$

PV $= (\$1,112.88)$

Based on this calculation, our estimate differs from the actual price by $1.30. Modified Duration is very effective for small changes in interest rates and is less effective for large changes in interest rates.

L. IMMUNIZATION

As we have emphasized, interest rate risk is one of the major concerns of fixed income investors, as well as managers of fixed income portfolios. As interest rates increase, the price of bonds decrease. However, an offsetting position must be considered. When interest rates increase, the reinvested coupon payments should be invested at higher rates, thus, offsetting the decline in the value of the bond. This offsetting of price and reinvested coupon payments is illustrated below:

Interest Rates Move	Value of Bond (Inverse to interest rates)	Value of Reinvested Coupon Payments (Direct to interest rates)
↑	↓	↑
↓	↑	↓

As you can see, when interest rates increase, the value of bonds decline, but the value of reinvested coupon payments increase. Similarly, as interest rates decline, bond prices increase and the value of reinvested coupon payments decreases. This offsetting is the basis for immunizing a bond or bond portfolio against interest rate risk.

Immunization is the concept of minimizing the impact of changes in interest rates on the value of investments. The goal of immunization is to protect a bond portfolio from interest rate fluctuations and reinvestment risk. Immunization should provide a stable compound rate of return that equals the calculated YTM at the purchase of the bond, despite interest rate fluctuations. The portfolio is considered immunized if the realized rate of return is at least as great as the YTM calculated at inception. Another way to think of immunization is that a bond portfolio is immunized when the actual future value is at least as great as it had been expected at inception. For example, the expected future value of a zero-coupon bond at maturity will be $1,000. If held to maturity, a zero-coupon bond will always have a future value of $1,000 and is, therefore, considered immunized at the point of maturity.

A bond portfolio is defined as being initially immunized at the point of duration. Therefore, if an investor were to match the duration of a bond portfolio to the time horizon of his goal, then his portfolio is initially immunized. This can be easily accomplished with a zero-coupon bond. An investor who had a cash need in five years could simply purchase a five-year, zero-coupon bond and eliminate all reinvestment risk.

The concept of immunization will be illustrated using the previous example and assuming that the client has a time horizon of four years.

Assumptions:

- Coupon rate of 6 percent, paid annually.

- Term of bond is 5 years.

- The yield on the bond equals 4.5 percent.

- The duration of the bond is approximately 4.4840 years.

- Time horizon of client's cash need is 4 years.

Immunization Example					
Assuming Interest Rates Remain at:		**Interest Rates Change to the Following:**			
	4.5%	**3.5%**	**4.0%**	**5.0%**	**5.5%**
Coupon Payment Reinvested					
PMT	$60.00	$60.00	$60.00	$60.00	$60.00
i	4.5%	3.5%	4.0%	5.0%	5.5%
n	4.000	4.000	4.000	4.000	4.000
FV @ 4 years	$256.69	$252.90	$254.79	$258.61	$260.54
Proceeds of Bond Sales @ 4th Year					
FV	$1,000.00	$1,000.00	$1,000.00	$1,000.00	$1,000.00
PMT	$60.00	$60.00	$60.00	$60.00	$60.00
i	4.5%	3.5%	4.0%	5.0%	5.5%
n	1.000	1.000	1.000	1.000	1.000
PV @ 4 years	$1,014.35	$1,024.15	$1,019.23	$1,009.52	$1,004.74
Reinvested Coupon Payments	$256.69	$252.90	$254.79	$258.61	$260.54
Bond Sale Proceeds	$1,014.35	$1,024.15	$1,019.23	$1,009.52	$1,004.74
Total @ 4 years	$1,271.04	$1,277.05	$1,274.02	$1,268.13	$1,265.28

HP 17bII/HP 17bII+		HP 12C		HP 10BII/HP 10BII+	
Keystrokes	*Display*	*Keystrokes*	*Display*	*Keystrokes*	*Display*
Step 1:					
[FIN]	SELECT A MENU	60 [CHS] [PMT]	–60.0000	60 [+/–] [PMT]	–60.0000
[TVM]	1 P/YR END MODE	4.5 [i]	4.5000	4.5 [I/YR]	4.5000
60 [+/–] [PMT]	PMT = –60.0000	4 [n]	4.0000	4 [N]	4.0000
4.5 [I%YR]	I%YR = 4.5000	0 [PV]	0.0000	0 [PV]	0.0000
4 [N]	N = 4.0000	[FV]	256.6915	[FV]	256.6915
0 [PV]	PV = 0.0000				
[FV]	FV = 256.6915				
Step 2:					
1000 [+/–] [FV]	FV = –1,000.0000	1000 [CHS] [FV]	–1,000.0000	1000 [+/–] [FV]	–1,000.0000
60 [+/–] [PMT]	PMT = –60.000	60 [CHS] [PMT]	–60.000	60 [+/–] [PMT]	–60.000
4.5 [I%YR]	I%YR = 4.5000	4.5 [i]	4.5000	4.5 [I/YR]	4.5000
1 [N]	N = 1.0000	1 [n]	1.0000	1 [N]	1.0000
[PV]	PV = 1,014.3541	[PV]	1,014.3541	[PV]	1,014.3541
Step 3:					
[EXIT] [EXIT]	1,014.3541	256.6915 [ENTER]	256.6915	256.6915 [+]	256.6915
[+] 256.6915 [=]	1,271.0456	1014.3540 [+]	1,271.0456	1014.3541 [=]	1,271.0456

TI BA II Plus		SHORTCUT	
Keystrokes	*Display*		
Step 1:			
60 [+/–] [PMT]	PMT = –60.0000	PMT	–60.0000
4.5 [I/Y]	I/Y = 4.5000	i	4.5000
4 [N]	N = 4.0000	n	4.0000
0 [PV]	PV = 0.0000	PV	0.0000
[CPT] [FV]	FV = 256.6915	FV	256.6915
Step 2:			
1000 [+/–] [FV]	FV = –1,000.0000	FV	–1,000.00000
60 [+/–] [PMT]	PMT = –60.000	PMT	–60.0000
4.5 [I/Y]	I/Y = 4.5000	i	4.5000
1 [N]	N = 1.0000	n	1.0000
[CPT] [PV]	PV = 1,014.3541	PV	1,014.3541
Step 3:			
256.6915 [+]	256.6915	256.6915 [+]	1,271.0456
1014.3541 [=]	1,271.0456	1,014.3541 [=]	

The previous example illustrates the concept of immunization. The investor should have $1,271.04 at the end of four years, assuming yields remain steady at 4.5 percent. The $1,271.04 consists of the reinvested coupon payments ($256.69) plus the sales proceeds of the bond ($1,014.35). Thus, $1,271.04 is the future value that we are expecting assuming no change in interest rates. This bond is considered immunized if the future value at other rates of return is at least as great as $1,271.04. As the chart illustrates, although the interest rate changes from 4.5 percent, the future value at the point of duration (4 years) for these other points is at least as great as the future value if the interest rates had remained at 4.5 percent. Therefore, at the point of duration (four years) this bond is considered immunized against changes in interest rates.

Matching the duration to the investor's cash need immunizes the portfolio against initial changes in interest rates. As time passes, however, the bond portfolio will need to be rebalanced so that the duration and remaining time continue to match. Rebalancing should be done once or twice per year. If rebalancing is performed more frequently than twice per year, then transaction costs will minimize any benefit derived by rebalancing.

M. SHORTCUT CALCULATION FOR DURATION

The duration formulas can be programmed into some calculators to provide a speedy and efficient way for individuals to calculate duration. Of the calculators featured in this book only the HP 12C and HP 17bII/HP 17bII+ have the capability of providing this shortcut. Their respective programs are as follows:

HP 12C Duration Formula

1. f, P/R	19. RCL 2
2. 1	20. × (TIMES)
3. ENTER	21. RCL 3
4. RCL 3	22. + (PLUS)
5. + (PLUS)	23. 1
6. ENTER	24. + (PLUS)
7. RCL 2	25. RCL 4
8. Y^x (Y Raised to the x power)	26. ÷ (DIVIDE)
9. 1	27. STO 4
10. – (MINUS)	28. RCL 3
11. RCL 1	29. 1
12. × (TIMES)	30. + (PLUS)
13. RCL 3	31. RCL 3
14. + (PLUS)	32. ÷ (DIVIDE)
15. STO 4	33. RCL 4
16. RCL 1	34. – (MINUS)
17. RCL 3	35. f, P/R
18. – (MINUS)	

To execute this program, all you need to do is enter the coupon rate, the years to maturity, and the yield to maturity. Both of the above interest rate variables should be entered as a decimal. Use the following example to verify that the program is working:

Consider a 6% coupon bond with 5 years until maturity and a 6.5% YTM. The keystrokes are as follows:

0.06 STO 1

5 STO 2

0.045 STO 3

R/S

The result is a duration of 4.4840 years.

HP 17bII/HP 17bII+ Duration Formula

From the main screen, press "solve" then "new." Then enter the following equation:

$(1+Y) \div Y - (((1+Y) + T \times (C-Y))) \div (C \times ((1+Y)^{\wedge} T - 1) + Y) = D$ using the keystrokes provided.

HP 17bII/HP 17bII+

Keystrokes	*Display*
[SOLVE]	{NEW}FOR NEW EQUATION
[NEW]	TYPE EQUATION; [INPUT]
(	(
[WXYZ]	WXYZ OTHER
[Y]	(Y
+	(Y +
1	(Y + 1
)	(Y + 1)
÷	(Y + 1) ÷
[WXYZ]	WXYZ OTHER
[Y]	(Y + 1) ÷ Y
–	(Y + 1) ÷ Y –
(	(Y + 1) ÷ Y – (
(	(Y + 1) ÷ Y – ((
(	(Y + 1) ÷ Y – (((
1	(Y + 1) ÷ Y – (((1
+	(Y + 1) ÷ Y – (((1 +
[WXYZ]	WXYZ OTHER
[Y]	(Y + 1) ÷ Y – (((1 + Y
)	(Y + 1) ÷ Y – (((1 + Y)
+	(Y + 1) ÷ Y – (((1 + Y) +
[RSTUV]	RSTUV OTHER
[T]	(Y + 1) ÷ Y – (((1 + Y) + T
x	(Y + 1) ÷ Y – (((1 + Y) + T x
(	(Y + 1) ÷ Y – (((1 + Y) + T x (
[ABCDE]	ABCDE OTHER
C	(Y + 1) ÷ Y – (((1 + Y) + T x (C
–	(Y + 1) ÷ Y – (((1 + Y) + T x (C –
[WXYZ]	WXYZ OTHER
[Y]	...+ 1) ÷ Y – (((1 + Y) + T x (C – Y
)	...1) ÷ Y – (((1 + Y) + T x (C – Y)
)	...)÷ Y – (((1 + Y) + T x (C – Y))
)	...÷ Y – (((1 + Y) + T x (C – Y)))
÷	...Y – (((1 + Y) + T x (C – Y))) ÷
(	...– (((1 + Y) + T x (C – Y))) ÷(
[ABCDE]	ABCDE OTHER
[C]	...(((1 + Y) + T x (C – Y))) ÷(C
x	...((1 + Y) + T x (C – Y))) ÷(C x
(	...(1 + Y) + T x (C – Y))) ÷(C x (
(	...1 + Y) + T x (C – Y))) ÷(C x ((
1	...+ Y) + T x (C – Y))) ÷(C x ((1
+	...Y) + T x (C – Y))) ÷(C x ((1 +

HP 17bII/HP 17bII+

Keystrokes	Display
[WXYZ]	WXYZ OTHER
[Y]	$\ldots) + T \times (C - Y))) \div (C \times ((1 + Y$
)	$\ldots + T \times (C - Y))) \div (C \times ((1 + Y)$
[■]Y^x	$\ldots T \times (C - Y))) \div (C \times ((1 + Y) \wedge$
[RSTUV]	RSTUV OTHER
[T]	$\ldots \times (C - Y))) \div (C \times ((1 + Y) \wedge T$
−	$\ldots (C - Y))) \div (C \times ((1 + Y) \wedge T -$
1	$\ldots C - Y))) \div (C \times ((1 + Y) \wedge T - 1$
)	$\ldots - Y))) \div (C \times ((1 + Y) \wedge T - 1)$
+	$\ldots - Y))) \div (C \times ((1 + Y) \wedge T - 1) +$
[WXYZ]	WXYZ OTHER
[Y]	$\ldots))) \div (C \times ((1 + Y) \wedge T - 1) + Y$
)	$\ldots)) \div (C \times ((1 + Y) \wedge T - 1) + Y)$
=	$\ldots) \div (C \times ((1 + Y) \wedge T - 1) + Y) =$
[ABCDE]	ABCDE OTHER
D	$\ldots \div (C \times ((1 + Y) \wedge T - 1) + Y) = D$
INPUT	$(Y + 1) \div Y - (((1 + Y) + T \times (C - Y \ldots$

To verify, calculate using the previous example:

[CALC]	VERIFYING EQUATION
	0.0000
.06[C]	C = 0.0600
5[T]	T = 5.0000
.045[Y]	Y = 0.0450
[D]	D = 4.4840

VI. PERFORMANCE MEASUREMENTS

A. HOLDING PERIOD RETURN

The holding period return (also known as the single period return) is the basic method to evaluate the speed at which an investment grows or declines. The holding period return is determined by dividing the change in wealth by the beginning value of the investment. The formula for the holding period return is:

$$HPR = \frac{\text{ending value of investment} - \text{beginning value of investment} + / - \text{cash flows}}{\text{beginning value of investment}}$$

However, the measurement has a major weakness because it fails to consider the timing of when the cash flows actually occurred. As a result, if the holding period of the investment is more than one year, the HPR overstates the true return of the investment on an annual basis. Conversely, if the investment's holding period is less than one year, the HPR understates the true return.

B. EXAMPLE

Bob purchases 100 shares of Davis stock for $40 per share. Two years later, Bob sells the 100 shares for $52 per share. In addition, Bob received a dividend of $2 per share in the first year and a dividend of $3 per share in the second year. His holding period return is calculated as follows:

Ending value of investment = $5,200 (100 × $52)

Beginning value of investment = $4,000 (100 × $40)

Cash flow = $500 = (100 × $2) + (100 × $3)

Therefore, the holding period return (HPR) is 42.5% [($5,200 – $4,000 + $500) ÷ $4,000].

HP 17bII/HP 17bII+		HP 12C		HP 10BII/HP 10BII+	
Keystrokes	Display	Keystrokes	Display	Keystrokes	Display
5200 [–]	5,200.0000–	5200 [ENTER]	5,200.0000	5200 [–]	5,200.0000
4000 [+]	1,200.0000+	4000 [–]	1,200.0000	4000 [+]	1,200.0000
500 [÷]	1,700.0000÷	500 [+]	1,700.0000	500 [÷]	1,700.0000
4000 [=]	0.4250	4000 [÷]	0.4250	4000 [=]	0.4250

TI BA II Plus		SHORTCUT
Keystrokes	Display	
5200 [–]	5,200.0000	5,200 – 4,000 + 500 = 1,700
4000 [+]	1,200.0000	1,700 ÷ 4,000 = **0.4250**
500 [÷]	1,700.0000	
4000 [=]	0.4250	

C. ARITHMETIC MEAN

The arithmetic mean is calculated by dividing the sum of the holding period returns for each period by the total number of periods being evaluated.

D. EXAMPLE 1

The arithmetic mean for the following set of data would be approximately 12.41%.

Year 1	Year 2	Year 3	Year 4	Year 5	Year 6	Year 7	Year 8
12.1%	10.0%	11.3%	15.2%	9.1%	6.5%	18.3%	16.8%

HP 17bII/HP 17bII+		HP 12C		HP 10BII/HP 10BII+	
Keystrokes	*Display*	*Keystrokes*	*Display*	*Keystrokes*	*Display*
[SUM]	ITEM(1)=?	[f][REG]		[■][C ALL]	0.0000
[■][CLR DATA]	CLEAR THE LIST?	12.1 [∑+]	1.0000	12.1 [∑+]	1.0000
[YES]	ITEM(1)=?	10.0 [∑+]	2.0000	10.0 [∑+]	2.0000
12.1[INPUT]	ITEM(2)=?	11.3 [∑+]	3.0000	11.3 [∑+]	3.0000
	TOTAL=12.1000	15.2 [∑+]	4.0000	15.2 [∑+]	4.0000
10[INPUT]	ITEM(3)=?	9.1 [∑+]	5.0000	9.1 [∑+]	5.0000
	TOTAL=22.1000	6.5 [∑+]	6.0000	6.5 [∑+]	6.0000
11.3[INPUT]	ITEM(4)=?	18.3 [∑+]	7.0000	18.3 [∑+]	7.0000
	TOTAL=33.4000	16.8 [∑+]	8.0000	16.8 [∑+]	8.0000
15.2[INPUT]	ITEM(5)=?	[g][x̄]	**12.4125**	[■][x̄ ȳ]	**12.4125**
	TOTAL=48.6000				
9.1[INPUT]	ITEM(6)=?				
	TOTAL=57.7000				
6.5[INPUT]	ITEM(7)=?				
	TOTAL=64.2000				
18.3[INPUT]	ITEM(8)=?				
	TOTAL=82.5000				
16.8[INPUT]	ITEM(9)=?				
	TOTAL=99.3000				
[EXIT]	ITEM(9)=?				
[CALC]	99.3000				
[MEAN]	MEAN=**12.4125**				

TI BA II Plus		SHORTCUT	
Keystrokes	*Display*		
12.1[+]	12.1000	12.1000 +	12.1000
10[+]	22.1000	10.0000 +	22.1000
11.3[+]	33.4000	11.3000 +	33.4000
15.2[+]	48.6000	15.2000 +	48.6000
9.1[+]	57.7000	9.1000 +	57.7000
6.5[+]	64.2000	6.5000 +	64.2000
18.3[+]	82.5000	18.3000 +	82.5000
16.8[÷]	99.3000	16.8000 +	99.3000
8[=]	**12.4125**	99.3000 ÷ 8	**12.4125**

NOTE: The arithmetic mean can be calculated using the plus (+) keys (as illustrated in the shortcut method). However, the above keystrokes (except for the TI BA II Plus) have been used to illustrate the summation feature for the calculators. This summation feature will be used for calculating the standard deviation of historical returns as described later in this book. The TI BA II Plus has an alternate method to calculate the mean; however, it requires a significant number of additional keystrokes. Please refer to the owner's manual for a complete description.

E.   EXAMPLE 2

What is the arithmetic mean for the following series of returns?

Year 1	Year 2	Year 3	Year 4	Year 5
15%	9%	(6.5%)	18%	16%

The arithmetic mean for this series of returns is 10.3%.

HP 17bII/HP 17bII+		HP 12C		HP 10BII/HP 10BII+	
Keystrokes	*Display*	*Keystrokes*	*Display*	*Keystrokes*	*Display*
[SUM]	ITEM(1)=?	[f][REG]	0.0000	[■][C ALL]	0.0000
[■] [CLR DATA]	CLEAR THE LIST?	15 [∑+]	1.0000	15[∑+]	1.0000
[YES]	ITEM(1)=?	9 [∑+]	2.0000	9 [∑+]	2.0000
15[INPUT]	ITEM(2)=?	6.5 [CHS][∑+]	3.0000	6.5 [+/–][∑+]	3.0000
	TOTAL=15.0000	18 [∑+]	4.0000	18 [∑+]	4.0000
9[INPUT]	ITEM(3)=?	16 [∑+]	5.0000	16 [∑+]	5.0000
	TOTAL=24.0000	[g][x̄]	10.3000	[■][x̄, ȳ]	10.3000
6.5[+/–][INPUT]	ITEM(4)=?				
	TOTAL=17.5000				
18[INPUT]	ITEM(5)=?				
	TOTAL=35.5000				
16[INPUT]	ITEM(6)=?				
	TOTAL=51.5000				
[EXIT]	ITEM(6)=?				
[CALC]	51.5000				
[MEAN]	MEAN=10.3000				

TI BA II Plus		SHORTCUT	
Keystrokes	*Display*		
15[+]	15.0000	15.0000[+]	15.0000
9[+]	24.0000	9.000[+]	24.0000
6.5[+/–][+]	17.5000	6.5000[+/–][+]	17.5000
18[+]	35.5000	18.0000[+]	35.5000
16[÷]	51.5000	16.0000[÷]	51.5000
5[=]	10.3000	5.0000[=]	10.3000

NOTE: The TI BA II Plus has an alternate method to calculate the mean; however, it requires a significant number of additional keystrokes. Please refer to the owner's manual.

F.   GEOMETRIC MEAN

Geometric mean is the average compounded rate of return or the internal rate of return (annualized return) for a set of returns over a period of time. This return is calculated by subtracting 1 from the nth root of the product of each period's return plus 1, where n is the number of periods over which the calculation is being made.

The formula is written as:

$$\text{Geometric mean} = \sqrt[n]{(1+r_1)(1+r_2)(1+r_3)...(1+r_n)} - 1$$

However, most financial calculators do not provide for a function to calculate the nth root of a number. Financial calculators do provide a function for raising a number to a power. The following equality will allow us to find the nth root of a number by using the power function:

$$\sqrt[n]{X} = X^{1/n}$$

The equality states that the nth root of x is equal to x raised to the 1/n power. Thus, the geometric mean can be solved by using the power function instead of finding the nth root.

G. EXAMPLE

What is the geometric mean for this five-year period?

Year 1	Year 2	Year 3	Year 4	Year 5
15%	9%	−6.5%	18%	16%

The geometric mean is equal to:

$[(1+.15) \times (1+.09) \times (1-.065) \times (1+.18) \times (1+.16)]^{1/5} - 1$, which equals **9.91%**.

HP 17bII/HP 17bII+		HP 12C		HP 10BII/HP 10BII+	
Keystrokes	*Display*	*Keystrokes*	*Display*	*Keystrokes*	*Display*
1.15 [x]	1.1500x	1.15 [ENTER]	1.1500	1.15 [x]	1.1500
1.09 [x]	1.2535x	1.09 [x]	1.2535	1.09 [x]	1.2535
.935 [x]	1.1720x	.935 [x]	1.1720	.935 [x]	1.1720
1.18 [x]	1.3830x	1.18 [x]	1.3830	1.18 [x]	1.3830
1.16 [=]	1.6043	1.16 [x]	1.6043	1.16 [=]	1.6043
[■][y^x]	1.6043^	[ENTER]	1.6043	[■][y^x]	1.6043
5 [■][$^1/x$]	1.6043^0.2000	5 [$^1/x$][y^x]	1.0991	5 [■][$^1/x$]	0.2000
[=]	1.0991	1 [−]	**0.0991**	[=]	1.0991
[−] 1 [=]	**0.0991**			[−] 1 [=]	**0.0991**

TI BA II Plus		SHORTCUT
Keystrokes	*Display*	
1.15 [x]	1.1500	$[1.15 \times 1.09 \times .935 \times 1.18 \times 1.16]^{1/5} - 1 = .0991$
1.09 [x]	1.2535	
.935 [x]	1.1720	
1.18 [x]	1.3830	
1.16 [=]	1.6043	
[y^x]	1.6043	
5 [$^1/x$]	0.2000	
[=]	1.0991	
[−] 1 [=]	**0.0991**	

NOTE: This calculation can also be solved by assuming a beginning balance of $1.00 and increasing it by the earnings rate each year. This will result in the ending balance, based on the earnings. The geometric mean can then be solved by using the time value of money (TVM) keys. Where PV = −1.0, FV = 1.60, n = 5, PMT = 0, and you solve for i.

H. REAL RETURN (INFLATION ADJUSTED)

The loss of purchasing power is one of the risks that investors must overcome in achieving their financial goals. Real returns reflect the earnings from an investment that are above the inflation rate. However, simply subtracting the rate of inflation from the nominal rate will not yield the real return.

I. EXAMPLE

Assume that $1,000 is invested at the beginning of the year and earns 10%, resulting in a balance at the end of the year of $1,100. Also assume that over the same period inflation has been 4%. Thus, $1,040 at the end of the year is equal to the initial investment of $1,000 at the beginning of the year. The real return is equal to the difference between the earnings ($100) and the increase as a result of inflation ($40), which is $60, divided by the initial investment adjusted for inflation ($1,040). This results in a return of 5.77%.

■ Conceptually, the return of 5.77% makes sense, in that the absolute return was 10% and the inflation was 4%, with the difference being 6%.

■ The nominal earnings for this investment is $60, while the real earnings are $57.69 (this is equivalent to $60 ÷ 1.04).

■ The real return can be calculated using the formula:

[[(1 + nominal return) ÷ (1 + inflation rate)] − 1] × 100

Nominal rate = The absolute return (in the example above, it was 10%)

Inflation rate = The rate of inflation for the period (in the example above it is 4%)

HP 17bII/HP 17bII+		HP 12C		HP 10BII/HP 10BII+	
Keystrokes	*Display*	*Keystrokes*	*Display*	*Keystrokes*	*Display*
1.1 [÷]	1.1000÷	1.1 [ENTER]	1.1000	1.1 [÷]	1.1000
1.04 [−]	1.0577−	1.04 [÷]	1.0577	1.04 [−]	1.0577
1 [x]	0.0577x	1 [−]	0.0577	1 [x]	0.0577
100 [=]	**5.7692**	100 [x]	**5.7692**	100 [=]	**5.7692**

TI BA II Plus		SHORTCUT	
Keystrokes	*Display*		
1.1 [÷]	1.1000	1.1000 [÷]	1.1000
1.04 [−]	1.0577	1.0400 [−]	1.0577
1 [x]	0.0577	1.0000 [x]	0.0577
100 [=]	**5.7692**	100.0000 [=]	**5.7692**

Alternative Method:

HP 17bII/HP 17bII+		HP 12C		HP 10BII/HP 10BII+	
Keystrokes	*Display*	*Keystrokes*	*Display*	*Keystrokes*	*Display*
[BUS]	SELECT A MENU	1.04 [ENTER]	1.0400	1.04 [INPUT]	1.0400
[%CHG]	0.0000	1.10[Δ%]	5.7692	1.10 [■][%CHG]	5.7692
1.04 [OLD]	OLD = 1.0400				
1.10 [NEW]	NEW = 1.1000				
[%CH]	%Change =5.7692				

TI BA II Plus		SHORTCUT
Keystrokes	*Display*	
[2nd][Δ%]	OLD= (Old work)	N/A
[2nd][CLR Work]	OLD= 0.0000	
1.04 [ENTER]	OLD= 1.0400	
[↓]	NEW= 0.0000	
1.10 [ENTER]	NEW= 1.1000	
[↓]	%CH= 0.0000	
[CPT]	%CH= 5.7692	

J.   TOTAL RETURN

Total return may be thought of as the sum of the capital appreciation/depreciation on the underlying principal of the investment and any income or earnings generated from that investment. For example, a typical annual dividend paid (income or earnings) on a stock is 2%. If, in addition, the market value of the stock increases 6% from the beginning of the year to year end, the investor would have a total return on the stock of 8% (2% income + 6% capital appreciation).

K.   THE SHARPE PERFORMANCE MEASURE

The Sharpe ratio is calculated as follows:

$$S_p = \frac{\overline{r}_p - \overline{r}_f}{\sigma_p}$$

where:
S_p = Sharpe ratio for portfolio p
$\overline{r}_p$ = the average rate of return
$\overline{r}_f$ = the risk-free rate of return
σ_p = the standard deviation for portfolio p

Sharpe based his ratio on the capital asset pricing model and the Capital Market Line. This ratio measures the risk-adjusted performance of a portfolio based on total risk (systematic risk and unsystematic risk). The Sharpe ratio uses standard deviation in its denominator and, therefore, may be used to compare the performance of all portfolios. Similar to the Treynor ratio, the Sharpe ratio is a relative performance measure, and the higher the ratio, the better the risk-adjusted performance.

L. EXAMPLE

The return for the portfolio is 7.5%, the risk-free rate is 2% and the standard deviation for the portfolio is 11%. What is the Sharpe ratio?

$$\text{Sharpe ratio} = \frac{.075 - .02}{.11} = .5$$

HP 17bII/HP 17bII+		HP 12C		HP 10BII/HP 10BII+	
Keystrokes	*Display*	*Keystrokes*	*Display*	*Keystrokes*	*Display*
.075 [−]	0.0750−	.075 [ENTER]	0.0750	.075 [−]	0.0750
.02 [÷]	0.0550÷	.02 [−]	0.0550	.02 [÷]	0.0550
.11 [=]	**0.5000**	.11 [÷]	**0.5000**	.11 [=]	**0.5000**

TI BA II Plus		SHORTCUT	
Keystrokes	*Display*		
.075 [−]	0.0750	.0750 [−]	0.0750
.02 [÷]	0.0550	.0200 [÷]	0.0550
.11 [=]	**0.5000**	.1100 [=]	**0.5000**

M. THE TREYNOR PERFORMANCE MEASURE

The Treynor ratio is calculated as follows:

$$T_p = \frac{\overline{r}_p - \overline{r}_f}{\beta_p}$$

where:
T_p = Treynor ratio for portfolio p
$\overline{r}_p$ = the average rate of return
$\overline{r}_f$ = the risk-free rate of return
β_p = the beta for portfolio p

Similar to the Sharpe ratio, Treynor's ratio is a relative measure of the risk-adjusted performance of a portfolio. However, this ratio uses beta in its denominator and, therefore, may be used only to compare the performance of diversified portfolios or stocks that constitute diversified portfolios. If a portfolio is fully diversified, both Sharpe and Treynor should yield the same result because diversification will eliminate all unsystematic risk from a portfolio.

N. EXAMPLE

The return for the portfolio is 8%, the risk-free rate is 2% and the Beta of the portfolio is 1.1. What is the Treynor ratio?

$$\text{Treynor ratio} = \frac{.08 - .02}{1.1} = .0546$$

HP 17bII/HP 17bII+		HP 12C		HP 10BII/HP 10BII+	
Keystrokes	*Display*	*Keystrokes*	*Display*	*Keystrokes*	*Display*
.08 [–]	0.0800–	.08 [ENTER]	0.0800	.08 [–]	0.0800
.02 [÷]	0.0600÷	.02 [–]	0.0600	.02 [÷]	0.0600
1.1 [=]	**0.0545**	1.1 [÷]	**0.0545**	1.1 [=]	**0.0545**

TI BA II Plus		SHORTCUT	
Keystrokes	*Display*		
.08 [–]	0.0800	.0800 [–]	0.0800
.02 [÷]	0.0600	.0200 [÷]	0.0600
1.1 [=]	**0.0545**	1.1000 [=]	**0.0545**

O. THE JENSEN PERFORMANCE MEASURE

Jensen's alpha is a measure of the risk-adjusted value added by a portfolio manager. Specifically, alpha is measured as the portfolio's actual or realized return in excess of (or deficient to) the return predicted by the capital asset pricing model (CAPM). A positive alpha means that the portfolio manager has added value on an absolute basis, compared with the required return based on the level of investment risk undertaken; a negative alpha means that the manager has underperformed. Because beta is used in calculating Jensen's alpha, it is only appropriate for evaluating diversified portfolios and stocks that constitute diversified portfolios.

The formula for Jensen's alpha is:

$$\alpha_p = \bar{r}_p - [\bar{r}_f + (\bar{r}_m - \bar{r}_f)\beta_p]$$

where:

α_p = alpha, which represents the return that is able to be earned above or below an unmanaged portfolio with identical market risk

β_p = the beta for portfolio p

$\bar{r}_m$ = the market's rate of return

$\bar{r}_f$ = the risk-free rate of return

NOTE: The last section of the equation, $[\bar{r}_f + (\bar{r}_m - \bar{r}_f)\beta_p]$, is equivalent to the capital asset pricing model. Thus, alpha is equal to the difference between the actual return and the expected return given the level of risk undertaken by the portfolio.

P.   EXAMPLE (SOLVING FOR ALPHA)

XYZ mutual fund had a return of 9%, while the market returned earnings of 10%. If the fund has a beta of .8 and the risk-free rate was 2%, then what is Jensen's alpha for this fund?

$$\alpha = .09 - [.02 + (.1 - .02).8]$$

$$\alpha = .09 - [.02 + (.08).8]$$

$$\alpha = .09 - [.084]$$

$$\alpha = .006 \text{ or } 0.6\%$$

HP 17bII/HP 17bII+		HP 12C		HP 10BII/HP 10BII+	
Keystrokes	*Display*	*Keystrokes*	*Display*	*Keystrokes*	*Display*
.1 [–]	0.1000–	.1 [ENTER]	0.1000	.1 [–]	0.1000
.02 [x]	0.0800x	.02 [–]	0.0800	.02 [x]	0.0800
.8 [+]	0.0640+	.8 [x]	0.0640	.8 [+]	0.0640
.02 [=]	0.0840	.02 [+]	0.0840	.02 [=]	0.0840
[+/–][+]	–0.0840+	[CHS]	–0.0840	[+/–][+]	–0.0840
.09 [=]	**0.0060**	.09 [+]	**0.0060**	.09 [=]	**0.0060**

TI BA II Plus		SHORTCUT	
Keystrokes	*Display*	*Keystrokes*	*Display*
.1 [–]	0.1000	.1000 [–]	0.1000
.02 [x]	0.0800	.0200 [x]	0.0800
.8 [+]	0.0640	.8000 [+]	0.0640
.02 [=]	0.0840	.0200 [=]	0.0840
[+/–][+]	–0.0840	[+/–][+]	–0.0840
.09 [=]	**0.0060**	.0900 [=]	**0.0060**

VII. TIME WEIGHTED VS. DOLLAR WEIGHTED

A. TIME WEIGHTED INTRODUCTION

A *time-weighted return* is determined without regard to the cash flows of the investor and is a measure of the performance of an investment over a period of time. Time-weighted returns only consider cash flows from both appreciation and dividends for a portfolio or stock. This measure can be used to determine how well an investment has done over a period of time. Most returns reported on mutual funds are time-weighted because the portfolio manager does not have any control over the future cash flows to the fund with respect to investor dollars.

B. EXAMPLE 1

Trent purchases 300 shares of TVM stock for $42 per share. Trent makes subsequent purchases at the end of the following years:

Year 1: 50 shares at $46/share

Year 2: 75 shares at $49/share

Year 3: 25 shares at $59/share

If it is now the end of the 4th year and no dividends have been paid and TVM stock is trading for $61/share, what is the annualized time-weighted return for TVM stock (assuming Trent were to sell at $61/share)?

HP 17bII/HP 17bII+		HP 12C		HP 10BII/HP 10BII+	
Keystrokes	*Display*	*Keystrokes*	*Display*	*Keystrokes*	*Display*
[FIN]	SELECT A MENU	42 [CHS][PV]	–42.0000	42 [+/–][PV]	–42.0000
[TVM]	1P/YREND MODE	4 [n]	4.0000	4 [N]	4.0000
42 [+/–][PV]	PV= –42.0000	0 [PMT]	0.0000	0 [PMT]	0.0000
4 [N]	N=4.0000	61 [FV]	61.0000	61 [FV]	61.0000
0 [PMT]	PMT=0.0000	[i]	**9.7792**	[I/YR]	**9.7792**
61 [FV]	FV=61.0000				
[I%YR]	I%YR=**9.7792**				

TI BA II Plus		SHORTCUT	
Keystrokes	*Display*		
42 [+/–][PV]	PV= –42.0000	PV	–42.0000
4 [N]	N=4.0000	*n*	4.0000
0 [PMT]	PMT=0.0000	PMT	0.0000
61 [FV]	FV=61.0000	FV	61.0000
[CPT][I/Y]	I/YR=**9.7792**	*i*	**9.7792**

C. EXAMPLE 2

Scott buys one share of XYZ stock for $80.50. One year later, he buys another share of XYZ stock for $90.00. XYZ stock pays a $3.00 dividend per share at the end of each year. If it is now two years from Scott's initial purchase, and the stock is trading at $100, what is the annualized time-weighted return for XYZ stock for the two-year period?

HP 17bII/HP 17bII+		HP 12C		HP 10BII/HP 10BII+	
Keystrokes	*Display*	*Keystrokes*	*Display*	*Keystrokes*	*Display*
[FIN]	SELECT A MENU	[f][REG]	0.0000	[■][C ALL]	0.0000
[CFLO]	FLOW(0)=?	80.5[CHS][g][CF$_0$]	–80.5000	80.5[+/–][CF$_j$]	–80.5000
[■][CLR DATA]	CLEAR THE LIST?	3[g][CF$_j$]	3.0000	3[CF$_j$]	3.0000
[YES]	FLOW(0)=?	103[g][CF$_j$]	103.0000	103[CF$_j$]	103.0000
80.5[+/–][INPUT]	FLOW(1)=?	[f][IRR]	**14.9938**	[■][IRR/YR]	**14.9938**
	–80.5000				
3[INPUT]	#TIMES(1)=1				
	1.0000				
[INPUT]	FLOW(2)=?				
	1.0000				
103[INPUT]	#TIMES(2)=1				
	1.0000				
[INPUT]	FLOW(3)=?				
	1.0000				
[EXIT]	FLOW(3)=?				
[CALC]	NPV, NUS, NFV NEED I%				
[IRR%]	IRR%=**14.9938**				

TI BA II Plus		SHORTCUT	
Keystrokes	*Display*		
[CF]	CF$_0$=(Old work)	CF$_0$	–80.5000
[2nd][CLR Work]	CF$_0$= 0.0000	CF$_1$	3.0000
80.5[+/–][ENTER]	CF$_0$=–80.5000	CF$_2$	103.0000 (100 + 3)
[↓] 3[ENTER]	C01=3.0000	IRR	**14.9938**
[↓][↓]	C02=0.0000		
103[ENTER]	C02=103.0000		
[IRR]	IRR=0.0000		
[CPT]	IRR=**14.9938**		

D. DOLLAR WEIGHTED INTRODUCTION

The dollar-weighted return is the compounded annual rate of return (internal rate of return) that discounts a portfolio's future value and cash flows to a present value. The dollar-weighted approach focuses on the return of the investor (not the investment, as in the time-weighted approach) over a period of time, and it usually results in a different rate of return than does the time-weighted method.

E.   EXAMPLE 1

Trent purchases 300 shares of TVM stock for $23 per share. Trent makes subsequent purchases at the end of the following years:

Year 1: 50 shares at $46/share

Year 2: 75 shares at $49/share

Year 3: 25 shares at $59/share

If it is now the end of the 4th year and no dividends have been paid and TVM stock is trading for $61/share. What is the annualized dollar-weighted return for Trent (assuming Trent were to sell at $61/share)?

The answer is 23.00%.

Year	Calculation	Cash Flow (CF_t)
0	300 × $23	($6,900)
1	50 × $46	($2,300)
2	75 × $49	($3,675)
3	25 × $59	($1,475)
4	450 × $61	$27,450
Solve for IRR = 23.0037		

HP 17bII/HP 17bII+		HP 12C		HP 10BII/HP 10BII+	
Keystrokes	*Display*	*Keystrokes*	*Display*	*Keystrokes*	*Display*
[FIN]	SELECT A MENU	[f][REG]	0.0000	[■][C ALL]	0.0000
[CFLO]	FLOW(0)=?	6900 [CHS]	−6,900.	6900 [+/−][CF$_j$]	−6,900.0000
[■][CLR DATA]	CLEAR THE LIST?	[g][CF$_0$]	−6,900.0000	2300 [+/−][CF$_j$]	−2,300.0000
[YES]	FLOW(0)=?	2300 [CHS]	−2,300.	3675 [+/−][CF$_j$]	−3,675.0000
6900 [+/−][INPUT]	FLOW(1)=?	[g][CF$_j$]	−2,300.0000	1475 [+/−][CF$_j$]	−1,475.0000
	−6,900.0000	3675 [CHS]	−3,675.	27450[CF$_j$]	27,450.0000
2300[+/−][INPUT]	#TIMES(1)=1	[g][CF$_j$]	−3,675.0000	[■][IRR/YR]	**23.0037**
	1.0000	1475 [CHS]	−1,475.		
[INPUT]	FLOW(2)=?	[g] [CF$_j$]	−1,475.0000		
	1.0000	27450[g][CF$_j$]	27,450.0000		
3675 [+/−][INPUT]	#TIMES(2)=1	[f] [IRR]	**23.0037**		
	1.0000				
[INPUT]	FLOW(3)=?				
	1.000				
1475 [+/−][INPUT]	#TIMES(3)=1				
	1.0000				
[INPUT]	FLOW(4)=?				
	1.0000				
27450 [INPUT]	#TIMES(4)=?				
	1.0000				
[EXIT]	#TIMES (4)=1				
[CALC]	NPV, NUS, NFV NEED I%				
[IRR%]	IRR%=**23.0037**				

TI BA II Plus		SHORTCUT	
Keystrokes	*Display*		
[CF]	CF$_0$=(OLD work)	CF$_0$	−$6,900.0000
[2nd][CLR Work]	CF$_0$=0.0000	CF$_1$	−$2,300.0000
6900[+/−][ENTER]	CF$_0$= −6,900.0000	CF$_2$	−$3,675.0000
[↓]2300[+/−][ENTER]	C01= −2,300.0000	CF$_3$	−$1,475.0000
[↓][↓]		CF$_4$	$27,450.0000
3675 [+/−][ENTER]	C02= −3,675.0000	IRR	**23.0037**
[↓][↓]			
1475 [+/−][ENTER]	C03= −1,475.0000		
[↓][↓]			
27450 [ENTER]	C04=27,450.0000		
[IRR][CPT]	IRR=**23.0037**		

F.   EXAMPLE 2

Scott buys one share of XYZ stock for $80.50. One year later, he buys another share of XYZ stock for $90.00. XYZ stock pays a $3.00 dividend per share at the end of each year. If it is now two years from Scott's initial purchase, and the stock is trading at $100, what is the annualized dollar-weighted return for XYZ stock for the two-year period?

HP 17bII/HP 17bII+		HP 12C		HP 10BII/HP 10BII+	
Keystrokes	*Display*	*Keystrokes*	*Display*	*Keystrokes*	*Display*
[FIN]	SELECT A MENU	[f][REG]	0.0000	[■][C ALL]	0.0000
[CFLO]	FLOW(0)=?	80.5[CHS][g][CF$_0$]	–80.5000	80.5[+/–][CF$_j$]	–80.5000
[■][CLR DATA]	CLEAR THE LIST?	87[CHS][g][CF$_j$]	–87.0000	87[+/–][CF$_j$]	–87.0000
[YES]	FLOW(0)=?	206[g][CF$_j$]	206.0000	206[CF$_j$]	206.0000
80.5[+/–][INPUT]	FLOW(1)=?	[f][IRR]	**14.8120**	[■][IRR/YR]	**14.8120**
	–80.5000				
87[+/–][INPUT]	#TIMES(1)=1				
	1.0000				
[INPUT]	FLOW(2)=?				
	1.0000				
206[INPUT]	#TIMES(2)=1				
	1.0000				
[INPUT]	FLOW(3)=?				
	1.0000				
[EXIT]	FLOW(3)=?				
[CALC]	NPV, NUS, NFV NEED I%				
[IRR%]	IRR%=**14.8120**				

TI BA II Plus		SHORTCUT		
Keystrokes	*Display*			
[CF]	CF$_0$=[Old work]	CF$_0$	–80.5000	
[2nd][CLR Work]	CF$_0$=0.0000	CF$_1$	–87.0000	
80.5[+/–][ENTER]	CF$_0$= –80.5000		(90.00 – 3.00)	
[↓] 87[+/–][ENTER]	C01= –87.0000	CF$_2$	206.0000	
[↓][↓]	C02=206.0000		[(100 + 3) × 2]	
206[ENTER]	IRR=0.0000	IRR	**14.8120**	
[IRR]	IRR=**14.8120**			
[CPT]				

VIII. MARGIN ACCOUNTS

A. INTRODUCTION

Margin accounts allow investors to borrow funds from the broker to purchase additional securities without adding additional cash to the account. Margin accounts allow investors flexibility and the ability to leverage the account.

Margin accounts require that the account owner pay for a certain percentage of the cost of an investment. The margin percentage that must be established for the purchase of a security is referred to as the **initial margin**. The Ferderal Reserve has set the initial margin percentage at 50 percent. Therefore, the initial purchase of a security requires that the investor put up at least 50 percent of the initial purchase.

In addition to the amount that must be initially put up by the investor, the investor must maintain an equity position in the account that equals or exceeds the **maintenance margin**. The maintenance margin is typically 35 percent, which means that the equity in the account must equal or exceed 35 percent. If the equity in the account drops below the maintenance margin, then the account holder receives a margin call from the broker. A margin call is a request for funds to restore the account equity to the maintenance margin.

B. DETERMINING THE PRICE FOR A MARGIN CALL

The account equity is defined as the market value of the securities in the account less the outstanding debt. The equity percentage equals the account equity divided by the market value of the securities. The price at which a margin call is received occurs at the point that the equity percentage drops below the maintenance margin.

This formula is used to determine when a margin call will occur:

$$\text{Margin call} = \frac{\text{debit balance}}{1 - \text{maintenance margin}}$$

Sometimes, this formula is also written as shown below:

$$\text{Margin call} = \frac{1 - \text{initial margin percentage}}{1 - \text{maintenance margin}} \times \text{purchase price of stock}$$

C.   EXAMPLE

Ben purchases one share of Tech Company for $130. Ben uses a margin account with a 50 percent initial margin for the purchase and is concerned about receiving a margin call. If the maintenance margin equals 35 percent, then Ben will receive a margin call if the stock declines below $100, as illustrated below:

$$\text{Margin call} = \frac{\text{debit balance}}{1 - \text{maintenance margin}}$$

$$\text{Margin call} = \frac{\$130 \times 50\%}{1 - 0.35} = \$100$$

HP 17bII/HP 17bII+		HP 12C		HP 10BII/HP 10BII+	
Keystrokes	*Display*	*Keystrokes*	*Display*	*Keystrokes*	*Display*
130 [x]	130.0000x	130 [ENTER]	130.0000	130 [x]	130.0000
.5 [=]	**65.0000**	.5 [x]	**65.0000**	.5 [=]	**65.0000**
1 [–]	1.0000–	1 [ENTER]	1.0000	1 [–]	1.0000
.35 [=]	**0.6500**	.35 [–]	**.6500**	.35 [=]	**0.6500**
- - - - - - - - - -	- - - - - - - - - -	- - - - - - - - - -	- - - - - - - - - -	- - - - - - - - - -	- - - - - - - - - -
65 [÷]	65.0000÷	65 [ENTER]	65.0000	65 [÷]	65.0000
.65 [=]	**100.0000**	.65 [÷]	**100.0000**	.65 [=]	**100.0000**

TI BA II Plus		SHORTCUT	
Keystrokes	*Display*		
130 [x]	130.0000	130 × 0.50 = **65.0000**	
.5 [=]	**65.0000**	1 − 0.35 = **0.6500**	
1 [–]	1.0000	65.0000 ÷ 0.6500 = 100.0000	
.35 [=]	**0.6500**		
- - - - - - - - - -	- - - - - - - - - -		
65 [÷]	65.0000		
0.65 [=]	**100.0000**		

D.   DETERMINING HOW MUCH TO PUT UP TO RESTORE THE ACCOUNT EQUITY

If the stock or account drops below the price at which there is a margin call, then the account owner must deposit sufficient funds to restore the account equity to the maintenance margin. Determining this amount can be accomplished by asking two questions. How much is the broker's equity requirement? How much is the investor's current equity? Using the previous example, assume that the stock drops in value to $90. In such a case, Ben would be required to put up $6.50 per share ($31.50 − $25.00).

Required Equity		Current Equity Position	
Current Value of Stock	$90.00	Current Value of Stock	$90.00
Equity %	35%	Loan Amount	(65.00)
Required Equity	$31.50	Current Equity	$25.00

Regardless of the price of the security (or account), the investor must maintain an equity position of 35 percent, which is the given maintenance margin. Therefore, because the price of the stock is currently $90, Ben must have $31.50 ($90 × 35%) of equity in his account. To determine Ben's current equity position, subtract the outstanding debt from the value of the stock. Because his current equity position equals $25.00 and he must have $31.50 of equity, Ben must fund the account with the difference of $6.50.

IX.   TAX-ADJUSTED RETURNS

A.   INTRODUCTION

A tax-adjusted return (after-tax rate of return) is the realized return multiplied by (1 – tax rate). When evaluating alternating investments, it is important to compare the after-tax rate of return for each potential investment. For example, the after-tax yield on a municipal bond may be higher than the after-tax yield for a corporate bond, even though the corporate bond carries a higher stated rate of return.

B.   EXAMPLE

Harry owns a taxable investment that earns 4% interest. He pays taxes at a marginal rate of 28%. What is the after-tax rate of return that Harry will receive on this investment?

The after-tax rate of return is .04 × (1 – .28) = 2.88%.

HP 17bII/HP 17bII+		HP 12C		HP 10BII/HP 10BII+	
Keystrokes	*Display*	*Keystrokes*	*Display*	*Keystrokes*	*Display*
1 [–]	1.0000–	1 [ENTER]	1.0000	1 [–]	1.0000
.28 [x]	0.7200x	.28 [–]	0.7200	.28 [x]	0.7200
.04 [=]	0.0288	.04 [x]	0.0288	.04 [=]	0.0288

TI BA II Plus		SHORTCUT	
Keystrokes	*Display*		
1 [–]	1.0000	1.0000 [–]	1.0000
.28 [x]	0.7200	.2800 [x]	0.7200
.04 [=]	0.0288	.0400 [=]	0.0288

C.   NONTAXABLE INCOME

1. Federal – The interest income from municipal bonds is not taxable by the federal government. In addition, unrealized appreciation is not taxable by the federal government (until realized).

2. Municipalities – The interest from Treasury bills, bonds, and notes, as well as savings bonds, is not taxable by municipalities. Additionally, most municipalities do not tax interest from municipal bonds issued by its own government.

Because the interest income of municipal bonds is not taxable by the federal government and is usually not taxed by the state in which the bond was issued, the issuer can usually pay a lower yield (coupon rate) on the bond. Investors in high tax brackets with a desire for current income or fixed income investments in their asset allocation will usually purchase municipal bonds.

The bonds are evaluated on their taxable equivalent yield. The taxable equivalent yield calculation is used to compare the yield on a non-taxable bond vs. a taxable bond.

D. EXAMPLE

Anna, who lives in Louisiana, owns a municipal bond issued by the State of Louisiana. The coupon rate on the bond is 4%. Her marginal state tax rate is 3% and her marginal federal tax rate is 28%. What is the taxable equivalent yield (TEY) of this bond for Anna?

TEY = tax-exempt yield ÷ (1 – combined federal and state tax rates)
TEY = .04 ÷ [1 – (.03 + .28)] = 5.80% (rounded)

HP 17bII/HP 17bII+		HP 12C		HP 10BII/HP 10BII+	
Keystrokes	*Display*	*Keystrokes*	*Display*	*Keystrokes*	*Display*
.03 [+]	0.0300+	.03 [ENTER]	0.0300	.03[+]	0.0300
.28 [=]	0.3100	.28 [+]	0.3100	.28[=]	0.3100
[+/–]	–0.3100	[CHS]	–0.3100	[+/–]	–0.3100
[+] 1[=]	**0.6900**	1 [+]	**0.6900**	[+]1[=]	**0.6900**
- - - - - - - - - - -	- - - - - - - - - - -	- - - - - - - - - - -	- - - - - - - - - - -	- - - - - - - - - - -	- - - - - - - - - - -
.04 [÷]	0.0400÷	.04 [ENTER]	0.0400	.04[÷]	0.0400
.69 [=]	**0.0580**	.69 [÷]	**0.0580**	.69[=]	**0.0580**

TI BA II Plus		SHORTCUT	
Keystrokes	*Display*		
.03 [+]	0.0300	.0300[+]	0.0300
.28 [=]	0.3100	.2800[=]	0.3100
[+/–]	–0.3100	[+/–]	–0.3100
[+] 1 [=]	**0.6900**	[+]1.0000[=]	**0.6900**
- - - - - - - - - - -	- - - - - - - - - - -	- - - - - - - - - - -	- - - - - - - - - - -
.04 [÷]	0.0400	.0400[÷]	0.0400
.69 [=]	**0.0580**	.6900[=]	**0.0580**

X. WEIGHTED AVERAGE RETURN

A. INTRODUCTION

The weighted average return represents the return for a set of securities, such as a portfolio, where each return is weighted by the proportion of the security to the entire group or portfolio.

B. EXAMPLE

Company	Market Price	Portfolio Return (%)	Product
A	$80.00	5%	$4.00
B	$35.00	25%	$8.75
C	$10.00	50%	$5.00
Total	$125.00	80%	$17.75
	Weighted return = $17.75 ÷ $125.00 = **14.20%**		

The simple average return for the portfolio above is 26.67% (80% return divided by 3 securities). Notice, however, that 64% of the portfolio had a return of only 5%. The weighted average return reflects the return that was received by the portfolio on a dollar-adjusted basis. The weighted average return is equal to 14.20% as depicted in the above table, significantly different than 26.67%.

HP 17bII/HP 17bII+		HP 12C		HP 10BII/HP 10BII+	
Keystrokes	*Display*	*Keystrokes*	*Display*	*Keystrokes*	*Display*
.64 [x]	0.6400x	.05 [ENTER]	0.0500	[■][C ALL]	0.0000
.05 [=]	**0.0320**	80 [∑+]	1.0000	.05 [INPUT]	0.0500
.28 [x]	0.2800x	.25 [ENTER]	0.2500	80 [∑+]	1.0000
.25 [=]	**0.0700**	35 [∑+]	2.0000	.25 [INPUT]	0.2500
.08 [x]	0.0800x	.5 [ENTER]	0.5000	35 [∑+]	2.0000
.5 [=]	**0.0400**	10 [∑+]	3.0000	.5 [INPUT]	0.5000
- - - - - - - -	- - - - - - - -	[g] [x̄ w]	**0.1420**	10 [∑+]	3.0000
.032 [+]	0.0320+	(located on the		[■][x̄ w]	**0.1420**
.07 [+]	0.1020+	[6] key)			
.04 [=]	**0.1420**				

TI BA II Plus

Keystrokes	Display
.64 [x]	0.6400
.05 [=]	**0.0320**
.28 [x]	0.2800
.25 [=]	**0.0700**
.08 [x]	0.0800
.5 [=]	**0.0400**
.032 [+]	0.0320
.07 [+]	0.1020
.04 [=]	**0.1420**

XI.   STANDARD DEVIATION

A.   INTRODUCTION

Standard deviation is a measurement of risk or dispersion of outcomes (returns) around the mean or expected mean. Observations will tend to cluster around the expected mean, and standard deviation is the measure of this dispersion. Because outcomes tend to cluster around the mean, the bell shaped curve is often used to represent the dispersion of outcomes, as illustrated below. The benefit of the bell shaped curve, or normal curve, is that the curve can be used to determine probabilities of outcomes.

B.   AREA UNDER THE CURVE

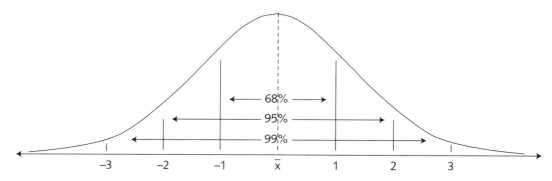

- ■ The bell shaped curve is symmetrical around the mean.

- ■ One half (50%) of the outcomes occur to the left of the mean and one half of the outcomes occur to the right of the mean.

- ■ The curve represents 100% of possible outcomes. These outcomes will tend to cluster around the mean; however, some occurrences will fall away from the mean (i.e., in the tails of the bell shaped curve).

- ■ Approximately 68% of outcomes will fall within one standard deviation (both above and below) of the mean.

- ■ For example, if the mean return for ABC stock is 18% and the standard deviation is 6%, the area under the bell shaped curve which represents one standard deviation would be from 12% (18% − 6%) to 24% (18% + 6%). Therefore, 68% of the outcomes will fall between 12% and 24%.

- ■ Approximately 95% of outcomes will fall within two standard deviations (both above and below) of the mean. Therefore, 95% of the outcomes will fall between 6% and 30% (18% ± 2 × 6%) for ABC stock.

- ■ Approximately 99% of outcomes will fall within three standard deviations (both above and below) of the mean. Therefore, 99% of the outcomes will fall between 0% and 36% (18% ± 3 × 6%) for ABC stock.

■ This information about the normal curve allows investors to determine the probability of specific outcomes. For example, an investor might want to know the probability of a negative return from ABC stock. To determine the probability of a negative return, the first step is to determine how many standard deviations from the mean is zero. Zero is 3 standard deviations from the mean [(18% – 0%) ÷ 6%]. Within 3 standard deviations from the mean will occur 99% of outcomes. Therefore, 1 percent of outcomes will fall below 0% and above 36%. Since the investor is concerned only with the likelihood that the return will be negative, simply divide the 1% in half. Thus, there is a 0.5% chance that an investor will have a negative return from ABC stock.

C. CALCULATION OF STANDARD DEVIATION

There are three different methods for calculating standard deviation of return. These include the calculation of:

1. Standard deviation of historical return.

2. Standard deviation of projected return.

3. Standard deviation of a two-asset portfolio.

D. HISTORICAL RETURNS

Standard deviation of historical returns is calculated by taking the square root of the sum of the squared differences between the average return and the individual returns divided by the number of returns minus one. This calculation is written as:

$$\sigma = \sqrt{\frac{\sum_{t=1}^{n}(r_t - \bar{r})^2}{n-1}}$$

where:
σ = standard deviation
n = number of observations
r_t = return at period t
$\bar{r}$ = average return

The calculation is performed in five steps:

1. For each observation, take the difference between the average return and the individual observations.

2. Square each difference.

3. Sum the squared differences.

4. Divide the sum in Step 3 by one less than the number of observations (if there are ten returns, divide by nine).

5. Take the square root of this division (Step 4).

NOTES:

1. Certain requirements must be met to use this technique with accuracy and are beyond the scope of this text.

2. The standard deviation equals the square root of the variance. Thus, the result of Step 4 is called the variance, and the result of Step 5 is called standard deviation.

E. EXAMPLE

Assume XYZ stock has historical returns over a 12-year period as indicated below. What is the standard deviation for XYZ stock over the 12-year period?

Year	Average Return*	Actual Return	Difference	Difference Squared
1	12%	13.5%	−1.5%	0.0002250
2	12%	12.0%	0.0%	−
3	12%	5.0%	7.0%	0.0049000
4	12%	−2.0%	14.0%	0.0196000
5	12%	7.0%	5.0%	0.0025000
6	12%	23.0%	−11.0%	0.0121000
7	12%	6.0%	6.0%	0.0036000
8	12%	10.0%	2.0%	0.0004000
9	12%	45.0%	−33.0%	0.1089000
10	12%	10.0%	2.0%	0.0004000
11	12%	0.5%	11.5%	0.0132250
12	12%	14.0%	−2.0%	0.0004000
The sum of the squared differences:				**0.1662500**

*The average return is simply the arithmetic average return for the 12-year period.

The standard deviation for XYZ stock will be 12.29% $[(0.16625 \div (12 - 1))]^{1/2}$. However, this calculation is performed much easier on a financial calculator.

HP 17bII/HP 17bII+		HP 12C		HP 10BII/HP 10BII+	
Keystrokes	*Display*	*Keystrokes*	*Display*	*Keystrokes*	*Display*
[SUM]	ITEM(1)=?	[f][REG]	0.0000	[■][C ALL]	0.0000
[■][CLR DATA]	CLEAR THE LIST?	13.5 [∑+]	1.0000	13.5 [∑+]	1.0000
[YES]	ITEM(1)=?	12 [∑+]	2.0000	12 [∑+]	2.0000
13.5[INPUT]	ITEM(2)=?	5 [∑+]	3.0000	5 [∑+]	3.0000
	TOTAL=13.5000	2 [CHS][∑+]	4.0000	2 [+/–][∑+]	4.0000
12[INPUT]	ITEM(3)=?	7 [∑+]	5.0000	7 [∑+]	5.0000
	TOTAL=25.5000	23 [∑+]	6.0000	23 [∑+]	6.0000
5[INPUT]	ITEM(4)=?	6 [∑+]	7.0000	6 [∑+]	7.0000
	TOTAL=30.5000	10 [∑+]	8.0000	10 [∑+]	8.0000
2[+/–][INPUT]	ITEM(5)=?	45 [∑+]	9.0000	45 [∑+]	9.0000
	TOTAL=28.5000	10 [∑+]	10.0000	10 [∑+]	10.0000
7[INPUT]	ITEM(6)=?	.5 [∑+]	11.0000	.5 [∑+]	11.0000
	TOTAL=35.5000	14 [∑+]	12.0000	14 [∑+]	12.0000
23[INPUT]	ITEM(7)=?	[g][s]	**12.2938**	[■][Sx,Sy]	**12.2938**
	TOTAL=58.5000	(located on the			
6[INPUT]	ITEM(8)=?	[.] key)			
	TOTAL=64.5000				
10[INPUT]	ITEM(9)=?				
	TOTAL=74.5000				
45[INPUT]	ITEM(10)=?				
	TOTAL=119.5000				
10[INPUT]	ITEM(11)=?				
	TOTAL=129.5000				
.5[INPUT]	ITEM(12)=?				
	TOTAL=130.0000				
14[INPUT]	ITEM(13)=?				
	TOTAL=144.0000				
[EXIT]	ITEM(13)=?				
[CALC]	144.0000				
[STDEV]	STDEV=**12.2938**				

TI BA II Plus		SHORTCUT
Keystrokes	*Display*	
[2ⁿᵈ][Data]	X01=(Old work)	N/A
[2ⁿᵈ][CLR Work]	X01 0.0000	
13.5[ENTER]	X01=13.50000	
[↓][↓]	X02=0.0000	
12[ENTER]	X02=12.0000	
[↓][↓]	X03=0.0000	
5[ENTER]	X03=5.0000	
[↓][↓]	X04=0.0000	
2[+/−][ENTER]	X04= −2.0000	
[↓][↓]	X05=0.0000	
7[ENTER]	X05=7.0000	
[↓][↓]	X06=0.0000	
23[ENTER]	X06=23.0000	
[↓][↓]	X07=0.0000	
6[ENTER]	X07=6.0000	
[↓][↓]	X08=0.0000	
10[ENTER]	X08=10.0000	
[↓][↓]	X09=0.0000	
45[ENTER]	X09=45.0000	
[↓][↓]	X10=0.0000	
10[ENTER]	X10=10.0000	
[↓][↓]	X11=0.0000	
.5[ENTER]	X11=0.5000	
[↓][↓]	X12=0.0000	
14[ENTER]	X12=14.0000	
[↓][↓]	X13=0.0000	
[2ⁿᵈ][Stat]	I–V	
[2ⁿᵈ][CLR Work]	LIN	
[2ⁿᵈ][SET]	Ln	
(Continue to press [2ⁿᵈ][SET] until I-V is displayed.)		
[↓][↓][↓]	Sx=**12.2938**	

F. PROJECTED RETURNS

A *probability distribution* can be thought of as a set of outcomes with assigned probabilities. Within investments, a probability distribution often consists of possible rates of return (outcomes) with assigned probabilities. The table below depicts an example of a probability distribution that lists the possible outcomes and assigned probabilities under different market conditions for a stock with a current market value of $100.

	Outcomes (Stock Price)	Probability	Single Period Rate of Return
Bull Market	$150	30%	50%
Slow Growth	$110	45%	10%
Bear Market	$85	25%	–15%

The *expected rate of return* $E(r)$ helps investors make decisions concerning where to invest their funds. The expected rate of return, which is the weighted average rate of return, can be calculated easily for a probability distribution:

■ Multiply each rate of return (percent) by the respective probability.

■ The expected rate of return is the total sum of the results.

■ As a formula, $E(r) = P_1(r_1) + P_2(r_2) + ... + P_t(r_t)$

where:

$E(r)$ = the expected return

P_t = the probability assigned to the rate of return for period t

r_t = the rate of return for period t

t   = the number of events that are being examined

G. EXAMPLE

The expected rate of return for the probability distribution in the table above is 15.75% [(30% × .50) + (45% × .10) + (25% ×(–.15))]. Therefore, an investment in this stock, priced at $100, should yield a rate of return of 15.75% or $15.75 per share based on the probability distribution.

HP 17bII/HP 17bII+		HP 12C		HP 10BII/HP 10BII+	
Keystrokes	*Display*	*Keystrokes*	*Display*	*Keystrokes*	*Display*
.3 [x]	0.3000x	.3 [ENTER]	0.3000	.3 [x]	0.3000
.5 [=]	**0.1500**	.5 [x]	**0.1500**	.5 [=]	**0.1500**
.45 [x]	0.4500x	.45 [ENTER]	0.4500	.45 [x]	0.4500
.1 [=]	**0.0450**	.1 [x]	**0.0450**	.1 [=]	**0.0450**
.25 [x]	0.2500x	.25 [ENTER]	0.2500	.25 [x]	0.2500
.15 [+/–][=]	**–0.0375**	.15 [CHS][x]	**–0.0375**	.15 [+/–][=]	**–0.0375**
.15 [+]	0.1500+	.15 [ENTER]	0.1500	.15 [+]	0.1500
.045 [+]	0.1950+	.045 [+]	0.1950	.045 [+]	0.1950
.0375 [+/–][=]	**0.1575**	.0375 [CHS][+]	**0.1575**	.0375 [+/–][=]	**0.1575**

TI BA II Plus		SHORTCUT		
Keystrokes	*Display*			
.3 [x]	0.3000			
.5 [=]	**0.1500**	**Probability**	**E(r)**	**E(r)w**
.45 [x]	0.4500	30%	50%	15.0000%
.1 [=]	**0.0450**	45%	10%	4.5000%
.25 [x]	0.2500	25%	–15%	–3.7500%
.15 [+/–][=]	**–0.0375**	100%		15.7500%
.15 [+]	0.1500			
.045 [+]	0.1950			
.0375 [+/–][=]	**0.1575**			

H. STANDARD DEVIATION FOR PROJECTED RETURNS

Standard deviation for projected returns equals the square root of the summation of products of the squared deviations of each possible rate of return from the expected rate of return multiplied by the corresponding probability factor.

$$\sigma = [P_1[r_1 - E(r)]^2 + P_2[r_2 - E(r)]^2 + \ldots + P_t[r_t - E(r)]^2]^{1/2}$$

where:

$E(r)$ = the expected return

P_t = the probability assigned to the rate of return for period t

r_t = the rate of return for period t

t   = the number of events that are being examined

I. EXAMPLE

Using the information from Sections F and G, calculate the standard deviation of the probability distribution.

$$\sigma^2 = P_1[r_1 - E(r)]^2 + P_2[r_2 - E(r)]^2 + P_3[r_3 - E(r)]^2$$

$$\sigma^2 = .3[.5 - .1575]^2 + .45[.1 - .1575]^2 + .25[-.15 - .1575]^2$$

$$\sigma^2 = .03519 + .00149 + .02364$$

$$\sigma^2 = .06032$$

$$\sigma = (.06032)^{1/2} = .2456 \text{ or } 24.56\%$$

HP 17bII/HP 17bII+		HP 12C		HP 10BII/HP 10BII+	
Keystrokes	*Display*	*Keystrokes*	*Display*	*Keystrokes*	*Display*
.5 [–]	0.5000–	.5 [ENTER]	0.5000	.5 [–]	0.5000
.1575 [=]	0.3425	.1575 [–][ENTER]	0.3425	.1575 [=]	0.3425
[■][yˣ] 2 [x]	0.1173x	2 [yˣ]	0.1173	[■][yˣ] 2 [x]	0.1173
.3 [=]	**0.0352**	.3 [x]	**0.0352**	.3 [=]	**0.0352**
.1 [–]	0.1000–	.1 [ENTER]	0.1000	.1 [–]	0.1000
.1575 [=]	–0.0575	.1575[–] [ENTER]	–0.0575	.1575 [=]	–0.0575
[■][yˣ] 2 [x]	0.0033x	2 [yˣ]	0.0033	[■][yˣ] 2 [x]	0.0033
.45 [=]	**0.0015**	.45 [x]	**0.0015**	.45 [=]	**0.0015**
.15 [+/–][–]	–0.1500–	.15[CHS][ENTER]	–0.0015	.15 [+/–][–]	–0.1500
.1575 [=]	–0.3075	.1575 [–][ENTER]	–0.3075	.1575 [=]	–0.3075
[■][yˣ] 2 [x]	0.0946x	2 [yˣ]	0.0946	[■][yˣ] 2 [x]	0.0946
.25 [=]	**0.0236**	.25 [x]	**0.0236**	.25 [=]	**0.0236**
.0352 [+]	0.0352+	.0352 [ENTER]	0.0352	.0352 [+]	0.0352
.0015 [+]	0.0367+	.0015 [+]	0.0367	.0015 [+]	0.0367
.0236 [=]	0.0603	.0236 [+]	0.0603	.0236 [=]	0.0603
[■] [$\sqrt{x}$]	**0.2456**	[g] [$\sqrt{x}$]	**0.2456**	[■] [$\sqrt{x}$]	**0.2456**

TI BA II Plus		SHORTCUT
Keystrokes	*Display*	
.5 [–]	0.5000	$(.1575 - .50)^2 \times (.30) = 0.0352$
.1575 [=]	0.3425	$(.1575 - .10)^2 \times (.45) = 0.0015$
[yˣ] 2 [x]	0.1173	$(.1575 - (.15))^2 \times (.25) = \underline{0.0236}$
.3 [=]	**0.0352**	$\sigma^2 = 0.0603$
.1 [–]	0.1000	$\sigma = \textbf{0.2456}$
.1575 [=]	–0.0575	
[yˣ] 2 [x]	0.0033	
.45 [=]	**0.0015**	
.15 [+/–][–]	–0.1500	
.1575 [=]	–0.3075	
[yˣ] 2 [x]	0.0946	
.25 [=]	**0.0236**	
.0352 [+]	0.0352	
.0015 [+]	0.0367	
.0236 [=]	0.0603	
[$\sqrt{x}$]	**0.2456**	

J.   STANDARD DEVIATION OF A TWO-ASSET PORTFOLIO

Diversification is the process by which different securities and asset classes are blended together within a portfolio to reduce risk. The reason diversification works is because different securities and asset classes are not perfectly correlated.

$$\sigma = \sqrt{W_A^2 \sigma_A^2 + W_B^2 \sigma_B^2 + 2W_A W_B [\sigma_A \sigma_B R_{AB}]}$$

where:

W_A = the percent of the portfolio that is invested in A
W_B = the percent of the portfolio that is invested in B
R_{AB} = the correlation between A and B
$\sigma_A \sigma_B R_{AB}$ = covariance between A and B

K.   EXAMPLE

Matt has two portfolios, A and B, with the following values and risk levels:

Portfolio	Value	Standard Deviation	% of Portfolio
A	7,000	18%	35%
B	13,000	24%	65%

If the correlation between Portfolio A and B is .4, what is the standard deviation of the two portfolios combined?

$$\sigma^2 = W_A^2 \sigma_A^2 + W_B^2 \sigma_B^2 + 2W_A W_B [\sigma_A \sigma_B R_{AB}]$$

$$\sigma^2 = (.35)^2 (.18)^2 + (.65)^2 (.24)^2 + 2(.35)(.65)[(.18)(.24)(.4)]$$

$$\sigma^2 = .0040 + .0243 + .0079 = .0362$$

$$\sigma = (.0362)^{1/2}$$

$$\sigma = 19.03\%$$

HP 17bII/HP 17bII+		HP 12C		HP 10BII/HP 10BII+	
Keystrokes	*Display*	*Keystrokes*	*Display*	*Keystrokes*	*Display*
.18[■][yˣ] 2 [=]	0.0324	.18 [ENTER]	0.1800	.18	.18
.35[■][yˣ] 2 [=]	0.1225	2 [yˣ]	0.0324	[■][yˣ] 2 [=]	0.0324
[x] .0324 [=]	**0.0040**	.35 [ENTER]	0.3500	.35	.35
- - - - - - - - -	- - - - - - - -	2 [yˣ]	0.1225	[■][yˣ] 2 [=]	0.1225
.24[■][yˣ] 2 [=]	0.0576	.0324 [x]	**0.0040**	[x] .0324 [=]	**0.0040**
.65[■][yˣ] 2 [=]	0.4225	- - - - - - - - -	- - - - - - - -	- - - - - - - -	- - - - - - - - -
[x] .0576 [=]	**0.0243**	.24 [ENTER]	0.2400	.24	0.24
- - - - - - - - -	- - - - - - -	2 [yˣ]	0.0576	[■][yˣ] 2 [=]	0.0576
.4 [x]	0.4000x	.65 [ENTER]	0.6500	.65	0.65
.24 [x]	0.0960x	2 [yˣ]	0.4425	[■][yˣ] 2 [=]	0.4225
.18 [x]	0.0173x	[ENTER]	0.4425	[x] .0576 [=]	**0.0243**
.65 [x]	0.0112x	.0576 [x]	**0.0243**		
.35 [x]	0.0039x	- - - - - - - - -	- - - - - - - -	- - - - - - - -	- - - - - - - - -
2 [=]	**0.0079**	.4 [ENTER]	0.4000	.4 [x]	0.4000
- - - - - - - - -	- - - - - - - -	.24 [x]	0.0960	.24 [x]	0.0960
.0079 [+]	0.0079+	.18 [x]	0.0173	.18 [x]	0.0173
.0243 [+]	0.0322+	.65 [x]	0.0112	.65 [x]	0.0112
.0040 [=]	0.0362	.35 [x]	0.0039	.35 [x]	0.0039
[■][√x̄]	**0.1903**	2 [x]	**0.0079**	2 [=]	**0.0079**
		- - - - - - - - -	- - - - - - - -	- - - - - - - -	- - - - - - - - -
		.0079 [ENTER]	0.0079	.0079 [+]	0.0079
		.0243 [+]	0.0322	.0243 [+]	0.0322
		.0040 [+]	0.0362	.0040 [=]	0.0362
		[g] [√x̄]	**0.1903**	[■][√x̄]	**0.1903**

TI BA II Plus	
Keystrokes	*Display*
.18	.18
[yˣ] 2 [=]	0.0324
.35	.35
[yˣ] 2 [=]	0.1225
[x] .0324 [=]	**0.0040**
- - - - - - - - - - - -	- - - - - - - - - - - -
.24	0.24
[yˣ] 2 [=]	0.0576
.65	0.65
[yˣ] 2 [=]	0.4225
[x] .0576 [=]	**0.0243**
- - - - - - - - - - - -	- - - - - - - - - - - -
.4 [x]	0.4000
.24 [x]	0.0960
.18 [x]	0.0173
.65 [x]	0.0112
.35 [x]	0.0039
2 [=]	**0.0079**
- - - - - - - - - - - -	- - - - - - - - - - - -
.0079 [+]	0.0079
.0243 [+]	0.0322
.0040 [=]	0.0362
[√x̄]	**0.1903**

Where keystrokes use y^x for the power key and $\sqrt{x}$ for the square root key.

XII.   VALUATION MODELS

A.   CONSTANT GROWTH DIVIDEND DISCOUNT MODEL

This model is used to determine the price for a security in which dividends are growing at a constant rate. The formula for this model is:

$$V = \frac{D_1}{r - g}$$

where:

V   =   price for the security

D_1 =   the dividend paid at period 1

r   =   the investor's required rate of return

g   =   the dividend growth rate

NOTES:

1. Problems will often provide the current dividend today, which is D_0. D_1 can be determined by multiplying D_0 by $(1 + g)$.

2. The model does not allow for the growth rate (g) to be greater than or equal to the required rate of return (r).

3. See perpetuities for stocks that pay a dividend that has a zero growth rate.

B.   EXAMPLE 1

Assume Francis Corporation is currently paying a dividend of $2.00 and the dividend is growing at a constant rate of 7%. What should the value of the security be if the investor's required rate of return is 11%?

$$V = \frac{D_1}{r - g}$$

$$V = \frac{2 \times (1.07)}{(.11 - .07)}$$

$$V = \frac{2.14}{(.04)}$$

$$V = \$53.50$$

NOTE: $[D_0 = \$2.00]$

Therefore, the investor should not pay more than $53.50 for this security.

HP 17bII/HP 17bII+		HP 12C		HP 10BII/HP 10BII+	
Keystrokes	*Display*	*Keystrokes*	*Display*	*Keystrokes*	*Display*
2 [x]	2.0000x	2 [ENTER]	2.0000	2 [x]	2.0000
1.07 [=]	**2.1400**	1.07 [x]	**2.1400**	1.07 [=]	**2.1400**
.11 [–]	0.1100–	.11 [ENTER]	0.1100	.11 [–]	0.1100
.07 [=]	0.0400	.07 [–]	**0.0400**	.07 [=]	**0.0400**
- - - - - - - - - -	- - - - - - - - - -	- - - - - - - - - -	- - - - - - - - - -	- - - - - - - - - -	- - - - - - - - - -
2.14 [÷]	2.1400÷	2.14 [ENTER]	2.1400	2.14 [÷]	2.1400
.04 [=]	**53.5000**	.04 [÷]	**53.5000**	.04 [=]	**53.5000**

TI BA II Plus		SHORTCUT	
Keystrokes	*Display*		
2 [x]	2.0000	2.0000 [x]	2.0000
1.07[=]	**2.1400**	1.0700 [=]	**2.1400**
.11[–]	0.1100	.1100 [–]	0.1100
.07 [=]	**0.0400**	.0700 [=]	**0.0400**
- - - - - - - - - -	- - - - - - - - - -	- - - - - - - - - -	- - - - - - - - - -
2.14 [÷]	2.1400	2.1400 [÷]	2.1400
.04 [=]	**53.5000**	.0400 [=]	**53.5000**

C.   EXAMPLE 2

Todd is considering buying a stock that is currently paying a dividend of $2.00. The dividend has been growing at 4%. If Todd's required rate of return is 12%, what is the most he should pay for this stock?

$$V = \frac{2 \times 1.04}{.12 - .04} = \frac{2.08}{.08} = \$26.00$$

HP 17bII/HP 17bII+		HP 12C		HP 10BII/HP 10BII+	
Keystrokes	*Display*	*Keystrokes*	*Display*	*Keystrokes*	*Display*
2 [x]	2.0000x	2 [ENTER]	2.0000	2 [x]	2.0000
1.04 [=]	**2.0800**	1.04 [x]	**2.0800**	1.04 [=]	**2.0800**
.12 [–]	0.1200–	.12 [ENTER]	0.1200	.12 [–]	0.1200
.04 [=]	**0.0800**	.04 [–]	**0.0800**	.04 [=]	**0.0800**
- - - - - - - - - -	- - - - - - - - - -	- - - - - - - - - -	- - - - - - - - - -	- - - - - - - - - -	- - - - - - - - - -
2.08 [÷]	2.0800÷	2.08 [ENTER]	2.0800	2.08 [÷]	2.0800
.08 [=]	**26.0000**	.08 [÷]	**26.0000**	.08 [=]	**26.0000**

TI BA II Plus		SHORTCUT	
Keystrokes	*Display*		
2 [x]	2.0000	2.0000 [x]	2.0000
1.04 [=]	**2.0800**	1.0400 [=]	**2.0800**
.12 [–]	0.1200	.1200 [–]	0.1200
.04 [=]	**0.0800**	.0400 [=]	**0.0800**
- - - - - - - - - - - -	- - - - - - - - - - - -	- - - - - - - - - - - -	- - - - - - - - - - - -
2.08[÷]	2.0800	2.0800 [÷]	2.0800
.08 [=]	**26.0000**	.0800 [=]	**26.0000**

D. MULTISTAGE GROWTH DIVIDEND DISCOUNT MODEL

The multistage (variable) growth dividend discount model assumes that the growth rate of the stock's dividend is not constant but rather changes (either up or down). To determine the intrinsic value of a stock using this model, you must follow a three-step process.

1. Calculate the value of each future dividend until the growth rate stabilizes.

2. Use the constant growth dividend discount model to calculate the remaining intrinsic value of the stock at the beginning of the year when the dividend growth rate stabilizes.

3. Use the uneven cash flow method to solve for the net present (intrinsic) value of the stock.

E. EXAMPLE

Assume ADM stock has a dividend that is expected to grow for three years at 6% annually and then at 7% annually thereafter. Furthermore, assume that the investor's required rate of return is 9%.

1. Calculate the value of each future dividend until the growth rate stabilizes (Years 1–3).

    $D_1 = \$2.00 \times 1.06 = \$2.1200$

    $D_2 = \$2.12 \times 1.06 = \$2.2472$

    $D_3 = \$2.2472 \times 1.06 = \$2.3820$

2. Use the constant growth dividend discount model to calculate the remaining intrinsic value of the stock at the beginning of the year when the dividend growth rate stabilizes (Year 4).

    $D_4 = \$2.3820 \times 1.07 = \$2.5488$

    $V = \$2.5488 \div (0.09 - 0.07) = \$127.4387$

3. Use the uneven cash flow method to solve for the net present (intrinsic) value of the stock.

$CF_0 = \$0$

$CF_1 = \$2.1200$

$CF_2 = \$2.2472$

$CF_3 = \$2.3820 + \$127.4387 = \$129.8207$

I/YR = 9%

Solve for NPV = \$104.0818

In this example, the intrinsic value of the stock is **\$104.08**.

HP 17bII/HP 17bII+		HP 12C	
Keystrokes	*Display*	*Keystrokes*	*Display*
2 [x]	2.0000x	2.00 [ENTER]	2.0000
1.06 [=]	**2.1200**	1.06 [x]	**2.1200**
2.12 [x]	2.1200x	2.1200 [ENTER]	2.1200
1.06 [=]	**2.2472**	1.06 [x]	**2.2472**
2.2472 [x]	2.2472x	2.2472 [ENTER]	2.2472
1.06 [=]	**2.3820**	1.06 [x]	**2.3820**
2.3820 [x]	2.3820x	2.3820 [ENTER]	2.3820
1.07 [=]	2.5488	1.07 [x]	**2.5488**
[÷][(][.09[−]	2.5488÷(0.0900−	2.5488 [ENTER]	2.5488
.07 [)]	2.5488÷0.0200	.09 [ENTER]	0.0900
[=]	**127.4387**	.07 [−] [÷]	**127.4387**
[FIN]	SELECT A MENU	0 [g] [CF0]	0.0000
[CFLO]	FLOW(0)=?	2.1200 [g] [CFj]	2.1200
[■][CLR DATA]	CLEAR THE LIST?	2.2472 [g] [CFj]	2.2472
[YES]	FLOW(0)=?	2.3820 [ENTER]	2.3820
0 [INPUT]	FLOW(1)=?	127.4387 [+] [g] [CFj]	129.8207
2.1200 [INPUT]	INPUT(1) =1	9 [i]	9.0000
	1.0000	[f] [NPV]	**104.0818**
[INPUT]	FLOW(2)=?		
2.2472 [INPUT]	#TIMES(2)=1		
	1.0000		
[INPUT]	FLOW(3)=?		
2.3820 [+]	2.3820		
127.4370 [=] [INPUT]	#TIMES(3)=1		
	1.0000		
[INPUT]	FLOW(3)=?		
	1.0000		
[EXIT]	FLOW(4)=?		
[CALC]	NPV, NUS, NFV NEED I%		
9[I%]	I% = 9.0000%		
[NPV]	**NPV=104.0805**		

HP 10BII/HP 10BII+		TI BA II Plus	
Keystrokes	*Display*	*Keystrokes*	*Display*
2 [x]	2.0000	2 [x]	2.0000
1.06 [=]	**2.1200**	1.06 [=]	**2.1200**
2.12 [x]	2.1200	2.12 [x]	2.1200
1.06 [=]	**2.2472**	1.06 [=]	**2.2472**
2.2472 [x]	2.2472	2.2472 [x]	2.2472
1.06 [=]	**2.3820**	1.06 [=]	**2.3820**
- - - - - - - - - - -	- - - - - - - - - - -	(Do not clear calculator)	
2.3820 [x]	2.3820	- - - - - - - - - - -	
1.07 [=]	2.5488	[x]	2.3820
[÷][■][(].09[−]	0.0900	1.07 [=]	2.5488
.07[■][)][=]	**127.4387**	[÷] [(] .09 [−]	0.0900
- - - - - - - - - - -	- - - - - - - - - - -	.07 [)] [=]	127.4387
0 [Cfj]	0.0000	- - - - - - - - - - -	
2.1200 [CFj]	2.1200	[CF]	CF$_0$ = (Old work)
2.2472 [CFj]	2.2472	[2nd] [CLR Work]	CF$_0$ = 0.0000
2.3820 [+]	2.3820	0 [ENTER]	CF$_0$ = 0.0000
127.4370 [CFj]	129.8207	[↓] 2.1200 [ENTER]	C01 = 2.1200
9 [I/YR]	9.0000	[↓] 1 [ENTER]	F01 = 1.0000
[■]NPV	**104.0818**	[↓] 2.2472 [ENTER]	C02 = 2.2472
		[↓] 1 [ENTER]	F02 = 1.0000
		[↓] 2.3820 + 127.4387 [ENTER]	C03 = 129.8207
		[↓] 1 [ENTER]	F03 = 1.0000
		[NPV]	I = 0.0000
		9 [ENTER]	I = 9.0000
		[↓] [CPT]	104.0818

F. PERPETUITIES

If the dividend growth rate is zero, then the dividend will be constant. To determine the value of this type of dividend stream, simply substitute zero for g in the previous model.

$$V = \frac{D_1}{(r - g)}$$

$$V = \frac{D_1}{(r - 0)}$$

$$V = \frac{D_1}{r}$$

The new formula is the dividend for the first period divided by the required rate of return. Because the dividend is constant, however, it could be the dividend for any period; therefore, D may be substituted for D_1 in the formula.

G. EXAMPLE

Assume Francis Corporation always pays a $2.00 dividend and the investor's required rate of return is 11%. The value of the security would be $18.18 ($2 ÷ .11). An example of a perpetuity is preferred stock which generally pays a set dividend each year.

HP 17bII/HP 17bII+		HP 12C		HP 10BII/HP 10BII+	
Keystrokes	Display	Keystrokes	Display	Keystrokes	Display
2 [÷]	2.0000÷	2 [ENTER]	2.0000	2 [÷]	2.0000
.11 [=]	**18.1818**	.11 [÷]	**18.1818**	.11 [=]	**18.1818**

TI BA II Plus		SHORTCUT	
Keystrokes	Display		
2 [÷]	2.0000	2.0000 [÷]	2.0000
.11 [=]	**18.1818**	.1100 [=]	**18.1818**

H.   CAPITALIZED EARNINGS

Capitalized earnings is a simplistic method to value a firm. The formula for capitalizing earnings is:

$$V = \frac{E}{R_d}$$

where:

V   =   the estimated value of the company or firm

E   =   the earnings used to value the firm

R_d =   the discount (capitalization) rate

This is the same basic formula used for valuing perpetuities.

Several problems exist with regard to the capitalized earnings method for valuing companies.

- ■ Earnings, as determined by Generally Accepted Accounting Principals (GAAP), do not necessarily represent cash flows. One of the problems with this method is determining what earnings should be capitalized and if any adjustments should be made to the earnings figure. These might include such adjustments as adding back to earnings any excessive salary or bonuses paid to owners.

- ■ An appropriate discount rate must be determined when using this formula. The discount rate should reflect a proper risk factor, an inflation factor, and various other adjustments to reflect the true cost of capital on a risk-adjusted basis.

I.   EXAMPLE

On December 31st of last year, it was calculated that Kristen Corporation had earnings of $50,000.00 for the entire year. The discount rate used to capitalize Kristen Corporation's earnings is 16%. What is the capitalized earnings value of Kristen Corporation?

V = $50,000 ÷ .16 = $312,500.

HP 17bII/HP 17bII+		HP 12C		HP 10BII/HP 10BII+	
Keystrokes	Display	Keystrokes	Display	Keystrokes	Display
50000 [÷]	50,000.0000÷	50000 [ENTER]	50,000.0000	50000 [÷]	50,000.0000
.16 [=]	**312,500.0000**	.16 [÷]	**312,500.0000**	.16 [=]	**312,500.0000**

TI BA II Plus		SHORTCUT	
Keystrokes	*Display*		
50000 [÷]	50,000.0000	50000 [÷]	50,000.0000
.16 [=]	**312,500.0000**	.1600 [=]	**312,500.0000**

XIII. REAL ESTATE VALUATION

A. REAL ESTATE INVESTMENTS

Real estate is property consisting of land, permanently attached structures, and accompanying rights and privileges (i.e. crops and mineral rights). Individuals often invest in real estate because it can provide the possibility of positive cash flow and the potential for significant appreciation. When purchasing real estate investments, clients will often need to know the market value of the investment in order to determine a fair purchase/sale price.

B. DIRECT CAPITALIZATION INCOME APPROACH

The direct capitalization income approach is one method of determining the market value of the real estate investment. This method appraises real estate based on the property's anticipated future income. The market value is seen as the present value of all of the future net operating income (NOI) amounts.

$$\text{Market value} = V = \frac{\text{NOI}}{\text{discount rate}}$$

NOI = gross potential revenue – vacancy and collection losses – property operating expenses

The discount rate is found by evaluating recent sales of income-producing properties and determining the rates of return required by those investors. A higher rate signals a riskier investment, thus the purchaser will often pay less for this type of investment. Conversely, an investment with a lower rate signifies that the investment is more stable and thus would require a higher purchase price.

C. EXAMPLE

A small, four-store shopping strip center has projected gross income of $200,000 per year. Calculate the market value of the property using the direct capitalization income approach assuming a discount rate of 10% given the following income statement:

EXHIBIT 1: Income Statement

Estimated gross income		$200,000
Less vacancy loss @ 8.5%		17,000
Effective gross income		183,000
Less expenses		
Depreciation	20,000	
Real estate taxes	1,345	
Insurance	2,567	
Maintenance	5,590	
Management fee	8,578	
Mortgage interest	17,000	55,080
Net income		$127,920

Step One – Calculate NOI

Net income	$127,920
Plus depreciation	20,000
Plus mortgage interest	17,000
Equals NOI	$164,920

Step Two – Calculate the market value.

$$\text{Market value} = \frac{\text{NOI}}{\text{discount rate}} = \frac{\$164,920}{.10} = \$1,649,200$$

Therefore, the appropriate market value of the shopping strip is $1,649,200. If an investor wanted to purchase this strip center they should expect a fair price to be around $1,649,200.

Note that depreciation and mortgage interest are added back when calculating NOI. Mortgage interest and principal are added back because the value of the property should not be impacted by the method the current owner has used to finance the property. Because depreciation is a non-cash expense, it is also added back to calculate NOI.

HP 17bII/HP 17bII+		HP 12C		HP 10BII/HP 10BII+	
Keystrokes	*Display*	*Keystrokes*	*Display*	*Keystrokes*	*Display*
127920 [+]	127,920.0000[+]	127920 [ENTER]	127,920.0000	127920 [+]	127,920.0000
20000 [+]	147,920.0000[+]	20000 [+]	147,920.0000	20000 [+]	147,920.0000
17000 [=]	164,920.0000	17000 [+]	164,920.0000	17000 [=]	164,920.0000
[÷].10 [=]	**1,649,200.0000**	.10[÷]	**1,649,200.0000**	[÷].10 [=]	**1,649,200.0000**

TI BA II Plus		SHORTCUT
Keystrokes	*Display*	
127920 [+]	127,920.0000	127,920 + 20,000 + 17,000 = 164,920.0000
20000 [+]	147,920.0000	164,920.0000 ÷ .10 = 1,649,200.0000
17000 [=]	164,920.0000	
[÷].10 [=]	**1,649,200.0000**	

Appendices

A. INVESTMENT FORMULAS

Constant Growth Dividend Discount Model

$$V = \frac{D_1}{r - g}$$

Expected Return Form of Dividend Discount Model

$$r = \frac{D_1}{P} + g$$

Covariance Between Two Sample Assets

$$COV_{ij} = \rho_{ij}\sigma_i\sigma_j$$

Standard Deviation of a Two-Asset Portfolio

$$\sigma_p = \sqrt{W_i^2\sigma_i^2 + W_j^2\sigma_j^2 + 2\,W_i\,W_j\,COV_{ij}}$$

Beta Coefficient of Sample Asset

$$\beta_i = \frac{COV_{im}}{\sigma_m^2} = \frac{\rho_{im}\sigma_i}{\sigma_m}$$

Population for Standard Deviation of a Single Asset

$$\sigma_r = \sqrt{\frac{\sum\limits_{t=1}^{n}\left(r_t - \bar{r}\right)^2}{n}}$$

Sample for Standard Deviation of a Single Asset

$$S_r = \sqrt{\frac{\sum\limits_{t=1}^{n}\left(r_t - \bar{r}\right)^2}{n-1}}$$

Conversion Value of a Convertible Bond

$$CV = \frac{Par}{CP} \times P_s$$

Capital Asset Pricing Model

$$r_i = r_f + \left(r_m - r_f\right)\beta_i$$

Capital Market Line

$$r_p = r_f + \sigma_p\left[\frac{r_m - r_f}{\sigma_m}\right]$$

Sharpe Ratio of Portfolio Performance

$$S_p = \frac{\bar{r}_p - \bar{r}_f}{\sigma_p}$$

Jensen's Alpha of Portfolio Performance

$$\alpha_p = \bar{r}_p - \left[\bar{r}_f + \left(\bar{r}_m - \bar{r}_f\right)\beta_p\right]$$

Treynor Ratio of Portfolio Performance

$$T_p = \frac{\bar{r}_p - \bar{r}_f}{\beta_p}$$

Macaulay Duration/Duration

$$D = \frac{\sum\limits_{t=1}^{n}\dfrac{c_t(t)}{\left(1+i\right)^t}}{\sum\limits_{t=1}^{n}\dfrac{c_t}{\left(1+i\right)^t}}$$

Macaulay Duration/Duration

$$D = \frac{1+y}{y} - \frac{\left(1+y\right)+t\left(c-y\right)}{c\left[\left(1+y\right)^t - 1\right]+y}$$

Estimate Change in Price of a Bond

$$\frac{\Delta P}{P} = -D\left[\frac{\Delta y}{1+y}\right]$$

Information Ratio

$$IR = \frac{R_P - R_B}{\sigma_A}$$

B. TIME VALUE OF MONEY TABLES

Present Value of $1

$$\left[\frac{1}{(1+i)^n}\right]$$

Period	1%	2%	3%	4%	5%	6%	7%	8%	9%	10%	11%	12%	13%
1	0.9901	0.9804	0.9709	0.9615	0.9524	0.9434	0.9346	0.9259	0.9174	0.9091	0.9009	0.8929	0.8850
2	0.9803	0.9612	0.9426	0.9246	0.9070	0.8900	0.8734	0.8573	0.8417	0.8264	0.8116	0.7972	0.7831
3	0.9706	0.9423	0.9151	0.8890	0.8638	0.8396	0.8163	0.7938	0.7722	0.7513	0.7312	0.7118	0.6931
4	0.9610	0.9238	0.8885	0.8548	0.8227	0.7921	0.7629	0.7350	0.7084	0.6830	0.6587	0.6355	0.6133
5	0.9515	0.9057	0.8626	0.8219	0.7835	0.7473	0.7130	0.6806	0.6499	0.6209	0.5935	0.5674	0.5428
6	0.9420	0.8880	0.8375	0.7903	0.7462	0.7050	0.6663	0.6302	0.5963	0.5645	0.5346	0.5066	0.4803
7	0.9327	0.8706	0.8131	0.7599	0.7107	0.6651	0.6227	0.5835	0.5470	0.5132	0.4817	0.4523	0.4251
8	0.9235	0.8535	0.7894	0.7307	0.6768	0.6274	0.5820	0.5403	0.5019	0.4665	0.4339	0.4039	0.3762
9	0.9143	0.8368	0.7664	0.7026	0.6446	0.5919	0.5439	0.5002	0.4604	0.4241	0.3909	0.3606	0.3329
10	0.9053	0.8203	0.7441	0.6756	0.6139	0.5584	0.5083	0.4632	0.4224	0.3855	0.3522	0.3220	0.2946
11	0.8963	0.8043	0.7224	0.6496	0.5847	0.5268	0.4751	0.4289	0.3875	0.3505	0.3173	0.2875	0.2607
12	0.8874	0.7885	0.7014	0.6246	0.5568	0.4970	0.4440	0.3971	0.3555	0.3186	0.2858	0.2567	0.2307
13	0.8787	0.7730	0.6810	0.6006	0.5303	0.4688	0.4150	0.3677	0.3262	0.2897	0.2575	0.2292	0.2042
14	0.8700	0.7579	0.6611	0.5775	0.5051	0.4423	0.3878	0.3405	0.2992	0.2633	0.2320	0.2046	0.1807
15	0.8613	0.7430	0.6419	0.5553	0.4810	0.4173	0.3624	0.3152	0.2745	0.2394	0.2090	0.1827	0.1599
16	0.8528	0.7284	0.6232	0.5339	0.4581	0.3936	0.3387	0.2919	0.2519	0.2176	0.1883	0.1631	0.1415
17	0.8444	0.7142	0.6050	0.5134	0.4363	0.3714	0.3166	0.2703	0.2311	0.1978	0.1696	0.1456	0.1252
18	0.8360	0.7002	0.5874	0.4936	0.4155	0.3503	0.2959	0.2502	0.2120	0.1799	0.1528	0.1300	0.1108
19	0.8277	0.6864	0.5703	0.4746	0.3957	0.3305	0.2765	0.2317	0.1945	0.1635	0.1377	0.1161	0.0981
20	0.8195	0.6730	0.5537	0.4564	0.3769	0.3118	0.2584	0.2145	0.1784	0.1486	0.1240	0.1037	0.0868
25	0.7798	0.6095	0.4776	0.3751	0.2953	0.2330	0.1842	0.1460	0.1160	0.0923	0.0736	0.0588	0.0471
30	0.7419	0.5521	0.4120	0.3083	0.2314	0.1741	0.1314	0.0994	0.0754	0.0573	0.0437	0.0334	0.0256
35	0.7059	0.5000	0.3554	0.2534	0.1813	0.1301	0.0937	0.0676	0.0490	0.0356	0.0259	0.0189	0.0139
40	0.6717	0.4529	0.3066	0.2083	0.1420	0.0972	0.0668	0.0460	0.0318	0.0221	0.0154	0.0107	0.0075
45	0.6391	0.4102	0.2644	0.1712	0.1113	0.0727	0.0476	0.0313	0.0207	0.0137	0.0091	0.0061	0.0041
50	0.6080	0.3715	0.2281	0.1407	0.0872	0.0543	0.0339	0.0213	0.0134	0.0085	0.0054	0.0035	0.0022

Present Value of $1

$$\left[\frac{1}{(1+i)^n}\right]$$

Period	14%	15%	16%	17%	18%	19%	20%	25%	30%	35%	40%	45%	50%
1	0.8772	0.8696	0.8621	0.8547	0.8475	0.8403	0.8333	0.8000	0.7692	0.7407	0.7143	0.6897	0.6667
2	0.7695	0.7561	0.7432	0.7305	0.7182	0.7062	0.6944	0.6400	0.5917	0.5487	0.5102	0.4756	0.4444
3	0.6750	0.6575	0.6407	0.6244	0.6086	0.5934	0.5787	0.5120	0.4552	0.4064	0.3644	0.3280	0.2963
4	0.5921	0.5718	0.5523	0.5337	0.5158	0.4987	0.4823	0.4096	0.3501	0.3011	0.2603	0.2262	0.1975
5	0.5194	0.4972	0.4761	0.4561	0.4371	0.4190	0.4019	0.3277	0.2693	0.2230	0.1859	0.1560	0.1317
6	0.4556	0.4323	0.4104	0.3898	0.3704	0.3521	0.3349	0.2621	0.2072	0.1652	0.1328	0.1076	0.0878
7	0.3996	0.3759	0.3538	0.3332	0.3139	0.2959	0.2791	0.2097	0.1594	0.1224	0.0949	0.0742	0.0585
8	0.3506	0.3269	0.3050	0.2848	0.2660	0.2487	0.2326	0.1678	0.1226	0.0906	0.0678	0.0512	0.0390
9	0.3075	0.2843	0.2630	0.2434	0.2255	0.2090	0.1938	0.1342	0.0943	0.0671	0.0484	0.0353	0.0260
10	0.2697	0.2472	0.2267	0.2080	0.1911	0.1756	0.1615	0.1074	0.0725	0.0497	0.0346	0.0243	0.0173
11	0.2366	0.2149	0.1954	0.1778	0.1619	0.1476	0.1346	0.0859	0.0558	0.0368	0.0247	0.0168	0.0116
12	0.2076	0.1869	0.1685	0.1520	0.1372	0.1240	0.1122	0.0687	0.0429	0.0273	0.0176	0.0116	0.0077
13	0.1821	0.1625	0.1452	0.1299	0.1163	0.1042	0.0935	0.0550	0.0330	0.0202	0.0126	0.0080	0.0051
14	0.1597	0.1413	0.1252	0.1110	0.0985	0.0876	0.0779	0.0440	0.0254	0.0150	0.0090	0.0055	0.0034
15	0.1401	0.1229	0.1079	0.0949	0.0835	0.0736	0.0649	0.0352	0.0195	0.0111	0.0064	0.0038	0.0023
16	0.1229	0.1069	0.0930	0.0811	0.0708	0.0618	0.0541	0.0281	0.0150	0.0082	0.0046	0.0026	0.0015
17	0.1078	0.0929	0.0802	0.0693	0.0600	0.0520	0.0451	0.0225	0.0116	0.0061	0.0033	0.0018	0.0010
18	0.0946	0.0808	0.0691	0.0592	0.0508	0.0437	0.0376	0.0180	0.0089	0.0045	0.0023	0.0012	0.0007
19	0.0829	0.0703	0.0596	0.0506	0.0431	0.0367	0.0313	0.0144	0.0068	0.0033	0.0017	0.0009	0.0005
20	0.0728	0.0611	0.0514	0.0433	0.0365	0.0308	0.0261	0.0115	0.0053	0.0025	0.0012	0.0006	0.0003
25	0.0378	0.0304	0.0245	0.0197	0.0160	0.0129	0.0105	0.0038	0.0014	0.0006	0.0002	0.0001	0.0000
30	0.0196	0.0151	0.0116	0.0090	0.0070	0.0054	0.0042	0.0012	0.0004	0.0001	0.0000	0.0000	0.0000
35	0.0102	0.0075	0.0055	0.0041	0.0030	0.0023	0.0017	0.0004	0.0001	0.0000	0.0000	0.0000	0.0000
40	0.0053	0.0037	0.0026	0.0019	0.0013	0.0010	0.0007	0.0001	0.0000	0.0000	0.0000	0.0000	0.0000
45	0.0027	0.0019	0.0013	0.0009	0.0006	0.0004	0.0003	0.0000	0.0000	0.0000	0.0000	0.0000	0.0000
50	0.0014	0.0009	0.0006	0.0004	0.0003	0.0002	0.0001	0.0000	0.0000	0.0000	0.0000	0.0000	0.0000

Future Value of $1

$$(1+i)^n$$

Period	1%	2%	3%	4%	5%	6%	7%	8%	9%	10%	11%	12%	13%
1	1.0100	1.0200	1.0300	1.0400	1.0500	1.0600	1.0700	1.0800	1.0900	1.1000	1.1100	1.1200	1.1300
2	1.0201	1.0404	1.0609	1.0816	1.1025	1.1236	1.1449	1.1664	1.1881	1.2100	1.2321	1.2544	1.2769
3	1.0303	1.0612	1.0927	1.1249	1.1576	1.1910	1.2250	1.2597	1.2950	1.3310	1.3676	1.4049	1.4429
4	1.0406	1.0824	1.1255	1.1699	1.2155	1.2625	1.3108	1.3605	1.4116	1.4641	1.5181	1.5735	1.6305
5	1.0510	1.1041	1.1593	1.2167	1.2763	1.3382	1.4026	1.4693	1.5386	1.6105	1.6851	1.7623	1.8424
6	1.0615	1.1262	1.1941	1.2653	1.3401	1.4185	1.5007	1.5869	1.6771	1.7716	1.8704	1.9738	2.0820
7	1.0721	1.1487	1.2299	1.3159	1.4071	1.5036	1.6058	1.7138	1.8280	1.9487	2.0762	2.2107	2.3526
8	1.0829	1.1717	1.2668	1.3686	1.4775	1.5938	1.7182	1.8509	1.9926	2.1436	2.3045	2.4760	2.6584
9	1.0937	1.1951	1.3048	1.4233	1.5513	1.6895	1.8385	1.9990	2.1719	2.3579	2.5580	2.7731	3.0040
10	1.1046	1.2190	1.3439	1.4802	1.6289	1.7908	1.9672	2.1589	2.3674	2.5937	2.8394	3.1058	3.3946
11	1.1157	1.2434	1.3842	1.5395	1.7103	1.8983	2.1049	2.3316	2.5804	2.8531	3.1518	3.4785	3.8359
12	1.1268	1.2682	1.4258	1.6010	1.7959	2.0122	2.2522	2.5182	2.8127	3.1384	3.4985	3.8960	4.3345
13	1.1381	1.2936	1.4685	1.6651	1.8856	2.1329	2.4098	2.7196	3.0658	3.4523	3.8833	4.3635	4.8980
14	1.1495	1.3195	1.5126	1.7317	1.9799	2.2609	2.5785	2.9372	3.3417	3.7975	4.3104	4.8871	5.5348
15	1.1610	1.3459	1.5580	1.8009	2.0789	2.3966	2.7590	3.1722	3.6425	4.1772	4.7846	5.4736	6.2543
16	1.1726	1.3728	1.6047	1.8730	2.1829	2.5404	2.9522	3.4259	3.9703	4.5950	5.3109	6.1304	7.0673
17	1.1843	1.4002	1.6528	1.9479	2.2920	2.6928	3.1588	3.7000	4.3276	5.0545	5.8951	6.8660	7.9861
18	1.1961	1.4282	1.7024	2.0258	2.4066	2.8543	3.3799	3.9960	4.7171	5.5599	6.5436	7.6900	9.0243
19	1.2081	1.4568	1.7535	2.1068	2.5270	3.0256	3.6165	4.3157	5.1417	6.1159	7.2633	8.6128	10.1974
20	1.2202	1.4859	1.8061	2.1911	2.6533	3.2071	3.8697	4.6610	5.6044	6.7275	8.0623	9.6463	11.5231
25	1.2824	1.6406	2.0938	2.6658	3.3864	4.2919	5.4274	6.8485	8.6231	10.8347	13.5855	17.0001	21.2305
30	1.3478	1.8114	2.4273	3.2434	4.3219	5.7435	7.6123	10.0627	13.2677	17.4494	22.8923	29.9599	39.1159
35	1.4166	1.9999	2.8139	3.9461	5.5160	7.6861	10.6766	14.7853	20.4140	28.1024	38.5749	52.7996	72.0685
40	1.4889	2.2080	3.2620	4.8010	7.0400	10.2857	14.9745	21.7245	31.4094	45.2593	65.0009	93.0510	132.7816
45	1.5648	2.4379	3.7816	5.8412	8.9850	13.7646	21.0025	31.9204	48.3273	72.8905	109.5302	163.9876	244.6414
50	1.6446	2.6916	4.3839	7.1067	11.4674	18.4202	29.4570	46.9016	74.3575	117.3909	184.5648	289.0022	450.7359

Future Value of $1

$$(1+i)^n$$

Period	14%	15%	16%	17%	18%	19%	20%	25%	30%	35%	40%	45%	50%
1	1.1400	1.1500	1.1600	1.1700	1.1800	1.1900	1.2000	1.2500	1.3000	1.3500	1.4000	1.4500	1.5000
2	1.2996	1.3225	1.3456	1.3689	1.3924	1.4161	1.4400	1.5625	1.6900	1.8225	1.9600	2.1025	2.2500
3	1.4815	1.5209	1.5609	1.6016	1.6430	1.6852	1.7280	1.9531	2.1970	2.4604	2.7440	3.0486	3.3750
4	1.6890	1.7490	1.8106	1.8739	1.9388	2.0053	2.0736	2.4414	2.8561	3.3215	3.8416	4.4205	5.0625
5	1.9254	2.0114	2.1003	2.1924	2.2878	2.3864	2.4883	3.0518	3.7129	4.4840	5.3782	6.4097	7.5938
6	2.1950	2.3131	2.4364	2.5652	2.6996	2.8398	2.9860	3.8147	4.8268	6.0534	7.5295	9.2941	11.3906
7	2.5023	2.6600	2.8262	3.0012	3.1855	3.3793	3.5832	4.7684	6.2749	8.1722	10.5414	13.4765	17.0859
8	2.8526	3.0590	3.2784	3.5115	3.7589	4.0214	4.2998	5.9605	8.1573	11.0324	14.7579	19.5409	25.6289
9	3.2519	3.5179	3.8030	4.1084	4.4355	4.7854	5.1598	7.4506	10.6045	14.8937	20.6610	28.3343	38.4434
10	3.7072	4.0456	4.4114	4.8068	5.2338	5.6947	61917	9.3132	13.7858	20.1066	28.9255	41.0847	57.6650
11	4.2262	4.6524	5.1173	5.6240	6.1759	6.7767	74301	11.6415	17.9216	27.1439	40.4957	59.5728	86.4976
12	4.8179	5.3503	5.9360	6.5801	7.2876	8.0642	8.9161	14.5519	23.2981	36.6442	56.6939	86.3806	129.7463
13	5.4924	6.1528	6.8858	7.6987	8.5994	9.5964	10.6993	18.1899	30.2875	49.4697	79.3715	125.2518	194.6195
14	6.2613	7.0757	7.9875	9.0075	10.1472	11.4198	12.8392	22.7374	39.3738	66.7841	111.1201	181.6151	291.9293
15	7.1379	8.1371	9.2655	10.5387	11.9737	13.5895	15.4070	28.4217	51.1859	90.1585	155.5681	263.3419	437.8939
16	8.1372	9.3576	10.7480	12.3303	14.1290	16.1715	18.4884	35.5271	66.5417	121.7139	217.7953	381.8458	656.8408
17	9.2765	10.7613	12.4677	14.4265	16.6722	19.2441	22.1861	44.4089	86.5042	164.3138	304.9135	553.6764	985.2613
18	10.5752	12.3755	14.4625	16.8790	19.6733	22.9005	26.6233	55.5112	112.4554	221.8236	426.8789	802.8308	1477.892
19	12.0557	14.2318	16.7765	19.7484	23.2144	27.2516	31.9480	69.3889	146.1920	299.4619	597.6304	1164.105	2216.838
20	13.7435	16.3665	19.4608	23.1056	27.3930	32.4294	38.3376	86.7362	190.0496	404.2736	836.6826	1687.952	3325.257
25	26.4619	32.9190	40.8742	50.6578	62.6686	77.3881	95.3962	264.6978	705.6410	1812.776	4499.880	10819.32	25251.17
30	50.9502	66.2118	85.8499	111.0647	143.3706	184.6753	237.3763	807.7936	2619.996	8128.550	24201.43	69348.98	191751.1
35	98.1002	133.1755	180.3141	243.5035	327.9973	440.7006	590.6682	2465.190	9727.860	36448.69	130161.1	444509	1456110
40	188.8835	267.8635	378.7212	533.8687	750.3783	1051.668	1469.772	7523.164	36118.86	163437.1	700037.7	2849181	11057332
45	363.6791	538.7693	795.4438	1170.479	1716.684	2509.651	3657.262	22958.87	134106.8	732857.6	3764971	18262495	83966617
50	700.2330	1083.657	1670.704	2566.215	3927.357	5988.914	9100.438	70064.92	497929.2	3286158	20248916	117057734	637621500

Present Value of Ordinary Annuity

$$\left[\frac{1 - \frac{1}{(1+i)^n}}{i} \right]$$

Period	1%	2%	3%	4%	5%	6%	7%	8%	9%	10%	11%	12%	13%
1	0.9901	0.9804	0.9709	0.9615	0.9524	0.9434	0.9346	0.9259	0.9174	0.9091	0.9009	0.8929	0.8850
2	1.9704	1.9416	1.9135	1.8861	1.8594	1.8334	1.8080	1.7833	1.7591	1.7355	1.7125	1.6901	1.6681
3	2.9410	2.8839	2.8286	2.7751	2.7232	2.6730	2.6243	2.5771	2.5313	2.4869	2.4437	2.4018	2.3612
4	3.9020	3.8077	3.7171	3.6299	3.5460	3.4651	3.3872	3.3121	3.2397	3.1699	3.1024	3.0373	2.9745
5	4.8534	4.7135	4.5797	4.4518	4.3295	4.2124	4.1002	3.9927	3.8897	3.7908	3.6959	3.6048	3.5172
6	5.7955	5.6014	5.4172	5.2421	5.0757	4.9173	4.7665	4.6229	4.4859	4.3553	4.2305	4.1114	3.9975
7	6.7282	6.4720	6.2303	6.0021	5.7864	5.5824	5.3893	5.2064	5.0330	4.8684	4.7122	4.5638	4.4226
8	7.6517	7.3255	7.0197	6.7327	6.4632	6.2098	5.9713	5.7466	5.5348	5.3349	5.1461	4.9676	4.7988
9	8.5660	8.1622	7.7861	7.4353	7.1078	6.8017	6.5152	6.2469	5.9952	5.7590	5.5370	5.3282	5.1317
10	9.4713	8.9826	8.5302	8.1109	7.7217	7.3601	7.0236	6.7101	6.4177	6.1446	5.8892	5.6502	5.4262
11	10.3676	9.7868	9.2526	8.7605	8.3064	7.8869	7.4987	7.1390	6.8052	6.4951	6.2065	5.9377	5.6869
12	11.2551	10.5753	9.9540	9.3851	8.8633	8.3838	7.9427	7.5361	7.1607	6.8137	6.4924	6.1944	5.9176
13	12.1337	11.3484	10.6350	9.9856	9.3936	8.8527	8.3577	7.9038	7.4869	7.1034	6.7499	6.4235	6.1218
14	13.0037	12.1062	11.2961	10.5631	9.8986	9.2950	8.7455	8.2442	7.7862	7.3667	6.9819	6.6282	6.3025
15	13.8651	12.8493	11.9379	11.1184	10.3797	9.7122	9.1079	8.5595	8.0607	7.6061	7.1909	6.8109	6.4624
16	14.7179	13.5777	12.5611	11.6523	10.8378	10.1059	9.4466	8.8514	8.3126	7.8237	7.3792	6.9740	6.6039
17	15.5623	14.2919	13.1661	12.1657	11.2741	10.4773	9.7632	9.1216	8.5436	8.0216	7.5488	7.1196	6.7291
18	16.3983	14.9920	13.7535	12.6593	11.6896	10.8276	10.0591	9.3719	8.7556	8.2014	7.7016	7.2497	6.8399
19	17.2260	15.6785	14.3238	13.1339	12.0853	11.1581	10.3356	9.6036	8.9501	8.3649	7.8393	7.3658	6.9380
20	18.0456	16.3514	14.8775	13.5903	12.4622	11.4699	10.5940	9.8181	9.1285	8.5136	7.9633	7.4694	7.0248
25	22.0232	19.5235	17.4131	15.6221	14.0939	12.7834	11.6536	10.6748	9.8226	9.0770	8.4217	7.8431	7.3300
30	25.8077	22.3965	19.6004	17.2920	15.3725	13.7648	12.4090	11.2578	10.2737	9.4269	8.6938	8.0552	7.4957
35	29.4086	24.9986	21.4872	18.6646	16.3742	14.4982	12.9477	11.6546	10.5668	9.6442	8.8552	8.1755	7.5856
40	32.8347	27.3555	23.1148	19.7928	17.1591	15.0463	13.3317	11.9246	10.7574	9.7791	8.9511	8.2438	7.6344
45	36.0945	29.4902	24.5187	20.7200	17.7741	15.4558	13.6055	12.1084	10.8812	9.8628	9.0079	8.2825	7.6609
50	39.1961	31.4236	25.7298	21.4822	18.2559	15.7619	13.8007	12.2335	10.9617	9.9148	9.0417	8.3045	7.6752

Present Value of Ordinary Annuity

$$\left[\dfrac{1-\dfrac{1}{(1+i)^n}}{i}\right]$$

Period	14%	15%	16%	17%	18%	19%	20%	25%	30%	35%	40%	45%	50%
1	0.8772	0.8696	0.8621	0.8547	0.8475	0.8403	0.8333	0.8000	0.7692	0.7407	0.7143	0.6897	0.6667
2	1.6467	1.6257	1.6052	1.5852	1.5656	1.5465	1.5278	1.4400	1.3609	1.2894	1.2245	1.1653	1.1111
3	2.3216	2.2832	2.2459	2.2096	2.1743	2.1399	2.1065	1.9520	1.8161	1.6959	1.5889	1.4933	1.4074
4	2.9137	2.8550	2.7982	2.7432	2.6901	2.6386	2.5887	2.3616	2.1662	1.9969	1.8492	1.7195	1.6049
5	3.4331	3.3522	3.2743	3.1993	3.1272	3.0576	2.9906	2.6893	2.4356	2.2200	2.0352	1.8755	1.7366
6	3.8887	3.7845	3.6847	3.5892	3.4976	3.4098	3.3255	2.9514	2.6427	2.3852	2.1680	1.9831	1.8244
7	4.2883	4.1604	4.0386	3.9224	3.8115	3.7057	3.6046	3.1611	2.8021	2.5075	2.2628	2.0573	1.8829
8	4.6389	4.4873	4.3436	4.2072	4.0776	3.9544	3.8372	3.3289	2.9247	2.5982	2.3306	2.1085	1.9220
9	4.9464	4.7716	4.6065	4.4506	4.3030	4.1633	4.0310	3.4631	3.0190	2.6653	2.3790	2.1438	1.9480
10	5.2161	5.0188	4.8332	4.6586	4.4941	4.3389	4.1925	3.5705	3.0915	2.7150	2.4136	2.1681	1.9653
11	5.4527	5.2337	5.0286	4.8364	4.6560	4.4865	4.3271	3.6564	3.1473	2.7519	2.4383	2.1849	1.9769
12	5.6603	5.4206	5.1971	4.9884	4.7932	4.6105	4.4392	3.7251	3.1903	2.7792	2.4559	2.1965	1.9846
13	5.8424	5.5831	5.3423	5.1183	4.9095	4.7147	4.5327	3.7801	3.2233	2.7994	2.4685	2.2045	1.9897
14	6.0021	5.7245	5.4675	5.2293	5.0081	4.8023	4.6106	3.8241	3.2487	2.8144	2.4775	2.2100	1.9931
15	6.1422	5.8474	5.5755	5.3242	5.0916	4.8759	4.6755	3.8593	3.2682	2.8255	2.4839	2.2138	1.9954
16	6.2651	5.9542	5.6685	5.4053	5.1624	4.9377	4.7296	3.8874	3.2832	2.8337	2.4885	2.2164	1.9970
17	6.3729	6.0472	5.7487	5.4746	5.2223	4.9897	4.7746	3.9099	3.2948	2.8398	2.4918	2.2182	1.9980
18	6.4674	6.1280	5.8178	5.5339	5.2732	5.0333	4.8122	3.9279	3.3037	2.8443	2.4941	2.2195	1.9986
19	6.5504	6.1982	5.8775	5.5845	5.3162	5.0700	4.8435	3.9424	3.3105	2.8476	2.4958	2.2203	1.9991
20	6.6231	6.2593	5.9288	5.6278	5.3527	5.1009	4.8696	3.9539	3.3158	2.8501	2.4970	2.2209	1.9994
25	6.8729	6.4641	6.0971	5.7662	5.4669	5.1951	4.9476	3.9849	3.3286	2.8556	2.4994	2.2220	1.9999
30	7.0027	6.5660	6.1772	5.8294	5.5168	5.2347	4.9789	3.9950	3.3321	2.8568	2.4999	2.2222	2.0000
35	7.0700	6.6166	6.2153	5.8582	5.5386	5.2512	4.9915	3.9984	3.3330	2.8571	2.5000	2.2222	2.0000
40	7.1050	6.6418	6.2335	5.8713	5.5482	5.2582	4.9966	3.9995	3.3332	2.8571	2.5000	2.2222	2.0000
45	7.1232	6.6543	6.2421	5.8773	5.5523	5.2611	4.9986	3.9998	3.3333	2.8571	2.5000	2.2222	2.0000
50	7.1327	6.6605	6.2463	5.8801	5.5541	5.2623	4.9995	3.9999	3.3333	2.8571	2.5000	2.2222	2.0000

Future Value of Ordinary Annuity

$$\left[\frac{(1+i)^n - 1}{i}\right]$$

Period	1%	2%	3%	4%	5%	6%	7%	8%	9%	10%	11%	12%	13%
1	1.0000	1.0000	1.0000	1.0000	1.0000	1.0000	1.0000	1.0000	1.0000	1.0000	1.0000	1.0000	1.0000
2	2.0100	2.0200	2.0300	2.0400	2.0500	2.0600	2.0700	2.0800	2.0900	2.1000	2.1100	2.1200	2.1300
3	3.0301	3.0604	3.0909	3.1216	3.1525	3.1836	3.2149	3.2464	3.2781	3.3100	3.3421	3.3744	3.4069
4	4.0604	4.1216	4.1836	4.2465	4.3101	4.3746	4.4399	4.5061	4.5731	4.6410	4.7097	4.7793	4.8498
5	5.1010	5.2040	5.3091	5.4163	5.5256	5.6371	5.7507	5.8666	5.9847	6.1051	6.2278	6.3528	6.4803
6	6.1520	6.3081	6.4684	6.6330	6.8019	6.9753	7.1533	7.3359	7.5233	7.7156	7.9129	8.1152	8.3227
7	7.2135	7.4343	7.6625	7.8983	8.1420	8.3938	8.6540	8.9228	9.2004	9.4872	9.7833	10.0890	10.4047
8	8.2857	8.5830	8.8923	9.2142	9.5491	9.8975	10.2598	10.6366	11.0285	11.4359	11.8594	12.2997	12.7573
9	9.3685	9.7546	10.1591	10.5828	11.0266	11.4913	11.9780	12.4876	13.0210	13.5795	14.1640	14.7757	15.4157
10	10.4622	10.9497	11.4639	12.0061	12.5779	13.1808	13.8164	14.4866	15.1929	15.9374	16.7220	17.5487	18.4197
11	11.5668	12.1687	12.8078	13.4864	14.2068	14.9716	15.7836	16.6455	17.5603	18.5312	19.5614	20.6546	21.8143
12	12.6825	13.4121	14.1920	15.0258	15.9171	16.8699	17.8885	18.9771	20.1407	21.3843	22.7132	24.1331	25.6502
13	13.8093	14.6803	15.6178	16.6268	17.7130	18.8821	20.1406	21.4953	22.9534	24.5227	26.2116	28.0291	29.9847
14	14.9474	15.9739	17.0863	18.2919	19.5986	21.0151	22.5505	24.2149	26.0192	27.9750	30.0949	32.3926	34.8827
15	16.0969	17.2934	18.5989	20.0236	21.5786	23.2760	25.1290	27.1521	29.3609	31.7725	34.4054	37.2797	40.4175
16	17.2579	18.6393	20.1569	21.8245	23.6575	25.6725	27.8881	30.3243	33.0034	35.9497	39.1899	42.7533	46.6717
17	18.4304	20.0121	21.7616	23.6975	25.8404	28.2129	30.8402	33.7502	36.9737	40.5447	44.5008	48.8837	53.7391
18	19.6147	21.4123	23.4144	25.6454	28.1324	30.9057	33.9990	37.4502	41.3013	45.5992	50.3959	55.7497	61.7251
19	20.8109	22.8406	25.1169	27.6712	30.5390	33.7600	37.3790	41.4463	46.0185	51.1591	56.9395	63.4397	70.7494
20	22.0190	24.2974	26.8704	29.7781	33.0660	36.7856	40.9955	45.7620	51.1601	57.2750	64.2028	72.0524	80.9468
25	28.2432	32.0303	36.4593	41.6459	47.7271	54.8645	63.2490	73.1059	84.7009	98.3471	114.4133	133.3339	155.6196
30	34.7849	40.5681	47.5754	56.0849	66.4388	79.0582	94.4608	113.2832	136.3075	164.4940	199.0209	241.3327	293.1992
35	41.6603	49.9945	60.4621	73.6522	90.3203	111.4348	138.2369	172.3168	215.7108	271.0244	341.5896	431.6635	546.6808
40	48.8864	60.4020	75.4013	95.0255	120.7998	154.7620	199.6351	259.0565	337.8824	442.5926	581.8261	767.0914	1013.704
45	56.4811	71.8927	92.7199	121.0294	159.7002	212.7435	285.7493	386.5056	525.8587	718.9048	986.6386	1358.230	1874.165
50	64.4632	84.5794	112.7969	152.6671	209.3480	290.3359	406.5289	573.7702	815.0836	1163.909	1668.771	2400.018	3459.507

Future Value of Ordinary Annuity

$$\left[\frac{(1+i)^n - 1}{i}\right]$$

Period	14%	15%	16%	17%	18%	19%	20%	25%	30%	35%	40%	45%	50%
1	1.0000	1.0000	1.0000	1.0000	1.0000	1.0000	1.0000	1.0000	1.0000	1.0000	1.0000	1.0000	1.0000
2	2.1400	2.1500	2.1600	2.1700	2.1800	2.1900	2.2000	2.2500	2.3000	2.3500	2.4000	2.4500	2.5000
3	3.4396	3.4725	3.5056	3.5389	3.5724	3.6061	3.6400	3.8125	3.9900	4.1725	4.3600	4.5525	4.7500
4	4.9211	4.9934	5.0665	5.1405	5.2154	5.2913	5.3680	5.7656	6.1870	6.6329	7.1040	7.6011	8.1250
5	6.6101	6.7424	6.8771	7.0144	7.1542	7.2966	7.4416	8.2070	9.0431	9.9544	10.9456	12.0216	13.1875
6	8.5355	8.7537	8.9775	9.2068	9.4420	9.6830	9.9299	11.2588	12.7560	14.4384	16.3238	18.4314	20.7813
7	10.7305	11.0668	11.4139	11.7720	12.1415	12.5227	12.9159	15.0735	17.5828	20.4919	23.8534	27.7255	32.1719
8	13.2328	13.7268	14.2401	14.7733	15.3270	15.9020	16.4991	19.8419	23.8577	28.6640	34.3947	41.2019	49.2578
9	16.0853	16.7858	17.5185	18.2847	19.0859	19.9234	20.7989	25.8023	32.0150	39.6964	49.1526	60.7428	74.8867
10	19.3373	20.3037	21.3215	22.3931	23.5213	24.7089	25.9587	33.2529	42.6195	54.5902	69.8137	89.0771	113.3301
11	23.0445	24.3493	25.7329	27.1999	28.7551	30.4035	32.1504	42.5661	56.4053	74.6967	98.7391	130.1618	170.9951
12	27.2707	29.0017	30.8502	32.8239	34.9311	37.1802	39.5805	54.2077	74.3270	101.8406	139.2348	189.7346	257.4927
13	32.0887	34.3519	36.7862	39.4040	42.2187	45.2445	48.4966	68.7596	97.6250	138.4848	195.9287	276.1151	387.2390
14	37.5811	40.5047	43.6720	47.1027	50.8180	54.8409	59.1959	86.9495	127.9125	187.9544	275.3002	401.3670	581.8585
15	43.8424	47.5804	51.6595	56.1101	60.9653	66.2607	72.0351	109.6868	167.2863	254.7385	386.4202	582.9821	873.7878
16	50.9804	55.7175	60.9250	66.6488	72.9390	79.8502	87.4421	138.1085	218.4722	344.8970	541.9883	846.3240	1311.682
17	59.1176	65.0751	71.6730	78.9792	87.0680	96.0218	105.9306	173.6357	285.0139	466.6109	759.7837	1228.170	1968.523
18	68.3941	75.8364	84.1407	93.4056	103.7403	115.2659	128.1167	218.0446	371.5180	630.9247	1064.697	1781.846	2953.784
19	78.9692	88.2118	98.6032	110.2846	123.4135	138.1664	154.7400	273.5558	483.9734	852.7483	1491.576	2584.677	4431.676
20	91.0249	102.4436	115.3797	130.0329	146.6280	165.4180	186.6880	342.9447	630.1655	1152.210	2089.206	3748.782	6648.513
25	181.8708	212.7930	249.2140	292.1049	342.6035	402.0425	471.9811	1054.791	2348.803	5176.504	11247.20	24040.72	50500.34
30	356.7868	434.7451	530.3117	647.4391	790.9480	966.7122	1181.882	3227.174	8729.985	23221.57	60501.08	154106.6	383500.1
35	693.5727	881.1702	1120.713	1426.491	1816.652	2314.214	2948.341	9856.761	32422.87	104136.3	325400.3	987794.5	2912217
40	1342.025	1779.090	2360.757	3134.522	4163.213	5529.829	7343.858	30088.66	120392.9	466960.4	1750092	6331512	22114663
45	2590.565	3585.128	4965.274	6879.291	9531.577	13203.42	18281.31	91831.50	447019.4	2093876	9412424	40583319	167933233
50	4994.521	7217.716	10435.65	15089.50	21813.09	31515.34	45497.19	280255.7	1659761	9389020	50622288	260128295	1275242998

Present Value of Annuity Due

$$\left[\frac{1-\dfrac{1}{(1+i)^{n-1}}}{i}+1\right]$$

Period	1%	2%	3%	4%	5%	6%	7%	8%	9%	10%	11%	12%	13%
1	1.0000	1.0000	1.0000	1.0000	1.0000	1.0000	1.0000	1.0000	1.0000	1.0000	1.0000	1.0000	1.0000
2	1.9901	1.9804	1.9709	1.9615	1.9524	1.9434	1.9346	1.9259	1.9174	1.9091	1.9009	1.8929	1.8850
3	2.9704	2.9416	2.9135	2.8861	2.8594	2.8334	2.8080	2.7833	2.7591	2.7355	2.7125	2.6901	2.6681
4	3.9410	3.8839	3.8286	3.7751	3.7232	3.6730	3.6243	3.5771	3.5313	3.4869	3.4437	3.4018	3.3612
5	4.9020	4.8077	4.7171	4.6299	4.5460	4.4651	4.3872	4.3121	4.2397	4.1699	4.1024	4.0373	3.9745
6	5.8534	5.7135	5.5797	5.4518	5.3295	5.2124	5.1002	4.9927	4.8897	4.7908	4.6959	4.6048	4.5172
7	6.7955	6.6014	6.4172	6.2421	6.0757	5.9173	5.7665	5.6229	5.4859	5.3553	5.2305	5.1114	4.9975
8	7.7282	7.4720	7.2303	7.0021	6.7864	6.5824	6.3893	6.2064	6.0330	5.8684	5.7122	5.5638	5.4226
9	8.6517	8.3255	8.0197	7.7327	7.4632	7.2098	6.9713	6.7466	6.5348	6.3349	6.1461	5.9676	5.7988
10	9.5660	9.1622	8.7861	8.4353	8.1078	7.8017	7.5152	7.2469	6.9952	6.7590	6.5370	6.3282	6.1317
11	10.4713	9.9826	9.5302	9.1109	8.7217	8.3601	8.0236	7.7101	7.4177	7.1446	6.8892	6.6502	6.4262
12	11.3676	10.7868	10.2526	9.7605	9.3064	8.8869	8.4987	8.1390	7.8052	7.4951	7.2065	6.9377	6.6869
13	12.2551	11.5753	10.9540	10.3851	9.8633	9.3838	8.9427	8.5361	8.1607	7.8137	7.4924	7.1944	6.9176
14	13.1337	12.3484	11.6350	10.9856	10.3936	9.8527	9.3577	8.9038	8.4869	8.1034	7.7499	7.4235	7.1218
15	14.0037	13.1062	12.2961	11.5631	10.8986	10.2950	9.7455	9.2442	8.7862	8.3667	7.9819	7.6282	7.3025
16	14.8651	13.8493	12.9379	12.1184	11.3797	10.7122	10.1079	9.5595	9.0607	8.6061	8.1909	7.8109	7.4624
17	15.7179	14.5777	13.5611	12.6523	11.8378	11.1059	10.4466	9.8514	9.3126	8.8237	8.3792	7.9740	7.6039
18	16.5623	15.2919	14.1661	13.1657	12.2741	11.4773	10.7632	10.1216	9.5436	9.0216	8.5488	8.1196	7.7291
19	17.3983	15.9920	14.7535	13.6593	12.6896	11.8276	11.0591	10.3719	9.7556	9.2014	8.7016	8.2497	7.8399
20	18.2260	16.6785	15.3238	14.1339	13.0853	12.1581	11.3356	10.6036	9.9501	9.3649	8.8393	8.3658	7.9380
25	22.2434	19.9139	17.9355	16.2470	14.7986	13.5504	12.4693	11.5288	10.7066	9.9847	9.3481	8.7843	8.2829
30	26.0658	22.8444	20.1885	17.9837	16.1411	14.5907	13.2777	12.1584	11.1983	10.3696	9.6501	9.0218	8.4701
35	29.7027	25.4986	22.1318	19.4112	17.1929	15.3681	13.8540	12.5869	11.5178	10.6086	9.8293	9.1566	8.5717
40	33.1630	27.9026	23.8082	20.5845	18.0170	15.9491	14.2649	12.8786	11.7255	10.7570	9.9357	9.2330	8.6268
45	36.4555	30.0800	25.2543	21.5488	18.6628	16.3832	14.5579	13.0771	11.8605	10.8491	9.9988	9.2764	8.6568
50	39.5881	32.0521	26.5017	22.3415	19.1687	16.7076	14.7668	13.2122	11.9482	10.9063	10.0362	9.3010	8.6730

Present Value of Annuity Due

$$\left[\dfrac{1-\dfrac{1}{(1+i)^{n-1}}}{i}+1\right]$$

Period	14%	15%	16%	17%	18%	19%	20%	25%	30%	35%	40%	45%	50%
1	1.0000	1.0000	1.0000	1.0000	1.0000	1.0000	1.0000	1.0000	1.0000	1.0000	1.0000	1.0000	1.0000
2	1.8772	1.8696	1.8621	1.8547	1.8475	1.8403	1.8333	1.8000	1.7692	1.7407	1.7143	1.6897	1.6667
3	2.6467	2.6257	2.6052	2.5852	2.5656	2.5465	2.5278	2.4400	2.3609	2.2894	2.2245	2.1653	2.1111
4	3.3216	3.2832	3.2459	3.2096	3.1743	3.1399	3.1065	2.9520	2.8161	2.6959	2.5889	2.4933	2.4074
5	3.9137	3.8550	3.7982	3.7432	3.6901	3.6386	3.5887	3.3616	3.1662	2.9969	2.8492	2.7195	2.6049
6	4.4331	4.3522	4.2743	4.1993	4.1272	4.0576	3.9906	3.6893	3.4356	3.2200	3.0352	2.8755	2.7366
7	4.8887	4.7845	4.6847	4.5892	4.4976	4.4098	4.3255	3.9514	3.6427	3.3852	3.1680	2.9831	2.8244
8	5.2883	5.1604	5.0386	4.9224	4.8115	4.7057	4.6046	4.1611	3.8021	3.5075	3.2628	3.0573	2.8829
9	5.6389	5.4873	5.3436	5.2072	5.0776	4.9544	4.8372	4.3289	3.9247	3.5982	3.3306	3.1085	2.9220
10	5.9464	5.7716	5.6065	5.4506	5.3030	5.1633	5.0310	4.4631	4.0190	3.6653	3.3790	3.1438	2.9480
11	6.2161	6.0188	5.8332	5.6586	5.4941	5.3389	5.1925	4.5705	4.0915	3.7150	3.4136	3.1681	2.9653
12	6.4527	6.2337	6.0286	5.8364	5.6560	5.4865	5.3271	4.6564	4.1473	3.7519	3.4383	3.1849	2.9769
13	6.6603	6.4206	6.1971	5.9884	5.7932	5.6105	5.4392	4.7251	4.1903	3.7792	3.4559	3.1965	2.9846
14	6.8424	6.5831	6.3423	6.1183	5.9095	5.7147	5.5327	4.7801	4.2233	3.7994	3.4685	3.2045	2.9897
15	7.0021	6.7245	6.4675	6.2293	6.0081	5.8023	5.6106	4.8241	4.2487	3.8144	3.4775	3.2100	2.9931
16	7.1422	6.8474	6.5755	6.3242	6.0916	5.8759	5.6755	4.8593	4.2682	3.8255	3.4839	3.2138	2.9954
17	7.2651	6.9542	6.6685	6.4053	6.1624	5.9377	5.7296	4.8874	4.2832	3.8337	3.4885	3.2164	2.9970
18	7.3729	7.0472	6.7487	6.4746	6.2223	5.9897	5.7746	4.9099	4.2948	3.8398	3.4918	3.2182	2.9980
19	7.4674	7.1280	6.8178	6.5339	6.2732	6.0333	5.8122	4.9279	4.3037	3.8443	3.4941	3.2195	2.9986
20	7.5504	7.1982	6.8775	6.5845	6.3162	6.0700	5.8435	4.9424	4.3105	3.8476	3.4958	3.2203	2.9991
25	7.8351	7.4338	7.0726	6.7465	6.4509	6.1822	5.9371	4.9811	4.3272	3.8550	3.4992	3.2219	2.9999
30	7.9830	7.5509	7.1656	6.8204	6.5098	6.2292	5.9747	4.9938	4.3317	3.8567	3.4999	3.2222	3.0000
35	8.0599	7.6091	7.2098	6.8541	6.5356	6.2489	5.9898	4.9980	4.3329	3.8570	3.5000	3.2222	3.0000
40	8.0997	7.6380	7.2309	6.8695	6.5468	6.2572	5.9959	4.9993	4.3332	3.8571	3.5000	3.2222	3.0000
45	8.1205	7.6524	7.2409	6.8765	6.5517	6.2607	5.9984	4.9998	4.3333	3.8571	3.5000	3.2222	3.0000
50	8.1312	7.6596	7.2457	6.8797	6.5539	6.2621	5.9993	4.9999	4.3333	3.8571	3.5000	3.2222	3.0000

Future Value of Annuity Due

$$\left[\frac{(1+i)^n - 1}{i}\right] \times [1+i]$$

Period	1%	2%	3%	4%	5%	6%	7%	8%	9%	10%	11%	12%	13%
1	1.0100	1.0200	1.0300	1.0400	1.0500	1.0600	1.0700	1.0800	1.0900	1.1000	1.1100	1.1200	1.1300
2	2.0301	2.0604	2.0909	2.1216	2.1525	2.1836	2.2149	2.2464	2.2781	2.3100	2.3421	2.3744	2.4069
3	3.0604	3.1216	3.1836	3.2465	3.3101	3.3746	3.4399	3.5061	3.5731	3.6410	3.7097	3.7793	3.8498
4	4.1010	4.2040	4.3091	4.4163	4.5256	4.6371	4.7507	4.8666	4.9847	5.1051	5.2278	5.3528	5.4803
5	5.1520	5.3081	5.4684	5.6330	5.8019	5.9753	6.1533	6.3359	6.5233	6.7156	6.9129	7.1152	7.3227
6	6.2135	6.4343	6.6625	6.8983	7.1420	7.3938	7.6540	7.9228	8.2004	8.4872	8.7833	9.0890	9.4047
7	7.2857	7.5830	7.8923	8.2142	8.5491	8.8975	9.2598	9.6366	10.0285	10.4359	10.8594	11.2997	11.7573
8	8.3685	8.7546	9.1591	9.5828	10.0266	10.4913	10.9780	11.4876	12.0210	12.5795	13.1640	13.7757	14.4157
9	9.4622	9.9497	10.4639	11.0061	11.5779	12.1808	12.8164	13.4866	14.1929	14.9374	15.7220	16.5487	17.4197
10	10.5668	11.1687	11.8078	12.4864	13.2068	13.9716	14.7836	15.6455	16.5603	17.5312	18.5614	19.6546	20.8143
11	11.6825	12.4121	13.1920	14.0258	14.9171	15.8699	16.8885	17.9771	19.1407	20.3843	21.7132	23.1331	24.6502
12	12.8093	13.6803	14.6178	15.6268	16.7130	17.8821	19.1406	20.4953	21.9534	23.5227	25.2116	27.0291	28.9847
13	13.9474	14.9739	16.0863	17.2919	18.5986	20.0151	21.5505	23.2149	25.0192	26.9750	29.0949	31.3926	33.8827
14	15.0969	16.2934	17.5989	19.0236	20.5786	22.2760	24.1290	26.1521	28.3609	30.7725	33.4054	36.2797	39.4175
15	16.2579	17.6393	19.1569	20.8245	22.6575	24.6725	26.8881	29.3243	32.0034	34.9497	38.1899	41.7533	45.6717
16	17.4304	19.0121	20.7616	22.6975	24.8404	27.2129	29.8402	32.7502	35.9737	39.5447	43.5008	47.8837	52.7391
17	18.6147	20.4123	22.4144	24.6454	27.1324	29.9057	32.9990	36.4502	40.3013	44.5992	49.3959	54.7497	60.7251
18	19.8109	21.8406	24.1169	26.6712	29.5390	32.7600	36.3790	40.4463	45.0185	50.1591	55.9395	62.4397	69.7494
19	21.0190	23.2974	25.8704	28.7781	32.0660	35.7856	39.9955	44.7620	50.1601	56.2750	63.2028	71.0524	79.9468
20	22.2392	24.7833	27.6765	30.9692	34.7193	38.9927	43.8652	49.4229	55.7645	63.0025	71.2651	80.6987	91.4699
25	28.5256	32.6709	37.5530	43.3117	50.1135	58.1564	67.6765	78.9544	92.3240	108.1818	126.9988	149.3339	175.8501
30	35.1327	41.3794	49.0027	58.3283	69.7608	83.8017	101.0730	122.3459	148.5752	180.9434	220.9132	270.2926	331.3151
35	42.0769	50.9944	62.2759	76.5983	94.8363	118.1209	147.9135	186.1021	235.1247	298.1268	379.1644	483.4631	617.7493
40	49.3752	61.6100	77.6633	98.8265	126.8398	164.0477	213.6096	279.7810	368.2919	486.8518	645.8269	859.1424	1145.486
45	57.0459	73.3306	95.5015	125.8706	167.6852	225.5081	305.7518	417.4261	573.1860	790.7953	1095.169	1521.218	2117.806
50	65.1078	86.2710	116.1808	158.7738	219.8154	307.7561	434.9860	619.6718	888.4411	1280.299	1852.336	2688.020	3909.243

Future Value of Annuity Due

$$\left[\frac{(1+i)^n - 1}{i}\right] \times [1+i]$$

Period	14%	15%	16%	17%	18%	19%	20%	25%	30%	35%	40%	45%	50%
1	1.1400	1.1500	1.1600	1.1700	1.1800	1.1900	1.2000	1.2500	1.3000	1.3500	1.4000	1.4500	1.5000
2	2.4396	2.4725	2.5056	2.5389	2.5724	2.6061	2.6400	2.8125	2.9900	3.1725	3.3600	3.5525	3.7500
3	3.9211	3.9934	4.0665	4.1405	4.2154	4.2913	4.3680	4.7656	5.1870	5.6329	6.1040	6.6011	7.1250
4	5.6101	5.7424	5.8771	6.0144	6.1542	6.2966	6.4416	7.2070	8.0431	8.9544	9.9456	11.0216	12.1875
5	7.5355	7.7537	7.9775	8.2068	8.4420	8.6830	8.9299	10.2588	11.7560	13.4384	15.3238	17.4314	19.7813
6	9.7305	10.0668	10.4139	10.7720	11.1415	11.5227	11.9159	14.0735	16.5828	19.4919	22.8534	26.7255	31.1719
7	12.2328	12.7268	13.2401	13.7733	14.3270	14.9020	15.4991	18.8419	22.8577	27.6640	33.3947	40.2019	48.2578
8	15.0853	15.7858	16.5185	17.2847	18.0859	18.9234	19.7989	24.8023	31.0150	38.6964	48.1526	59.7428	73.8867
9	18.3373	19.3037	20.3215	21.3931	22.5213	23.7089	24.9587	32.2529	41.6195	53.5902	68.8137	88.0771	112.3301
10	22.0445	23.3493	24.7329	26.1999	27.7551	29.4035	31.1504	41.5661	55.4053	73.6967	97.7391	129.1618	169.9951
11	26.2707	28.0017	29.8502	31.8239	33.9311	36.1802	38.5805	53.2077	73.3270	100.8406	138.2348	188.7346	256.4927
12	31.0887	33.3519	35.7862	38.4040	41.2187	44.2445	47.4966	67.7596	96.6250	137.4848	194.9287	275.1151	386.2390
13	36.5811	39.5047	42.6720	46.1027	49.8180	53.8409	58.1959	85.9495	126.9125	186.9544	274.3002	400.3670	580.8585
14	42.8424	46.5804	50.6595	55.1101	59.9653	65.2607	71.0351	108.6868	166.2863	253.7385	385.4202	581.9821	872.7878
15	49.9804	54.7175	59.9250	65.6488	71.9390	78.8502	86.4421	137.1085	217.4722	343.8970	540.9883	845.3240	1310.6817
16	58.1176	64.0751	70.6730	77.9792	86.0680	95.0218	104.9306	172.6357	284.0139	465.6109	758.7837	1227.1699	1967.5225
17	67.3941	74.8364	83.1407	92.4056	102.7403	114.2659	127.1167	217.0446	370.5180	629.9247	1063.697	1780.8463	2952.7838
18	77.9692	87.2118	97.6032	109.2846	122.4135	137.1664	153.7400	272.5558	482.9734	851.7483	1490.576	2583.6771	4430.6756
19	90.0249	101.4436	114.3797	129.0329	145.6280	164.4180	185.6880	341.9447	629.1655	1151.210	2088.206	3747.7818	6647.5135
20	103.7684	117.8101	133.8405	152.1385	173.0210	196.8474	224.0256	428.6809	819.2151	1555.484	2924.889	5435.7336	9972.7702
25	207.3327	244.7120	289.0883	341.7627	404.2721	478.4306	566.3773	1318.489	3053.444	6988.280	15746.08	34859.038	75750.5049
30	406.7370	499.9569	615.1616	757.5038	933.3186	1150.387	1418.258	4033.968	11348.98	31349.12	84701.51	223454.60	575250.178
35	790.6729	1013.346	1300.027	1668.994	2143.649	2753.914	3538.009	12320.95	42149.73	140583.9	455560.4	1432302.0	4368325.82
40	1529.909	2045.954	2738.478	3667.391	4912.591	6580.496	8812.629	37610.82	156510.7	630396.5	2450128	9180692.2	33171994.0
45	2953.244	4122.898	5759.718	8048.770	11247.26	15712.07	21937.57	114789.4	581125.2	2826733	13177394	58845813	251899849
50	5693.75	8300.37	12105.35	17654.72	25739.45	37503.25	54596.63	350319.6	2157689	12675177	70871203	377186028	1912864498

C.   TROUBLESHOOTING GUIDE

Listed below are the more common errors that may be encountered while using your financial calculator. Although there are possible errors that are not listed below, the following are the most common errors that occur during the operation of the calculators in this text. For each of the calculators, you can exit from the error alert by pressing the clear button. If you encounter an error that is not listed, you should refer to the owner's manual for your calculator.

1.   Hewlett Packard 17bII/17bII+

   The HP 17bII/HP 17bII+ has various error messages. These are the most common TVM error messages that you may encounter. Consult your owner's manual for further explanations.

   a.   **Invalid N** – When calculating for I/YR one of the following values for n may have been attempted:

   ■   Less than or equal to .99999. This gives a payment of less than one. There must be at least one payment.

   ■   More than or equal to 1E10. This gives a payment of more than 10,000,000,000. There must be less than 10,000,000,000 payments.

   b.   **Many or No Solutions** – An internal rate of return error occurred because there is no solution for the numbers entered. This often occurs because at least one positive cash flow and one negative cash flow have not been entered.

   c.   **Many/No Solution; Key In Guess** – An internal rate of return error occurred that may involve several answers. An estimate must be input before the calculator will continue.

   d.   **No Solution** – There is no solution for the numbers entered. This is often the case because there has been an error made when inputting the numbers. Check the signs of the cash flows and other monetary units.

   e.   **N! N<0 or N Noninteger** – Calculate n! using n<0 or n that is a noninteger. The symbol, n! refers to when a number n is multiplied by every number less than the number n. Therefore, if n = 5 then the result would be (5*4*3*2*1). The number n cannot be less than zero and should be an integer or a whole number (1, 2, 3). An input of 1.2, 6.8 or any other fractional number, will result in an error.

2.   Hewlett Packard 12C

   The HP 12C has error messages that range from 0-9. The ones listed below are the TVM errors that may be encountered. Consult your owner's manual for further explanations.

   a.   **Error 0** – A mathematics error has occurred, such as:

   ■   Dividing by zero. You cannot divide any number by zero. Likewise, any formula that is entered that will result in trying to divide by zero will result in an error.

   ■   Attempting to calculate the square root of a negative number. The square root of a negative number does not exist, therefore, the calculator will be unable to process this request.

b. **Error 1** – There is a storage register overflow. This is when any calculation results in a number exceeding the range of $9.99999999 * 10^{99}$.

c. **Error 3** – There is an internal rate of return error that may involve several answers. An estimate must be input before the calculator will continue the calculation.

d. **Error 5** – There may be one of the following errors:

   ■ No solution exists for n based on the current i, PV, or FV.

   ■ All of the cash flows have the same sign. There must be at least one positive cash flow and one negative cash flow.

   ■ The interest factor is less than or equal to –100%. An interest rate equal to –100% would result in zero as the solution. Therefore, if you have a –100% return or less, then you would get a return of zero.

e. **Error 6** – A storage error has occurred. IRR and NPV may have been calculated using an n value that is:

   ■ Less than 0. This gives a payment of less than zero. There cannot be less than zero payments.

   ■ Greater than 20. There cannot be more than 20 payments.

   ■ A noninteger. The n should be an integer, or a whole number (1, 2, 3). If 1.2, 6.8 or any other fractional number is entered, the calculator will result in an error.

f. **Error 7** – There is an internal rate of return error because there is no answer for the numbers entered. This is often the case because there has been a mistake made when inputting the numbers. There must be at least one positive cash flow and one negative cash flow.

3. Hewlett Packard 10BII/10BII+

   The HP 10BII/HP 10BII+ have various error messages. These are the most common TVM error messages that you may encounter. Consult your owner's manual for further explanations.

   a. **Error- Func** – One of the following has been attempted:

      ■ Divide by zero. You cannot divide any number by zero. Likewise, any formula that is entered that will result in trying to divide by zero will result in an error.

      ■ Calculate the square root of a negative number. The square root of a negative number does not exist, therefore, the calculator will be unable to process this request.

      ■ Calculate n! (factorial) using n<0 or n that is a noninteger. The symbol n! refers to the product of the integers ranging from 1 to n. For example, if n = 5, then the factorial would be (5*4*3*2*1). With this function, n cannot be less than zero and must be a positive integer. Inputting fractions, decimals or negative numbers will result in an error.

   b. **Error- Full** – More than 15 cash flow groups have been entered. The calculator is only equipped to handle 15 cash flow groups. If there are more than 15 groups, try to break up the problem to accommodate this limit.

c. **Error- Int** – The interest factor is less than or equal to –100%. An interest rate equal to –100% would result in zero as the solution. Therefore, if you have a –100% return or less, then you would get a return of zero.

d. **Error- n** – When calculating for I/YR the n value may be:

■ Less than or equal to .99999. This gives a payment of less than one. There must be at least one payment.

■ More than or equal to 1E10. This gives a payment of more than 10,000,000,000. There must be less than 10,000,000,000 payments.

e. **Error- P_Yr** – In regards to the P/YR (Payments per Year) feature there may be:

■ A number outside the legal range of 1 to 999. The calculator has a limit as to the number of payments that may be entered. For this calculator, there must be at least one but less than 1,000 payments.

■ A number that is not an integer. There must be full payments. Regardless of the amount of money you send to a creditor, you still make a full payment. There will always be whole number payments.

f. **Error- PEr** – In regards to the N_j there may be:

■ A number outside the legal range of 1 to 999. The calculator has a limit as to the number of payments that may be entered. For this calculator, there must be at least one but less than 1,000 payments.

■ A number that is not an integer. There must be full payments. Regardless of the amount of money sent to a creditor, a full payment must be made. There will always be whole number payments.

g. **Error- Sol** – There is an internal rate of return error that may involve several answers. An estimate must be given before the calculator will continue.

h. **Error- No Sol** – There is an internal rate of return error because there is no answer for the numbers entered. This often occurs because there was a mistake inputting the numbers. There must be at least one positive cash flow and one negative cash flow in order to solve this calculation.

i. **Error- Stat** – Incorrect data used in a statistics calculation.

j. **Error- TVM** – There is a TVM error (such as solving for P/YR).

k. **OFLO** – The magnitude of the answer is too large. This is when any calculation results in a number exceeding the range of + $-9.99999999999*10^{99}$.

l. **UFLO** – The intermediate result in the TVM is too small for the calculator to process.

4. TI BA II Plus

For this calculator, there are many reasons you could get the following error messages. Listed are the most common TMV error messages. Consult your owner's manual for further explanations.

a. **Error 1** – One of the following has been attempted:

- Divide by zero. You cannot divide any number by zero. Likewise, any formula that is entered that will result in trying to divide by zero will result in an error.

- A value outside the range of $-9.9999999999999E^{99}$ to $+9.9999999999999E^{99}$.

b. **Error 2** – One of the following has been attempted:

- Calculate the square root of a negative number. The square root of a negative number is not a real number; therefore, the calculator will be unable to process this request.

- Calculate n! using n<0 or n that is a noninteger. The symbol, n! refers to when a number n is multiplied by every number less than the number n. Therefore, if n = 5, then the result would be (5*4*3*2*1). The number n cannot be less than zero and should be an integer or a whole number (1, 2, 3). An input of 1.2, 6.8, or any other fractional number, will result in an error.

c. **Error 3** – One of the following has been attempted:

- More than 15 active levels of parentheses have been entered. The calculator is only equipped to handle 15 levels. If there are more than 15 levels, try to break up the problem to accommodate the limit.

- More than 8 pending operations have been entered. The calculator is only equipped to handle 8 operations at a time. If there are more than 8 operations, try to break up the problem to accommodate the limit.

d. **Error 4** – This is an out-of-range error. One of the following may have been tried:

- In regards to the P/YR (Payments per Year) feature, there may be a number less than or equal to zero. For this calculator, there must be at least one P/YR.

- In cash flows, you may have tried to enter a FNN (frequency) that is outside the legal range of 1 to 9,999. For this calculator, there must be at least one but less than 9,000.

e. **Error 5** – You have an internal rate of return error because there is no answer for the numbers entered. This is often the case because there has been a mistake made when inputting the numbers. There must be at least one positive cash flow and one negative cash flow.

Student Workbook

Basic Functions

I. SIMPLE ARITHMETIC CALCULATIONS

A. ADDITION

1. Calculate 93.2 + 46.5

2. Calculate 22.1 + 81.2

3. Calculate 14.0 + 13.9

B. SUBTRACTION

4. Calculate 90.00 – 27.42

5. Calculate 100.00 – 142.30

6. Calculate –21.50 – 78.50

C. MULTIPLICATION

7. Calculate 21 × 14

8. Calculate 12 × 11

9. Calculate –29 × –8

D.   DIVISION

10. Calculate $36 \div .6$

11. Calculate $-52 \div 12$

12. Calculate $-90 \div -6$

II.   CHAIN CALCULATIONS

13. Calculate $[(250 - 70) \div 9.3] \times (93 \div 18)$

14. Calculate $[(63 \div .025) + 9] - [(48 \div .075) + 39]$

15. Calculate $[(36.2 \times 48.5) \div 1.1] + [(14.5 - .89) + 2]$

III.   POWERS

16. Calculate 2^{30}

17. Calculate -6^3

18. Calculate $.2^3$

IV.   ROOTS

A.   SQUARE ROOTS

19. Calculate $\sqrt{400}$

20. Calculate $\sqrt{64}$

21. Calculate $\sqrt{.04}$

B.   ROOTS GREATER THAN 2 (N^TH ROOT OF X)

22. Calculate $\sqrt[3]{91,125}$

23. Calculate $\sqrt[3]{-64}$

24. Calculate $\sqrt[10]{40,658.6896}$

V.   RECIPROCAL

25. Calculate the reciprocal of 9

26. Calculate the reciprocal of 25

27. Calculate the reciprocal of 0.025

Basic Time Value of Money Calculations

I. PRESENT VALUE (PV) OF A SUM CERTAIN

A. ANNUAL INTEREST

28. Calculate the present value of $5 million to be received in 40 years assuming an annual interest rate of 10%.

29. Calculate the present value of $50,000 to be received in 15 years assuming an annual interest rate of 6%.

30. Calculate the present value of $100,000 to be received in 10 years assuming an annual interest rate of 4%.

B. MONTHLY INTEREST

31. Calculate the present value of $25,000 to be received in 5 years assuming an annual interest rate of 12%, compounded monthly.

32. Calculate the present value of $500,000 to be received in 7 years assuming an annual interest rate of 6%, compounded monthly.

33. Calculate the present value of $1,000,000 to be received in 20 years assuming an annual interest rate of 5%, compounded monthly.

II.   FUTURE VALUE (FV) OF A SUM CERTAIN

A.   ANNUAL INTEREST

34. Calculate the future value of $5,000 invested for 30 years assuming an annual interest rate of 12%.

35. Calculate the future value of $13,500 invested for 10 years assuming an annual interest rate of 6%.

36. Calculate the future value of $1,000 invested for 5 years assuming an annual interest rate of 20%.

B.   MONTHLY INTEREST

37. Calculate the future value of $12,000 invested for 18 years assuming an annual interest rate of 12%, compounded monthly.

38. Calculate the future value of $1,000 invested for 100 years assuming an annual interest rate of 8%, compounded monthly.

39. Calculate the future value of $6,000 invested for 360 months assuming an annual interest rate of 9%, compounded monthly.

III.   PRESENT VALUE (PV) OF AN ORDINARY ANNUITY

40. Calculate the present value of an ordinary annuity of $2,000 received annually for 5 years assuming a discount rate of 10%.

41. Calculate the present value of an ordinary annuity of $12,500 received quarterly for 30 years assuming a discount rate of 8%.

42. Calculate the present value of an ordinary annuity of $4,000 received monthly for 10 years assuming a discount rate of 12%.

IV.   PRESENT VALUE (PV) OF AN ANNUITY DUE

43. Calculate the present value of an annuity of $100,000 received annually that begins today and continues for 8 years, assuming a discount rate of 7.5%.

44. Calculate the present value of an annuity of $6,000 received quarterly that begins today and continues for 25 years, assuming a discount rate of 8%.

45. Calculate the present value of an annuity of $10,000 received monthly that begins today and continues for 20 years, assuming a discount rate of 6%.

V. FUTURE VALUE (FV) OF AN ORDINARY ANNUITY

46. Calculate the future value of an ordinary annuity of $3,500 paid annually for 18 years, assuming an annual earnings rate of 8%.

47. Calculate the future value of an ordinary annuity of $2,000 paid every quarter for 10 years, assuming an annual earnings rate of 7%.

48. Calculate the future value of an ordinary annuity of $250 paid every month for 30 years, assuming an annual earnings rate of 6%.

VI.   FUTURE VALUE (FV) OF AN ANNUITY DUE

49. Calculate the future value of an annual annuity of $1,200 beginning today and continuing for 21 years, assuming an earnings rate of 7.5%.

50. Calculate the future value of a quarterly annuity of $2,000 beginning today and continuing for 10 years, assuming an annual earnings rate of 7%.

51. Calculate the future value of a monthly annuity of $10 beginning today and continuing for 100 years, assuming an annual earnings rate of 7%.

VII.   ORDINARY ANNUITY (PMT)

52. Calculate the annual payment that can be received over 30 years from a single investment of $1,000,000 earning 9%, compounded annually.

53. Calculate the quarterly payment to be received over 5 years from a single investment of $50,000.00 earning 8%, compounded quarterly.

54. Calculate the monthly payment to be received over 15 years from a single investment of $250,000.00 earning 7%, compounded monthly.

VIII.   ANNUITY DUE (PMT)

55. Calculate the payment to be received at the beginning of each year for 5 years from an investment of $250,000.00 earning 8.75%, compounded annually.

56. Calculate the payment to be received at the beginning of each quarter for 6 years from an investment of $15,000.00 earning 7%, compounded quarterly.

57. Calculate the payment to be received at the beginning of each month for 15 years from an investment of $250,000.00 earning 7%, compounded monthly.

IX.   AMORTIZATION

58. Calculate the monthly payment for a home loan of $100,000 financed at 7% over 30 years.

59. Calculate the monthly payment for a home loan of $150,000 financed at 6.75% over 15 years.

60. Calculate the monthly payment for a home loan of $200,000 financed at 5% over 20 years.

X. NET PRESENT VALUE OF A SERIES OF UNEVEN CASH FLOWS (NPV)

61. Calculate the NPV of a machine which is bought for $5,000.00, sold at the end of year 5 for $2,500.00, and produces the following cash flows: year 1) +$700; year 2) +$600; year 3) +$500; year 4) +$400; year 5) +$300, assume the cost of capital is 6%.

62. Calculate the NPV of a machine which is bought for $10,000.00, sold at the end of year 5 for $3,500.00, and produces the following cash flows: year 1) +$300; year 2) +$600; year 3) +$1,200; year 4) +$2,400; year 5) +$4,800, assume the cost of capital is 6%.

63. Calculate the NPV of a machine which is bought for $6,000.00, sold at the end of year 5 for $2,000.00, and produces the following cash flows: year 1) +$2,000; year 2) +$1,750; year 3) +$1,500; year 4) +$1,000; year 5) +$500, assume the cost of capital is 8%.

XI.   INTERNAL RATE OF RETURN – IRR (I)

64. Calculate the IRR of a project that requires an initial cash outflow of $5,000.00 and will be sold at the end of year 5 for $2,500.00. The project produces the following cash flows: year 1) +$700; year 2) +$600; year 3) +$500; year 4) +$400; year 5) +$300.

65. Calculate the IRR of a project that requires an initial cash outflow of $10,000.00 and will be sold at the end of year 5 for $3,500.00. The project produces the following cash flows: year 1) +$300; year 2) +$600; year 3) +$1,200; year 4) +$2,400; year 5) +$4,800.

66. Calculate the IRR of a project that requires an initial cash outflow of $6,000.00 and will be sold at the end of year 5 for $2,000.00. The project produces the following cash flows: year 1) +$2,000; year 2) +$1,750; year 3) +$1,500; year 4) +$1,000; year 5) +$500.

XII.   SOLVING FOR TERM OR PERIODS (N)

67. Calculate the number of years it will take $2,500 to grow to $25,000 assuming an annual rate of return of 7%.

68. Calculate the number of months it will take $10,000 to grow to $1,000,000 assuming an annual rate of return of 6%, compounded monthly.

69. Calculate the number of years it will take $100,000 to grow to $5,000,000 assuming an annual rate of return of 7%, compounded monthly.

Time Value of Money & Fundamentals Problems

I. FUTURE VALUE – COMPOUNDED ANNUALLY

70. Today John Doe purchased an antique car for $150,000. He expects it to increase in value at a rate of 9% compounded annually for the next 10 years. How much will the car be worth at the end of the 10th year if his expectations are correct?

71. Today Jim Jones purchased a new sports car for $80,000. He expects it to decrease in value at a rate of 6% compounded annually for the next 5 years. How much will the car be worth at the end of the 5th year if his expectations are correct?

72. Today Tom Smith purchased an apartment building for $1,000,000. He expects it to increase in value at a rate of 7.5% compounded annually for the next 20 years. How much will the building be worth at the end of the 20th year if his expectations are correct?

II.   FUTURE VALUE – COMPOUNDED MONTHLY

73. A client invests $30,000 in common stock of ABC Company which is appreciating at an annual rate of 8% compounded monthly. How much will the stock be worth when he retires in 15 years?

74. Tina, who just turned 18, deposits a $20,000 gift into an interest-bearing account earning a 2% annual rate of interest compounded monthly. How much will she have in the account when she retires at age 60 assuming all interest is reinvested at the 2% rate?

75. Bob bought an oil well for $9,000. It has been appreciating at 9% per year compounded monthly. How much will the oil well be worth in 10 years assuming it grows at the same rate?

III.   PRESENT VALUE – COMPOUNDED ANNUALLY

76. Mindy wants to give $50,000 to the Special charity when she retires in 15 years. How much should she invest today at an annual interest rate of 2% compounded annually to have $50,000 in 15 years?

77. Billy wants to give his daughter $150,000 on her graduation day in 5 years. How much should he invest today at an annual interest rate of 3% compounded annually to have $150,000 in 5 years?

78. Ashby wants to give her mother $25,000 to buy a new car in 3 years. How much should she invest today at an annual interest rate of 2.5% compounded annually to have $25,000 in 3 years?

IV.   PRESENT VALUE – COMPOUNDED SEMIANNUALLY

79. Barney expects to receive $50,000 from a trust fund in 10 years. What is the current value of this fund if it is discounted at 6% compounded semiannually?

80. Mike expects to receive $100,000 from the sale of his business in 5 years. What is the current value of his business if it is discounted at 9% compounded semiannually?

81. Candy expects to receive $1,000,000 when her rich Uncle Fred dies in 20 years. What is the current value of her inheritance if it is discounted at 8.5% compounded semiannually?

V.   PRESENT VALUE – COMPOUNDED MONTHLY

82. Donna expects to receive $60,000 in 8 years. Her opportunity cost is 7% compounded monthly. What is this sum worth to Donna today?

83. Jack expects to receive $1,000,000 in 40 years. His opportunity cost is 6% compounded monthly. What is this sum worth to Jack today?

84. Billy Bob expects to receive a gold watch worth $25,000 in 5 years. His opportunity cost is 8% compounded monthly. What is this watch worth to Billy Bob today?

VI.   INTEREST CALCULATION – COMPOUNDED ANNUALLY

85. Ron purchased 700 shares of Growth stock for $25 per share 5 years ago. Today he sold all 100 shares for $25,000. What was his average annual compound rate of return on this investment before tax?

86. Randy purchased 10 zero-coupon bonds at 10% of par 30 years ago. Today the bonds matured. What was his average annual compound rate of return on this investment before tax?

87. Cindy purchased 100 shares of a closed-end fund for $24 per share 15 years ago. Today she sold all 100 shares for $10,000. What was her average annual compound rate of return on this investment before tax?

VII.   INTEREST CALCULATION

88.   Jake borrowed $18,000 from his father to purchase a camper. Jake paid back $25,000 to his father at the end of 6 years. What was the average annual compound rate of interest on Jake's loan from his father?

89.   Sarah borrowed $10,000 from her aunt to donate to charity. Sarah paid back $7,000 to her aunt at the end of 3 years. What was the average annual compound rate of interest on Sarah's loan from her aunt?

90.   Mike borrowed $120,000 from his father, the banker, to purchase a house. Mike paid back $300,000 to his father at the end of 20 years. What was the average annual compound rate of interest on Mike's loan from his father?

91. Sue purchased a zero-coupon bond 20 years ago for $250. If the bond matures today and the face value is $1,000, what is the average annual compound rate of return, assuming semiannual compounding, that Sue realized on her investment?

92. Billy purchased a certificate of deposit 5 years ago for $1,700. If the certificate of deposit is due today in the amount of $2,000, what is the average annual compound rate of return, assuming monthly compounding, that Billy realized on his investment?

93. Jethro purchased a diamond 7 years ago for $800. If the diamond could be sold today for $1,200, what is the average annual compound rate of return that Jethro realized on his investment?

VIII.   TERM CALCULATION

94. Kerry purchased an antique for $12,000. Today, he sold the antique for $69,975.49. Kerry estimated the average annual compound rate of return on the antique was 8%. Approximately how many years did Kerry own the antique? (rounded to the nearest .000)

95. Gilbert purchased several gold coins for $30,000. Today, he sold the coins for $55,045.91. Gilbert estimated the average annual rate of return (compounded monthly) on the coins was 9%. Approximately how many years did Gilbert own the coins? (rounded to the nearest .000)

96. Sam purchased a certificate of deposit yielding 3% annually for $6,000. Today, it matured for $12,004.25. Approximately how many years did Sam own the certificate of deposit? (rounded to the nearest .000)

IX.   FUTURE VALUE OF AN ORDINARY ANNUITY (END)

97. Harriet has been investing $200 at the end of each month for the past 25 years in an equity mutual fund. How much is the fund worth assuming she has earned a 7% annual return compounded monthly on her investment?

98. Carol has been investing $5,000 in her Section 401(k) plan at the end of each year for the past 10 years in an equity mutual fund. How much is the fund worth assuming she has earned 6% compounded annually on her investment?

99. Scott has been investing $5 at the end of each day for the past 12 years in an equity mutual fund. How much is the fund worth assuming he has earned a 9% return compounded daily on his investment?

X.   FUTURE VALUE OF AN ANNUITY DUE (BEG)

100.   Ron has been investing $3,500 at the beginning of each year for the past 18 years for his daughter's college education. How much has he accumulated assuming he has earned 6% compounded annually on his investment?

101.   Bill has been investing $10,000 at the beginning of each year for the past 5 years. How much has he accumulated assuming he has earned 7% compounded annually on his investment?

102.   Kelli has been investing $250 at the beginning of each month for the past 20 years. How much has she accumulated assuming she has earned an 8% annual return compounded monthly on her investment?

XI.   PRESENT VALUE OF AN ORDINARY ANNUITY (END)

103. Stacy expects to receive $25,000 at the end of each of the next 4 years from an annuity. Her opportunity cost is 8% compounded annually. What are these payments worth today?

104. Stan expects to receive $20,000 at the end of each month for the next 25 years from a trust fund. His opportunity cost is 7% compounded monthly. What are these payments worth today?

105. Smiley expects to receive $12,000 annually from Social Security for the next 30 years. His opportunity cost is 6% compounded annually. What are these payments worth today?

XII.   PRESENT VALUE OF AN ANNUITY DUE (BEG)

106. Jan wants to withdraw $1,000 at the beginning of each month for the next 10 years. She wants to have $50,000 left at the end of the 10 years. She expects to earn 8% compounded monthly on her investment. What lump sum should Jan deposit today?

107. Cathy wants to purchase an annuity where she can withdraw $15,000 at the beginning of each year for the next 20 years. She expects to earn 8% compounded annually on her investment. How much should she pay for the annuity?

108. Beverly wants to donate $10,000 to charity at the beginning of each year for the next 15 years. She wants to have $50,000 left at the end of the 15 years. She expects to earn 6% compounded annually on her investment. What lump sum should Beverly deposit today?

XIII.   ANNUITY DUE (BEG) WITH LUMP-SUM DEPOSIT

109. Albert has received an inheritance of $1,500,000. He wants to withdraw equal periodic payments at the beginning of each month for the next 30 years. He expects to earn 7.2% compounded monthly on his investments. How much can he receive each month?

110. Alvin has retired with a savings of $5,000,000. He wants to withdraw equal periodic payments at the beginning of each month for the next 20 years. He expects to earn 6% compounded monthly on his investments. How much can he receive each month?

111. Bo has an IRA with a balance of $700,000. He wants to withdraw equal periodic payments at the beginning of each year for the next 5 years. He expects to earn 8% compounded annually on his IRA. How much can he receive each year?

XIV. PRESENT VALUE OF INFLATION-ADJUSTED RETIREMENT NEEDS OF AN ANNUITY DUE (BEG)

112. Mike and Judy are planning for their retirement. They want to receive the equivalent of $100,000 in today's dollars at the beginning of each year for the next 25 years. They assume inflation will average 3% over the long run, and they can earn 8% (compounded annually) on their investments. How much will they need to have when they retire?

113. John and Patty are ready to retire. They want to receive the equivalent of $50,000 in today's dollars at the beginning of each year for the next 30 years. They assume inflation will average 2% over the long run, and they can earn 7% (compounded annually) on their investments. What lump sum do they need to invest today to attain their goal?

114. Kevin and Jennifer are ready to retire. They want to receive the equivalent of $40,000 in today's dollars at the beginning of each year for the next 50 years. They assume inflation will average 3% over the long run, and they can earn 8% (compounded annually) on their investments. What lump sum do they need to invest today to attain their goal?

XV. SERIAL PAYMENTS TO ACHIEVE A FUTURE SUM – COMPOUNDED ANNUALLY

115. Pat wants to start his own business in 5 years. He needs to accumulate $500,000 (in today's dollars) in 5 years to sufficiently finance his business. He assumes inflation will average 2%, and he can earn a 6% (compounded annually) after-tax return on investments. What serial payment should Pat invest at the end of the first year to attain his goal?

116. Harold wants to start saving for his retirement in 15 years. He needs to accumulate $1,500,000 (in today's dollars) in 15 years to have enough to retire. He assumes inflation will average 3%, and he can earn a 7% (compounded annually) after-tax return on investments. What serial payment should Harold invest at the end of the first year to attain his goal?

117. John wants to buy a house in 10 years. He needs to accumulate $150,000 (in today's dollars) in 10 years for his down payment. He assumes inflation will average 4%, and he can earn a 9% (compounded annually) after-tax return on investments. What serial payment should John invest at the end of the first year to attain his goal?

XVI.   MORTGAGES – MONTHLY PAYMENT

118.   Lee recently purchased his house for $400,000. He put down 30% and financed the balance over 30 years at 6%. How much will Lee's monthly mortgage payment be?

119.   Clay recently purchased his house for $200,000. He put down 5% and financed the balance over 15 years at 5%. How much will Clay's monthly mortgage payment be?

120.   Bunny recently purchased her house for $150,000. She put down 20% and financed the balance over 30 years at 6%. How much will Bunny's monthly mortgage payment be?

XVII. MORTGAGES – INTEREST

121. Lee recently purchased his house for $400,000. He put down 30% and financed the balance over 30 years at 5%. If Lee's first payment is due on July 1st of the current year, how much interest can he deduct in the current year? How much interest can Lee deduct next year?

122. Clay recently purchased his house for $200,000. He put down 5% and financed the balance over 15 years at 4.5%. If Clay's first payment is due on January 1st of the current year, how much interest can he deduct in the current year? How much interest can Clay deduct next year?

123. Bunny recently purchased her house for $150,000. She put down 20% and financed the balance over 30 years at 6%. If Bunny's first payment is due on November 1st of the current year, how much interest can she deduct in the current year? How much interest can Bunny deduct next year?

124. Lee recently purchased his house for $400,000. He put down 30% and financed the balance over 30 years at 5.5%. How much interest will he pay over the life of the loan?

125. Clay recently purchased his house for $200,000. He put down 5% and financed the balance over 15 years at 9%. How much interest will he pay over the life of the loan?

126. Bunny recently purchased her house for $150,000. She put down 20% and financed the balance over 30 years at 4.5%. How much interest will she pay over the life of the loan?

XVIII. EDUCATION CALCULATION (THE UNEVEN CASH FLOW METHOD)

127. James and Staci would like to plan for their son's college education. They would like their son, who was born today, to attend a private university for 6 years beginning at age 18. Tuition is currently $30,000 a year and has increased at an annual rate of 5%, while inflation has only increased at 2% per year. They can earn an after-tax rate of return of 7%. How much must they save at the end of each year if they would like to make the last payment at the beginning of their son's first year of college?

128. David would like to plan for his son's college education. He would like his son, who was born exactly 2 years ago, to attend a private university for 4 years beginning at age 18. Tuition is currently $20,000 a year and has increased at an annual rate of 6%, while inflation has only increased at 3.5% per year. David can earn an after-tax rate of return of 8%. How much must David save at the end of each year if he would like to make his last payment at the beginning of his son's last year of college?

129. Fred would like to plan for his son's college education. He would like his son, who was born today, to attend a public university for 5 years beginning at age 18. Tuition is currently $15,000 a year and has increased at an annual rate of 5%, while inflation has only increased at 2% per year. Fred can earn an after-tax rate of return of 9%. How much must Fred save at the beginning of each year if he would like to make his last payment at the beginning of his son's last year of college?

XIX. RETIREMENT NEEDS ANALYSIS

130. Lesli, a single woman who is age 25, has come to you for help in determining her financial needs in retirement. She would like to retire at age 65, and expects to live to age 95. Her current income is $50,000 per year. She estimates that she will need 80% of her current income annually while in retirement. Lesli expects that her Social Security benefit will be $12,000 per year (in today's dollars). Inflation is expected to average 4%. Lesli expects to make 8% annual return on her investments. How much must Lesli save at the end of each year, beginning now, to meet her retirement goals?

131. Rod, who is age 35, has come to you for help in determining his financial needs in retirement. He would like to retire at age 60, and expects to live to age 100. His current income is $60,000 per year. He estimates that he will need 80% of his current income annually while in retirement. Rod expects that his Social Security benefit will be $16,000 per year (in today's dollars). Inflation is expected to average 3%. Rod expects to make an 7% annual return on his investments. How much must Rod save at the end of each year, beginning now, to meet his retirement goals?

132. Tina, a single woman who is age 40, has come to you for help in determining her financial needs in retirement. She would like to retire at age 62, and expects to live to age 90. Her current income is $35,000 per year. She estimates that she will need 70% of her current income annually while in retirement. Tina expects that her Social Security benefit will be $9,000 per year (in today's dollars). Inflation is expected to average 3.5%. Tina expects to make an 8% annual return on her investments. How much must Tina save at the end of each year, beginning now, to meet her retirement goals?

Investment Planning Concepts & Calculations

I. INTERNAL RATE OF RETURN (IRR)

133. Kary owns 100 shares of ABC Company stock. She purchased these shares three years ago for $25 per share. The current market value of the stock is $42 per share. Since buying the stock, the following dividends have been paid:

Dividend year 1 (end)	$1.50 per share
Dividend year 2 (end)	$1.75 per share
Dividend year 3 (end)	$2.25 per share

    What is the IRR that Kary earned on her investment?

134. Connie owns 100 shares of Silky stock. She purchased these shares four years ago for $150 per share. The current market value of the stock is $225 per share. Since buying the stock, the following dividends have been paid:

Dividend year 1 (end)	$2.00 per share
Dividend year 2 (end)	$3.00 per share
Dividend year 3 (end)	$3.50 per share
Dividend year 4 (end)	$3.75 per share

    What is the IRR that Connie earned on her investment?

135. Laura owns 200 shares of Growth stock. She purchased these shares five years ago for $56 per share. The current market value of the stock is $60 per share. Since buying the stock, the following dividends have been paid:

Dividend year 1 (end)	$1.00 per share
Dividend year 2 (end)	$1.25 per share
Dividend year 3 (end)	$1.75 per share
Dividend year 4 (end)	$2.00 per share
Dividend year 5 (end)	$2.00 per share

What is the IRR that Laura earned on her investment?

II.   YIELD TO MATURITY (YTM)

136. Tina is considering purchasing a 30-year corporate bond that is selling for $838.39. What is the YTM for this bond if it has a 5% coupon, paid semiannually?

137. Toyna is considering purchasing a 20-year zero-coupon bond that is selling for $266.78. What is the YTM for this bond (use semiannually compounding)?

138. Toni is considering purchasing a 10-year bond that is selling for $934.96. What is the YTM for this bond if it has a 4% coupon, paid semiannually?

III.   YIELD TO CALL

139.   Top Company issues a 20-year bond paying a 6% coupon paid semiannually and selling at par ($1,000). If Top Co. has the option to call the bonds in 5 years for 105% of face, what is the yield to call?

140.   Middle Company issues a 30-year bond paying a 5% coupon paid semiannually and selling for $950. If Middle Co. has the option to call the bonds in 5 years for 103% of face, what is the yield to call?

141.   Bottom Company issues a 10-year bond paying a 5.5% coupon paid semiannually and selling for $1,100. If Bottom Co. has the option to call the bonds in 5 years for 106% of face, what is the yield to call?

IV.   DURATION

142. Rachel purchased a 5-year bond today for $971.62. Calculate the duration of the bond assuming that it has a YTM of 4.14% and a Coupon Rate of 3.5% (assume annual coupon payments).

143. Lucy purchased a 3-year junk bond today for $990.97. Calculate the duration of the bond assuming that it has a YTM of 6.34% and a coupon rate of 6% (assume annual coupon payments).

144. David purchased a 25-year bond today for $1,002.73. Calculate the duration of the bond assuming that it has a YTM of 4.98% and a coupon rate of 5% (assume annual coupon payments).

145. Rachel purchased a 5-year bond today for $971.62. Calculate the modified duration of the bond that has a YTM of 4.14% and a coupon rate of 3.5%.

146. Lucy purchased a 3-year junk bond today for $990.97. Calculate the percentage change in price of the bond that has a YTM of 6.34% and a coupon rate of 6% assuming the YTM increases 1.5%.

147. David purchased a 25-year bond today for $1,002.73. Calculate the new price of the bond that has a YTM of 4.98% and a coupon rate of 5% assuming the YTM decreases by 1%.

V. PERFORMANCE MEASUREMENTS: HOLDING PERIOD RETURN

148. Tom purchases 100 shares of Davis stock for $50 per share. Five years later, Tom sells the 100 shares for $65 per share. In addition, Tom received a dividend of $1 per share each year (including the year of the sale). What is his holding period return?

149. Donna bought a house for $69,000 in May. She sold it the next December for $75,000 and collected rents of $10,000 over that time. What is Donna's holding period return?

150. Mary bought a wrecked vintage car for $2,000 and fixed it up at a cost of $1,800. She sold it two years later for $7,000. What is her holding period return?

VI.   PERFORMANCE MEASUREMENTS: ARITHMETIC MEAN

151. What is the arithmetic mean for these years of returns?

Year 1	Year 2	Year 3	Year 4	Year 5	Year 6	Year 7	Year 8
5.2%	7.0%	9.3%	25.4%	18.0%	7.0%	12.0%	14.6%

152. What is the arithmetic mean for these years of returns?

Year 1	Year 2	Year 3	Year 4	Year 5
12.6%	(18.0%)	10.0%	32.0%	16.0%

153. What is the arithmetic mean for these years of returns?

Year 1	**Year 2**	**Year 3**	**Year 4**	**Year 5**
12.5%	29.2%	(14.0%)	38.0%	13.3%

VII.   PERFORMANCE MEASUREMENTS: GEOMETRIC MEAN

154. What is the geometric mean for this five-year period?

Year 1	Year 2	Year 3	Year 4	Year 5
10.0%	15.0%	39.0%	(12.0%)	3.0%

155. What is the geometric mean for this five-year period?

Year 1	Year 2	Year 3	Year 4	Year 5
25.0%	17.0%	(4.0%)	0.0%	9.0%

156. What is the geometric mean for this four-year period?

Year 1	Year 2	Year 3	Year 4
(6.0%)	2.0%	(4.0%)	46.0%

VIII. THE SHARPE PERFORMANCE MEASURE

157. The return for the portfolio is 6%, the risk-free rate is 2%, and the standard deviation for the portfolio is 9%. What is the Sharpe ratio?

158. The return for the portfolio is 5%, the risk-free rate is 1.5%, and the standard deviation for the portfolio is 7%. What is the Sharpe ratio?

159. The return for the portfolio is 10%, the risk-free rate is 3%, and the standard deviation for the portfolio is 15%. What is the Sharpe ratio?

IX.   THE TREYNOR PERFORMANCE MEASURE

160. The return for the portfolio is 8%, the risk-free rate is 1%, and the beta of the portfolio is 1.25. What is the Treynor ratio?

161. The return for the portfolio is 6%, the risk-free rate is 1.5%, and the beta of the portfolio is 0.8. What is the Treynor ratio?

162. The return for the portfolio is 10%, the risk-free rate is 2.5%, and the beta of the portfolio is 0.9. What is the Treynor ratio?

X.   THE JENSEN PERFORMANCE MEASURE

163. Growth Fund had a return of 8% for this year, while the market returned 10%. If the fund has a beta of 0.8 and the risk-free rate was 2%, what is the alpha for this fund?

164. Sector Fund had a return of 10%, while the market returned 12%. If the fund has a beta of 1.25 and the risk-free rate was 1.5%, what is the alpha for this fund?

165. Contrarian Fund had a return of 5%, while the market returned 10%. If the fund has a beta of 1.1 and the risk-free rate was 2%, what is the alpha for this fund?

XI. TIME-WEIGHTED RETURN VS. DOLLAR-WEIGHTED RETURN

A. TIME-WEIGHTED RETURN

166. Brent purchases 100 shares of stock for $25 per share. The stock pays dividend as follows:

   Year 1: $0.50 per share

   Year 2: $0.75 per share

   Year 3: $0.50 per share

   Year 4: $0.50 per share

   If it is now the end of the 4th year the stock is trading for $50 per share, what is the annualized time-weighted return for the stock?

167. Elmer purchases 350 shares of Value stock for $100 per share. He makes subsequent purchases at the end of the following years:

   Year 1:   50 shares at $110/share

   Year 2:   75 shares at $115/share

   Year 3:   25 shares at $120/share

   If it is now the end of the 4th year and no dividends have been paid and Value stock is trading for $130 per share, what is the annualized time-weighted return for Value stock for the four-year period?

168. Bob buys 100 shares of XYZ stock for $45.00 per share. One year later, he buys another 100 shares of XYZ stock for $52.00 per share. XYZ stock pays a $1.50 dividend per share at the end of each year. If it is now two years from Bob's initial purchase, and the stock is trading at $60, what is the annualized time-weighted return for XYZ stock for the two-year period?

B.   DOLLAR-WEIGHTED RETURN

169. Ted purchases 200 shares of ABC stock for $20 per share. Ted makes subsequent purchases at the end of the following years:

      Year 1:   50 shares at $30/share

      Year 2:   75 shares at $35/share

      Year 3:   25 shares at $45/share

If it is now the end of the 4th year and no dividends have been paid and TVM stock is trading for $55 per share. What is the dollar-weighted return for Ted's stock (assuming Ted were to sell at $55 per share)?

170. Steve buys one share of XYZ stock for $45. One year later, he buys another share of XYZ stock for $52. XYZ stock pays a $1.50 dividend per share at the end of each year. If it is now two years from Steve's initial purchase, and the stock is trading at $60 per share, what is the dollar-weighted return for Steve's stock for the two-year period?

171. Dan buys one share of BQS stock for $75. One year later, he buys another share of BQS stock for $80.00. BQS stock pays a $2.00 dividend per share at the end of each year. If it is now two years from Dan's initial purchase, and the stock is trading at $95 per share, what is the dollar-weighted return for BQS stock for the two-year period?

XII. MARGIN ACCOUNTS – CALCULATING MARGIN CALL

172. Frank purchased 100 shares of Fox Company stock for $100.75 per share. To purchase this stock Frank used a margin account with a 60% initial margin and a maintenance margin equal to 35%. Below what price must the stock decline for Frank to receive a margin call?

173. Paula purchased 150 shares of Nolan Company stock for $12 per share. To purchase this stock Paula used a margin account with a 50% initial margin and a maintenance margin equal to 40%. Below what price must the stock decline for Paula to receive a margin call?

174. Richard purchased 200 shares of HighPrice Inc. stock for $325 per share. To purchase this stock Richard used a margin account with a 70% initial margin and a maintenance margin equal to 50%. Below what price must the stock decline for Richard to receive a margin call?

XIII.   MARGIN ACCOUNTS – CALCULATING MARGIN DEPOSIT

175.   Fred purchased 100 shares of Nanez stock on a margin account. The price of the stock was $120, the initial margin for the purchase was 50%, and the maintenance margin was 45%. If the stock falls to $80 and Fred receives a margin call, how much will Fred have to deposit per share?

176.   Cody purchased 100 shares of Falling Inc. stock on a margin account. The price of the stock was $50, the initial margin for the purchase was 65%, and the maintenance margin was 35%. If the stock falls to $25 and Cody receives a margin call, how much will Cody have to deposit per share?

177.   Grover purchased 150 shares of Cleveland Inc. stock on a margin account. The price of the stock was $100 per share, the initial margin for the purchase was 70%, and the maintenance margin was 35%. If the stock falls to $40 per share and Grover receives a margin call, how much will Grover have to deposit?

XIV.   TAX-ADJUSTED RETURNS

178. If Sandra earns a total return of 8% (6% from unrealized appreciation and 2% dividends) from her equity portfolio and her marginal tax bracket is 28%, then what is her after-tax return?

179. If Dawn earns a total return of 7.5% (6.5% from unrealized appreciation and 1% dividends) from her equity portfolio and her marginal tax bracket is 35%, then what is her after-tax return?

180. Andrea, who lives in Texas, owns a municipal bond issued by the State of California. The coupon rate on the bond is 3%. Her marginal federal tax rate is 33%. What is the taxable equivalent yield of this bond for Andrea?

XV.   WEIGHTED AVERAGE RETURN

181. Terry has a portfolio with securities A, B, and C valued at $100, $70, and $50 respectively. These securities have expected returns of 14%, 10%, and 6% respectively. If Terry has 100 shares of each security, what is the weighted average return for his portfolio?

182. Roger has a portfolio with securities A, B, and C valued at $80, $95, and $120 respectively. These securities have expected returns of 8%, 10%, and 12% respectively. If Roger has 100 shares of each security, what is the weighted average return for his portfolio?

183. Brian has a portfolio with securities A, B, and C valued at $65, $30, and $45 respectively. These securities have expected returns of 9%, 16%, and 14% respectively. If Brian has 100 shares of each security, what is the weighted average return for his portfolio?

XVI.   STANDARD DEVIATION: HISTORICAL RETURN

184. Assume ABC Company has the following returns:

Year 1	Year 2	Year 3	Year 4	Year 5
9.3%	25.4%	18.0%	7.0%	12.0%

What is the standard deviation for these returns?

185. Assume ABC Company has the following returns:

Year 1	Year 2	Year 3	Year 4	Year 5
12.6%	(18.0%)	10.0%	32.0%	16.0%

What is the standard deviation for these returns?

186. Assume ABC Company has the following returns:

Year 1	Year 2	Year 3	Year 4	Year 5
12.5%	29.2%	(14.0%)	38.0%	13.3%

What is the standard deviation for these returns?

XVII. STANDARD DEVIATION: PROJECTED RETURNS

Assume the following probability distribution for Stocks A, B, and C.

	Slow Market	Normal Market	Growth Market
Probability	20%	40%	40%
Stock A	(20%)	10%	20%
Stock B	(5%)	5%	10%
Stock C	(10%)	15%	10%

187. What is the standard deviation for Stock A?

188. What is the standard deviation for Stock B?

189. What is the standard deviation for Stock C?

XVIII. STANDARD DEVIATION OF A TWO-ASSET PORTFOLIO

Matt has two portfolios, A and B, with the following values and risk levels:

Portfolio	Value	Standard Deviation
A	8,000	18%
B	12,000	24%

190. If the correlation between Portfolio A and B is 0.4, then what is the standard deviation of the two portfolios combined?

191. If the correlation between Portfolio A and B is 0, then what is the standard deviation of the two portfolios combined?

192. If the correlation between Portfolio A and B is –0.8, then what is the standard deviation of the two portfolios combined?

XIX.   CONSTANT GROWTH DIVIDEND DISCOUNT MODEL

193.   Assume Big Corporation is currently paying a dividend of $3.50 and the dividend will grow at a constant rate of 3%. What should the value of the security be if the investor's required rate of return is 7.5%?

194.   Assume Small Company is currently paying a dividend of $4.00 and the dividend will grow at a constant rate of 4%. What should the value of the security be if the investor's required rate of return is 8%?

195.   Fred is considering buying a stock that is currently paying a dividend of $3.00. The dividend has been growing at 5%. If Fred's required rate of return is 10%, what is the most he should pay for the stock?

XX.   PERPETUITIES

196. Assume XYZ Company always pays a $3.00 dividend and the investor's required rate of return is 8%. What would the value of the security be?

197. Assume ABC Corporation always pays a $4.00 dividend and the investor's required rate of return is 5%. What would the value of the security be?

198. Assume Thomson Corporation always pays a $2.50 dividend and the investor's required rate of return is 7.5%. What would the value of the security be?

XXI.   CAPITALIZED EARNINGS

199.   On December 31st of last year, it was calculated that Profitable Corporation had earnings of $150,000 for the entire year. What is the value of Profitable Corporation using a 12% discount ratio?

200.   On December 31st of last year, it was calculated that Samson Corporation had earnings of $2,000,000 for the entire year. What is the value of Samson Corporation using a 10% discount rate?

201.   On December 31st of last year, it was calculated that Kendal Corporation had earnings of $750,000 for the entire year. What is the value of Kendal Corporation using an 8% discount rate?

XXII. REAL ESTATE – CALCULATING MARKET VALUATION

202. Calculate the market value of a rental property assuming the annual NOI is $200,000 and the market capitalization rate is 10%.

203. Calculate the market value of a rental property assuming the estimated gross income is $500,000, the vacancy loss is 10%, the annual expenses are $45,000 and the market capitalization rate is 12%.

204. The owners of GoodBrand Inc. have come to you and want to know the current market value of their rental property. Assuming the following information, what is the estimated market value?

Insurance Expense	$2,142
Real Estate Taxes	$999
Maintenance Expense	$4,865
Depreciation Expense	$16,000
Estimated Gross Income	$150,000
Management Fee	$7,894
Mortgage Interest	$12,000
Less Vacancy Loss	9%
Capitalization Rate	11%

XXIII. ADVANCED SECTION

205. Calculate the Sharpe ratio of a stock with a beta of 1.0, a Treynor ratio of .10, a risk-free rate of 0.04 and a standard deviation of 0.20.

206. Teddy invests $6,000 of his $10,000 available assets into Portfolio A with the remainder in the S&P 500. Portfolio A and the S&P 500 are positively correlated. Changes in the S&P 500 account for or explain 16% of the returns for Portfolio A. If Portfolio A has a standard deviation of 25% and the S&P 500 has a standard deviation of 10%, what is the standard deviation of the combined $10,000 portfolio?

207. Robert invests $15,000 of his $40,000 available assets into the Smooth Return Fund with the remainder in the Dow Jones Industrial Average. The Smooth Return Fund and the S&P 500 are positively correlated. Changes in the Dow Jones explain 36% of the returns for the Smooth Return Fund. If the Smooth Return Fund has a standard deviation of 16% and the Dow Jones has a standard deviation of 12%, what is the standard deviation of the combined portfolio?

208. Assume ABC stock's annual dividend is $1.35 and expected to grow for 3 years at 1.5%. After 3 years, the dividend is expected to grow at a 1.7% rate. Your required rate of return is 7.0%. What is the intrinsic value of ABC stock?

209. Sara received a bond from her brother, Kent, 2 years ago as a birthday present. Kent purchased the bond with a 10-year maturity 3 years before giving it to Sara. The interest rate when Kent purchased this bond was about 8%. Sara has just determined that her bond is worth $896.11. If the interest rates below are indications of the current prevailing market interest rates for this type of bond, how much did Kent originally purchase the bond for in the secondary market? (Assume annual coupon payments.)

Maturities	1 year	2 years	3 years	5 years	10 years	30 years
Interest Rates	4.5%	5%	5.5%	6.5%	7.5%	9.5%

210. Micah and Jenny Stewart have two children, ages 15 and 11. The Stewarts want to start saving for their children's education. Each child will spend 4 years at a private college and will begin at age 18. College currently costs $35,000 per year and is expected to increase at 5% per year. Assuming the Stewarts can earn an after-tax annual compound return of 8% and inflation is 3%, how much must the Stewarts deposit at the end of each year to pay for their children's education requirements until the youngest goes to school? Assume that education expenses are withdrawn at the beginning of each year and that the last deposit will be made at the beginning of the first year of the youngest child.

211. Brian and Wendy Genz have three children, ages 10, 7, and 1. The Genzs want to start saving for their children's education. Each child will spend 5 years at a state college and will begin at age 18. College currently costs $15,000 per year and is expected to increase at 6% per year. Assuming the Genzs can earn an after-tax annual compound return of 9% and inflation is 3%, how much must the Genzs deposit at the end of each year to pay for their children's education requirements? Assume that education expenses are withdrawn at the beginning of each year and that the last deposit will be made at the end of the youngest child's fourth year of college.

212. Michael and Sheila Madary have four children, ages 12, 10, 8, and 5. The Madarys want to start saving for their children's education. Each child will spend 3 years at a community college and will begin at age 18. College currently costs $10,000 per year and is expected to increase at 4% per year. Assuming the Madarys can earn an after-tax annual compound return of 8% and inflation is 3%, how much must the Madarys deposit at the end of each year to pay for their children's education requirements if paid over the next ten years? Assume that education expenses are withdrawn at the beginning of each year and that the last deposit will be made ten years from today.

213. Ross and Marcel plan to retire in 25 years, when their life expectancy is 30 years. They will need $78,000 (in today's dollars) at the beginning of each year during retirement. Social Security will provide $20,400 per year. Both Ross and Marcel expect to earn 8% on their investment both before and during retirement. Inflation is expected to be 3%. How much must they save at the end of each year to reach their goal assuming they have already saved $15,000?

214. Chris and Kristi plan to retire in 17 years, when Chris turns 63. Both Chris and Kristi plan for a retirement of 32 years. They will need $96,000 (in today's dollars) at the beginning of each year during retirement. Social Security will provide $26,400 per year. They expect to earn 10% on their investment both before and during retirement. Inflation is expected to be 4%. How much must they save at the end of each year to reach their goal assuming they have already saved $40,000?

215. Dave and Michelle plan to retire in 32 years. They both plan for a fruitful retirement of 25 years. They will need $57,600 (in today's dollars) at the beginning of each year during retirement. Social Security will provide $32,400 per year. They expect to earn 7% on their investment both before and during retirement. Inflation is expected to be 3%. How much must they save at the end of each quarter to reach their goal assuming they have already saved $5,000?

Student Workbook Solutions

Student Workbook Solutions

1.	139.7000	31.	(13,761.2404)	61.	(976.6548)
2.	103.3000	32.	(328,867.3939)	62.	(72.1725)
3.	27.9000	33.	368,644.5289	63.	979.4310
4.	62.5800	34.	149,799.6106	64.	0.0000
5.	(42.3000)	35.	24,176.4439	65.	5.8229
6.	(100.0000)	36.	2,488.3200	66.	14.0273
7.	294.0000	37.	102,943.2756	67.	34.0324
8.	132.0000	38.	2,902,858.6226	68.	923.3347
9.	232.0000	39.	88,383.4567	69.	56.0489
10.	60.0000	40.	(7,581.5735)	70.	355,104.5512
11.	(4.3333)	41.	(566,942.3563)	71.	58,712.3218
12.	15.0000	42.	(278,802.0881)	72.	4,247,851.1002
13.	100.0000	43.	(629,660.1321)	73.	99,207.6443
14.	1,850.0000	44.	(263,761.9120)	74.	46,294.9577
15.	1,611.7009	45.	(1,402,786.7554)	75.	22,062.2137
16.	1,073,741,824	46.	131,075.8531	76.	(37,150.7365)
17.	(216.0000)	47.	114,468.2678	77.	(129,391.3177)
18.	0.0080	48.	251,128.7606	78.	(23,214.9853)
19.	20.0000	49.	61,342.7668	79.	(27,683.7877)
20.	8.0000	50.	116,471.4625	80.	(64,392.7682)
21.	0.2000	51.	1,851,116.4474	81.	(189,215.8244)
22.	45.0000	52.	97,336.3514	82.	(34,328.3510)
23.	(4.0000)	53.	3,057.8359	83.	(91,262.0788)
24.	2.8901	54.	2,247.0707	84.	(16,780.2611)
25.	0.1111	55.	58,718.8363	85.	7.3941
26.	0.0400	56.	757.5280	86.	7.9775
27.	40.0000	57.	2,234.0388	87.	9.9814
28.	(110,474.6408)	58.	(665.3025)	88.	5.6277
29.	(20,863.2530)	59.	(1,327.3642)	89.	(11.2096)
30.	(67,556.4169)	60.	(1,319.9115)	90.	4.6880

91.	7.0530	127.	(12,160.5325)	163.	(.4%)
92.	3.2548	128.	(6,007.4161)	164.	(4.63%)
93.	5.9634	129.	(3,405.0445)	165.	(5.80%)
94.	22.9108	130.	(9,494.7905)	166.	20.7088
95.	6.7694	131.	(22,163.8903)	167.	6.7790
96.	23.4618	132.	(9,955.5193)	168.	18.5831
97.	162,014.3386	133.	24.9580%	169.	27.2275
98.	65,903.9747	134.	12.3876%	170.	18.4792
99.	39,425.8310	135.	4.1325%	171.	17.0268
100.	114,659.9710	136.	6.1920%	172.	$62.00
101.	61,532.9074	137.	6.7170%	173.	$10.00
102.	148,236.8046	138.	4.8276%	174.	$195.00
103.	(82,803.1710)	139.	6.8553%	175.	$16.00
104.	(2,829,738.0677)	140.	6.7085%	176.	$1.25
105.	(165,177.9738)	141.	4.3410%	177.	$600
106.	(105,497.1305)	142.	4.6676	178.	7.44%
107.	(159,053.9880)	143.	2.8326	179.	6.65%
108.	(123,813.0923)	144.	14.8129	180.	4.48%
109.	10,121.0966	145.	4.4820	181.	10.91%
110.	35,643.3362	146.	(4%)	182.	10.27%
111.	162,332.8872	147.	1,144.2152	183.	12.11%
112.	(1,499,625.2161)	148.	40%	184.	7.42%
113.	(815,389.9161)	149.	23.1884%	185.	18.09%
114.	(783,241.6935)	150.	160%	186.	19.86%
115.	(94,307.5331)	151.	12.3125%	187.	14.73%
116.	(77,829.3541)	152.	10.5200%	188.	5.48%
117.	(12,514.4735)	153.	15.8000%	189.	9.33%
118.	(1,678.7415)	154.	9.7703%	190.	18.49%
119.	(1,502.5079)	155.	8.8827%	191.	16.09%
120.	(719.4606)	156.	7.6683%	192.	9.64%
121.	13,801.8257	157.	0.4444	193.	80.1111
122.	7,947.2720	158.	0.5000	194.	104.0000
123.	7,145.1402	159.	0.4667	195.	63.0000
124.	292,331.3134	160.	0.0560	196.	37.5000
125.	107,918.7189	161.	0.0563	197.	80.0000
126.	98,888.0538	162.	0.0833	198.	33.3333

199.	1,250,000	206.	17.00%	213.	($25,632.7208)
200.	20,000,000	207.	12.08%	214.	($46,131.1148)
201.	9,375,000	208.	$25.67	215.	($2,173.6613)
202.	$2,000,000	209.	($731.60)		
203.	$3,375,000	210.	($44,874.8864)		
204.	$1,096,364	211.	($16,483.3175)		
205.	0.5000	212.	($12,209.7794)		

Basic Functions

I.   SIMPLE ARITHMETIC CALCULATIONS

A.   ADDITION

Answer 1.	Answer 2.	Answer 3.
139.7000	103.3000	27.9000

B.   SUBTRACTION

Answer 4.	Answer 5.	Answer 6.
62.5800	(42.3000)	(100.0000)

C.   MULTIPLICATION

Answer 7.	Answer 8.	Answer 9.
294.0000	132.0000	232.0000

D.   DIVISION

Answer 10.	Answer 11.	Answer 12.
60.0000	(4.3333)	15.0000

II.   CHAIN CALCULATIONS

Answer 13.	Answer 14.	Answer 15.
100.0000	1,850.0000	1,611.7009

III.   POWERS

Answer 16.	Answer 17.	Answer 18.
1,073,741,824	(216.0000)	0.0080

IV.   ROOTS

A.   SQUARE ROOTS

Answer 19.	Answer 20.	Answer 21.
$[400]^{1/2}$ = 20.0000	$[64]^{1/2}$ = 8.0000	$[.04]^{1/2}$ = 0.2000

B.   ROOTS GREATER THAN 2 (NTH ROOT OF X)

Answer 22.	Answer 23.	Answer 24.
$[91,125]^{1/3}$ = 45.0000	$[-64]^{1/3}$ = (4.0000)*	$[40,658.6896]^{1/10}$ = 2.8901

NOTE: The HP12C, HP10BII, and HP17BII calculators do not calculate the root of a negative number correctly. Negative 4 is the correct solution: $-4 \times -4 \times -4 = -64$

V.   RECIPROCAL

Answer 25.	Answer 26.	Answer 27.
1/9 = 0.1111	1/25 = 0.0400	1/.025 = 40.0000

Basic Time Value of Money Calculations

I. PRESENT VALUE (PV) OF A SUM CERTAIN

A. ANNUAL INTEREST

	Answer 28.		Answer 29.		Answer 30.
n	40.0000	n	15.0000	n	10.0000
i	10.0000	i	6.0000	i	4.0000
PMT	0.0000	PMT	0.0000	PMT	0.0000
FV	5,000,000.0000	FV	50,000.0000	FV	100,000.0000
PV	(110,474.6408)	PV	(20,863.2530)	PV	(67,556.4169)

B. MONTHLY INTEREST

	Answer 31.		Answer 32.		Answer 33.
n	60.0000 (5 × 12)	n	84.0000 (7 × 12)	n	240.0000 (20 × 12)
i	1.0000 (12 ÷ 12)	i	0.5000 (6 ÷ 12)	i	0.4167 (5 ÷ 12)
PMT	0.0000	PMT	0.0000	PMT	0.0000
FV	25,000.0000	FV	500,000.0000	FV	1,000,000.0000
PV	(13,761.2404)	PV	(328,867.3939)	PV	368,644.5289

II. FUTURE VALUE (FV) OF A SUM CERTAIN

A. ANNUAL INTEREST

	Answer 34.		Answer 35.		Answer 36.
PV	(5,000.0000)	PV	(13,500.0000)	PV	(1,000.0000)
n	30.0000	n	10.0000	n	5.0000
i	12.0000	i	6.0000	i	20.0000
PMT	0.0000	PMT	0.0000	PMT	0.0000
FV	149,799.6106	FV	24,176.4439	FV	2,488.3200

B.   MONTHLY INTEREST

	Answer 37.		Answer 38.		Answer 39.
PV	(12,000.0000)	PV	(1,000.0000)	PV	(6,000.0000)
n	216.0000 (18 × 12)	n	1,200.0000 (100 × 12)	n	360.0000 (months)
i	1.0000 (12 ÷ 12)	i	0.6667 (8 ÷ 12)	i	0.7500 (9 ÷ 12)
PMT	0.0000	PMT	0.0000	PMT	0.0000
FV	102,943.2756	FV	2,902,858.6226	FV	88,383.4567

III.   PRESENT VALUE (PV) OF AN ORDINARY ANNUITY

	Answer 40.		Answer 41.		Answer 42.
n	5.0000	n	120.0000 (30 × 4)	n	120.0000 (10 × 12)
i	10.0000	i	2.0000 (8 ÷ 4)	i	1.0000 (12 ÷ 12)
PMT_{OA}	2,000.0000	PMT_{OA}	12,500.0000	PMT_{OA}	4,000.0000
FV	0.0000	FV	0.0000	FV	0.0000
PV_{OA}	(7,581.5735)	PV_{OA}	(566,942.3563)	PV_{OA}	(278,802.0881)

IV.   PRESENT VALUE (PV) OF AN ANNUITY DUE

(Remember to select begin mode.)

	Answer 43.		Answer 44.		Answer 45.
n	8.0000	n	100.0000 (25 × 4)	n	240.0000 (20 × 12)
i	7.5000	i	2.0000 (8 ÷ 4)	i	0.5000 (6 ÷ 12)
PMT_{AD}	100,000.0000	PMT_{AD}	6,000.0000	PMT_{AD}	10,000.0000
FV	0.0000	FV	0.0000	FV	0.0000
PV_{AD}	(629,660.1321)	PV_{AD}	(263,761.9120)	PV_{AD}	(1,402,786.7554)

V.   FUTURE VALUE (FV) OF AN ORDINARY ANNUITY

	Answer 46.		Answer 47.		Answer 48.
PV	0.0000	PV	0.0000	PV	0.0000
n	18.0000	n	40.0000 (10 × 4)	n	360.0000 (30 × 12)
i	8.0000	i	1.7500 (7 ÷ 4)	i	0.5000 (6 ÷ 12)
PMT_{OA}	(3,500.0000)	PMT_{OA}	(2,000.0000)	PMT_{OA}	(250.0000)
FV_{OA}	131,075.8531	FV_{OA}	114,468.2678	FV_{OA}	251,128.7606

VI.   FUTURE VALUE (FV) OF AN ANNUITY DUE

(Remember to select begin mode.)

Answer 49.		Answer 50.		Answer 51.	
PV	0.0000	PV	0.0000	PV	0.0000
n	21.0000	n	40.0000 (10 × 4)	n	1,200.0000
i	7.5000	i	1.7500 (7 ÷ 4)		(100 × 12)
PMT_{AD}	(1,200.0000)	PMT_{AD}	(2,000.0000)	i	0.5833 (7 ÷ 12)
FV	**61,342.7668**	FV	**116,471.4625**	PMT_{AD}	(10.0000)
				FV	**1,851,116.4474**

NOTE for #50: $114,468.2678 (from Question 47) increased by 1.75% to equal 116,471.4625

VII.   ORDINARY ANNUITY (PMT)

Answer 52.		Answer 53.		Answer 54.	
PV	(1,000,000.0000)	PV	(50,000.0000)	PV	(250,000.0000)
FV	0.0000	FV	0.0000	FV	0.0000
i	9.0000	i	2.0000 (8 ÷ 4)	i	0.5833 (7 ÷ 12)
n	30.0000	n	20.0000 (5 × 4)	n	180.0000 (15 × 12)
PMT_{OA}	**97,336.3514**	PMT_{OA}	**3,057.8359**	PMT_{OA}	**2,247.0707**

VIII.   ANNUITY DUE (PMT)

(Remember to select begin mode.)

Answer 55.		Answer 56.		Answer 57.	
PV	(250,000.0000)	PV	(15,000.0000)	PV	(250,000.0000)
n	5.0000	n	24.0000 (6 × 4)	n	180.0000 (15 × 12)
i	8.7500	i	1.7500 (7 ÷ 4)	i	0.5833 (7 ÷ 12)
FV	0.0000	FV	0.0000	FV	0.0000
PMT_{AD}	**58,718.8363**	PMT_{AD}	**757.5280**	PMT_{AD}	**2,234.0388**

IX. AMORTIZATION

Answer 58.		Answer 59.		Answer 60.	
PV	100,000.0000	PV	150,000.0000	PV	200,000.0000
n	360.0000 (30 × 12)	n	180.0000 (15 × 12)	n	240.0000 (20 × 12)
i	0.5833 (7 ÷ 12)	i	0.5625 (6.75 ÷ 12)	i	0.4167 (5 ÷12)
FV	0.0000	FV	0.0000	FV	0.0000
PMT_{OA}	**(665.3025)**	PMT_{OA}	**(1,327.3642)**	PMT_{OA}	**(1,319.9115)**

X. NET PRESENT VALUE OF A SERIES OF UNEVEN CASH FLOWS (NPV)

Answer 61.		Answer 62.		Answer 63.	
CF_0	(5,000.0000)	CF_0	(10,000.0000)	CF_0	(6,000.0000)
CF_1	700.0000	CF_1	300.0000	CF_1	2,000.0000
CF_2	600.0000	CF_2	600.0000	CF_2	1,750.0000
CF_3	500.0000	CF_3	1,200.0000	CF_3	1,500.0000
CF_4	400.0000	CF_4	2,400.0000	CF_4	1,000.0000
CF_5	2,800.0000	CF_5	8,300.0000	CF_5	2,500.0000
	(2,500 + 300)		(4,800 + 3,500)		(2,000 + 500)
i	6.0000	i	6.0000	i	8.0000
NPV	**(976.6548)**	NPV	**(72.1725)**	NPV	**979.4310**

XI. INTERNAL RATE OF RETURN – IRR (I)

Answer 64.		Answer 65.		Answer 66.	
CF_0	(5,000.0000)	CF_0	(10,000.0000)	CF_0	(6,000.0000)
CF_1	700.0000	CF_1	300.0000	CF_j	2,000.0000
CF_2	600.0000	CF_2	600.0000	CF_2	1,750.0000
CF_3	500.0000	CF_3	1,200.0000	CF_3	1,500.0000
CF_4	400.0000	CF_4	2,400.0000	CF_4	1,000.0000
CF_5	2,800.0000	CF_5	8,300.0000	CF_5	2,500.0000
	(2,500 + 300)		(4,800 + 3,500)		(2,000 + 500)
IRR	**0.0000**	IRR	**5.8229**	IRR	**14.0273**

XII.   SOLVING FOR TERM OR PERIODS (N)

Answer 67.		Answer 68.		Answer 69.	
PV	(2,500.0000)	PV	(10,000.0000)	PV	(100,000.0000)
i	7.0000	i	0.5000 (6 ÷12)	i	0.5833 (7 ÷12)
PMT	0.0000	PMT	0.0000	PMT	0.0000
FV	25,000.0000	FV	1,000,000.0000	FV	5,000,000.0000
n	**34.0324**	n	**923.3347**	n	672.5866 months
					= **56.0489** years
HP 12C shows	35.0000	HP 12C shows	924.0000	HP 12C shows	673 which is 56 years and 1 month

Time Value of Money & Fundamentals Problems

I. FUTURE VALUE – COMPOUNDED ANNUALLY

Answer 70.		Answer 71.		Answer 72.	
PV	(150,000.0000)	PV	(80,000.0000)	PV	(1,000,000.0000)
n	10.0000	n	5.0000	n	20.0000
i	9.0000	i	–6.0000	i	7.5000
PMT	0.0000	PMT	0.0000	PMT	0.0000
FV	355,104.5512	FV	58,712.3218	FV	4,247,851.1002

II. FUTURE VALUE – COMPOUNDED MONTHLY

Answer 73.		Answer 74.		Answer 75.	
PV	(30,000.0000)	PV	(20,000.0000)	PV	(9,000.0000)
n	180.0000 (15 × 12)	n	504.0000 (42 × 12)	n	120.0000 (10 × 12)
i	0.6667 (8 ÷ 12)	i	0.1667 (2 ÷ 12)	i	0.7500 (9 ÷ 12)
PMT	0.0000	PMT	0.0000	PMT	0.0000
FV	99,207.6443	FV	46,294.9577	FV	22,062.2137

III. PRESENT VALUE – COMPOUNDED ANNUALLY

Answer 76.		Answer 77.		Answer 78.	
FV	50,000.0000	FV	150,000.0000	FV	25,000.0000
n	15.0000	n	5.0000	n	3.0000
i	2.0000	i	3.0000	i	2.5000
PMT	0.0000	PMT	0.0000	PMT	0.0000
PV	(37,150.7365)	PV	(129,391.3177)	PV	(23,214.9853)

IV.   PRESENT VALUE – COMPOUNDED SEMIANNUALLY

Answer 79.		Answer 80.		Answer 81.	
FV	50,000.0000	FV	100,000.0000	FV	1,000,000.0000
n	20.0000 (10 × 2)	n	10.0000 (5 × 2)	n	40.0000 (20 × 2)
i	3.0000 (6 ÷ 2)	i	4.5000 (9 ÷ 2)	i	4.2500 (8.5 ÷ 2)
PMT	0.0000	PMT	0.0000	PMT	0.0000
PV	**(27,683.7877)**	PV	**(64,392.7682)**	PV	**(189,215.8244)**

V.   PRESENT VALUE – COMPOUNDED MONTHLY

Answer 82.		Answer 83.		Answer 84.	
FV	60,000.0000	FV	1,000,000.0000	FV	25,000.0000
n	96.0000 (8 × 12)	n	480.0000 (40 × 2)	n	60.0000 (5 × 12)
i	0.5833 (7 ÷ 12)	i	0.5000 (6 ÷ 12)	i	0.6667 (8 ÷ 12)
PMT	0.0000	PMT	0.0000	PMT	0.0000
PV	**(34,328.3510)**	PV	**(91,262.0788)**	PV	**(16,780.2611)**

VI.   INTEREST CALCULATION – COMPOUNDED ANNUALLY

Answer 85.		Answer 86.		Answer 87.	
n	5.0000	n	30.0000	n	15.0000
PV	(17,500.00)	PV	(1,000.0000)	PV	(2,400.0000)
PMT	0.0000	PMT	0.0000	PMT	0.0000
FV	25,000.0000	FV	10,000.0000	FV	10,000.0000
i	**7.3941**	i	**7.9775**	i	**9.9814**

VII. INTEREST CALCULATION

Answer 88.		Answer 89.		Answer 90.	
n	6.0000	n	3.0000	n	20.0000
PV	18,000.0000	PV	10,000.0000	PV	120,000.0000
PMT	0.0000	PMT	0.0000	PMT	0.0000
FV	(25,000.0000)	FV	(7,000.0000)	FV	(300,000.0000)
i	**5.6277**	i	**(11.2096)**	i	**4.6880**

Answer 91.		Answer 92.		Answer 93.	
n	40.0000 (20 × 2)	n	60.0000 (5 × 12)	n	7.0000
PV	(250.0000)	PV	(1,700.0000)	PV	(800.0000)
PMT	0.0000	PMT	0.0000	PMT	0.0000
FV	1,000.0000	FV	2,000.0000	FV	1,200.0000
i	3.5265	i	0.2712	i	**5.9634**
× 2	**7.0530**	× 12	**3.2548**		

VIII. TERM CALCULATION

Answer 94.		Answer 95.		Answer 96.	
i	8.0000	i	0.7500 (9 ÷ 12)	i	3.0000
PV	(12,000.0000)	PV	(30,000.0000)	PV	(6,000.0000)
PMT	0.0000	PMT	0.0000	PMT	0.0000
FV	69,975.49	FV	55,045.9100	FV	12,004.2500
n	**22.9108**	n	81.2325 = **6.7694** years	n	**23.4618**
HP 12C shows	23.0000	HP 12C shows	82.0000	HP 12C shows	24.0000

IX.   FUTURE VALUE OF AN ORDINARY ANNUITY (END)

	Answer 97.		Answer 98.		Answer 99.
n	300.0000 (25 × 12)	n	10.0000	n	4,380.0000 (12 × 365)
i	0.5833 (7 ÷ 12)	i	6.0000	i	0.0247 (9 ÷ 365)
PV	0.0000	PV	0.0000	PV	0.0000
PMT_{OA}	(200.0000)	PMT_{OA}	(5,000.0000)	PMT_{OA}	(5.0000)
FV	**162,014.3386**	FV	**65,903.9747**	FV	**39,425.8310**

X.   FUTURE VALUE OF AN ANNUITY DUE (BEG)

(Remember to select begin mode.)

	Answer 100.		Answer 101.		Answer 102.
n	18.0000	n	5.0000	n	240.0000 (20 × 12)
i	6.0000	i	7.0000	i	0.6667 (8 ÷ 12)
PV	0.0000	PV	0.0000	PV	0.0000
PMT_{AD}	(3,500.0000)	PMT_{AD}	(10,000.0000)	PMT_{AD}	(250.0000)
FV	**114,659.9710**	FV	**61,532.9074**	FV	**148,236.8046**

XI.   PRESENT VALUE OF AN ORDINARY ANNUITY (END)

	Answer 103.		Answer 104.		Answer 105.
n	4.0000	n	300.0000 (25 × 12)	n	30.0000
i	8.0000	i	0.5833 (7 ÷ 12)	i	6.0000
FV	0.0000	FV	0.0000	FV	0.0000
PMT_{OA}	25,000.0000	PMT_{OA}	20,000.0000	PMT_{OA}	12,000.0000
PV	**(82,803.1710)**	PV	**(2,829,738.0677)**	PV	**(165,177.9738)**

XII.   PRESENT VALUE OF AN ANNUITY DUE (BEG)

(Remember to select begin mode.)

	Answer 106.		Answer 107.		Answer 108.
n	120.0000 (10 × 12)	n	20.0000	n	15.0000
i	0.6667 (8 ÷ 12)	i	8.0000	i	6.0000
PMT_{AD}	1,000.0000	PMT_{AD}	15,000.0000	PMT_{AD}	10,000.0000
FV	50,000.0000	FV	0.0000	FV	50,000.0000
PV_{AD}	(105,497.1305)	PV_{AD}	(159,053.9880)	PV_{AD}	(123,813.0923)

XIII.   ANNUITY DUE (BEG) WITH LUMP SUM DEPOSIT

(Remember to select the begin mode.)

	Answer 109.		Answer 110.		Answer 111.
n	360.0000 (30 × 12)	n	240.0000 (20 × 12)	n	5.0000
i	0.6000 (7.2 ÷ 12)	i	0.5000 (6 ÷ 12)	i	8.0000
PV	(1,500,000.0000)	PV	(5,000,000.0000)	PV	(700,000.0000)
FV	0.0000	FV	0.0000	FV	0.0000
PMT_{AD}	10,121.0966	PMT_{AD}	35,643.3362	PMT_{AD}	162,332.8872

XIV.   PRESENT VALUE OF INFLATION-ADJUSTED RETIREMENT NEEDS OF AN ANNUITY DUE (BEG)

(Remember to select begin mode.)

	Answer 112.		Answer 113.		Answer 114.
n	25.0000	n	30.0000	n	50.0000
PMT	100,000.0000	PMT	50,000.0000	PMT	40,000.0000
i	4.8544 =	i	4.9020 =		4.8544 =
	[(1.08 ÷ 1.03)–1] × 100		[(1.07 ÷ 1.02)–1] × 100	i	[(1.08 ÷ 1.03)–1] × 100
FV	0.0000	FV	0.0000	FV	0.0000
PV_{AD}	(1,499,625.2161)	PV_{AD}	(815,389.9161)	PV_{AD}	(783,241.6935)

XV.   SERIAL PAYMENTS TO ACHIEVE A FUTURE SUM –
COMPOUNDED ANNUALLY

	Answer 115.		Answer 116.		Answer 117.
FV	500,000.0000	FV	1,500,000.0000	FV	150,000.0000
n	5.0000	n	15.0000	n	10.0000
PV	0.0000	PV	0.0000	PV	0.0000
i	3.9216 =	i	3.8835 =	i	4.8077 =
	$[(1.06 \div 1.02) - 1] \times 100$		$[(1.07 \div 1.03) - 1] \times 100$		$[(1.09 \div 1.04) - 1] \times 100$
PMT	(92,458.3658)	PMT	(75,562.4797)	PMT	(12,033.1476)
1.02 x	**(94,307.5331)**	1.03 x	**(77,829.3541)**	1.04 x	**(12,514.4735)**

XVI.   MORTGAGES – MONTHLY PAYMENT

	Answer 118.		Answer 119.		Answer 120.
PV	280,000.0000 =	PV	190,000.0000 =	PV	120,000.0000 =
	(400,000 × .70)		(200,000 × .95)		(150,000 × .80)
n	360.0000 (30 × 12)	n	180.0000 (15 × 12)	n	360.0000 (30 × 12)
i	0.5000 (6 ÷ 12)	i	0.4167 (5 ÷ 12)	i	0.5000 (6 ÷ 12)
FV	0.0000	FV	0.0000	FV	0.0000
PMT	**(1,678.7415)**	PMT	**(1,502.5079)**	PMT	**(719.4606)**

XVII. MORTGAGES – INTEREST

First Method:

Answer 121.		Answer 122.		Answer 123.	
Step 1: Calculate the monthly payment.					
PV	280,000.0000 = (400,000 × .70)	PV	190,000.0000 = (200,000 × .95)	PV	120,000.0000 = (150,000 × .80)
n	360.0000 (30 × 12)	*n*	180.0000 (15 × 12)	*n*	360.0000 (30 × 12)
i	0.4167 (5 ÷ 12)	*i*	0.3750 (4.5 ÷ 12)	*i*	0.5000 (6 ÷ 12)
FV	0.0000	FV	0.0000	FV	0.0000
PMT	(1,503.1005)	PMT	(1,453.4872)	PMT	(719.4606)
Step 2: Calculate the PV of the mortgage at the end of the current year.					
n	354.0000 (360 – 6)	*n*	168.0000 (180 – 12)	*n*	358.0000 (360 – 2)
PV	277,960.2524	PV	180.922.4468	PV	119,760.4814

Step 3: Calculate the amount of deductible interest at the end of the current year.

Payments	Principal		Payments	Principal		Payments	Principal	
1,503.1005	280,000.0000		1,453.4872	190,000.0000		719.4606	120,000.0000	
× 6	(277,960.2524)		× 12	(180,922.4468)		× 2	(119,760.4814)	
9,018.6033	2,039.7476		17,441.8470	9,077.5532		1,438.9212	239.5186	
(2,039.7476)	Less Principal		(9,077.5532)	Less Principal		(239.5186)	Less Principal	
6,978.8557	Interest*		8,364.2938	Interest*		**1,199.4026**	Interest*	

Answer 121.		Answer 122.		Answer 123.	
Step 4: Calculate the PV of the mortgage at the end of next year.					
n	342.0000 (360 – 18)	*n*	156.0000 (180 – 24)	*n*	346.0000 (360 – 14)
PV	273,724.8721	PV	171,427.8724	PV	118,272.0944

Step 5: Calculate the amount of deductible interest at the end of next year.

Payments	Principal		Payments	Principal		Payments	Principal	
1,503.1005	277,960.2524		1,453.4872	180,922.4468		719.4606	119,760.4814	
× 12	(273,724.8721)		× 12	(171,427.8724)		× 12	(118,272.0944)	
18,037.2060	4,235.3803		17,441.8464	9,494.5744		8,633.5272	1,488.3870	
(4,235.3803)	Less Principal		(9,494.5744)	Less Principal		(1,488.3870)	Less Principal	
13,801.8257	Interest*		**7,947.2720**	Interest*		**7,145.1402**	Interest*	

* Slight differences in the interest calculated may occur due to rounding when calculating by hand instead of using a financial calculator.

Second Method:

Answer 121.		Answer 122.		Answer 123.	
Step 1: Calculate the monthly payment.					
PV	280,000.0000 =	PV	190,000.0000 =	PV	120,000.0000 =
	(400,000 × .70)		(200,000 × .95)		(150,000 × .80)
n	360.0000 (30 × 12)	*n*	180.0000 (15 × 12)	*n*	360.0000 (30 × 12)
i	0.4167 (5 ÷ 12)	*i*	0.3750 (4.5 ÷ 12)	*i*	0.5000 (6 ÷ 12)
FV	0.0000	FV	0.0000	FV	0.0000
PMT	(1,503.1005)	PMT	(1,453.4872)	PMT	(719.4606)
Step 2: Calculate the amount of deductible interest at the end of the current year.					
6 (Amort)	6,978.8558	12 (Amort)	8,364.2929	2 (Amort)	1,199.4027
Step 3: Calculate the amount of deductible interest at the end of next year.					
12 (Amort)	**13,801.8262**	12 (Amort)	**7,947.2736**	12 (Amort)	**7,145.1405**

Answer 124.		Answer 125.		Answer 126.	
PV	280,000.0000 =	PV	190,000.0000 =	PV	120,000.0000 =
	(400,000 × .70)		(200,000 × .95)		(150,000 × .80)
n	360.0000 (30 × 12)	*n*	180.0000 (15 × 12)	*n*	360.0000 (30 × 12)
i	0.4583 (5.5 ÷ 12)	*i*	0.5417 (6.5 ÷ 12)	*i*	0.3750 (4.5 ÷ 12)
FV	0.0000	FV	0.0000	FV	0.0000
PMT	(1,589.8092)	PMT	(1,655.1040)	PMT	(608.0224)
x 360 +	(572,331.3134)	x 180 +	(297,918.7189)	x 360 +	(218,888.0538)
280,000 =	**292,331.3134**	190,000 =	**107,918.7189**	120,000 =	**98,888.0538**

XVIII. EDUCATION CALCULATION (THE UNEVEN CASH FLOW METHOD)

	Answer 127.		Answer 128.		Answer 129.
Step 1: Determine the present value of the years of tuition at the age of entrance.					
$CF_{0\ to\ 17}$	0.0000	$CF_{0\ to\ 15}$	0.0000	$CF_{0\ to\ 17}$	0.0000
$CF_{18\ to\ 23}$	30,000.0000	$CF_{16\ to\ 19}$	20,000.0000	$CF_{18\ to\ 22}$	15,000.0000
i	1.9048 =	i	1.8868 =	i	3.8095 =
	$[(1.07 \div 1.05) - 1] \times 100$		$[(1.08 \div 1.06) - 1] \times 100$		$[(1.09 \div 1.05) - 1] \times 100$
NPV	122,323.8531	NPV	57,692.8165	NPV	35,556.9230
Step 2: Determine the annual payments needed to fund college tuition costs.					
PV_0	122,323.8531	PV_0	57,692.8165	PV_0	35,556.9230
n	18.0000	n	19.0000 (21 – 2)	n	23.0000
i	7.0000	i	8.0000	i	9.0000
PMT_{OA}	(12,160.5325)	PMT_{OA}	(6,007.4161)	PMT_{AD}	(3,405.0445)

XIX.   RETIREMENT NEEDS ANALYSIS

Answer 130.	Answer 131.	Answer 132.
Step 1: Determine the present value of annual income needed in retirement.		
Income 50,000.0000	Income 60,000.0000	Income 35,000.0000
WRR × 80 %	WRR × 80 %	WRR × 70 %
Retirement Income 40,000.0000	Retirement Income 48,000.0000	Retirement Income 24,500.0000
Social Security −12,000.0000	Social Security −16,000.0000	Social Security −9,000.0000
Amount Needed 28,000.0000	Amount Needed 32,000.0000	Amount Needed 15,500.0000
Step 2: Inflate the PV of the annual income needed in retirement to a FV at retirement based on the expected inflation rate.		
PV 28,000.0000	PV 32,000.0000	PV 15,500.0000
n 40.0000 (65 − 25)	n 25.0000 (60 − 35)	n 22.0000 (62 − 40)
i 4.0000	i 3.0000	i 3.5000
PMT 0.0000	PMT 0.0000	PMT 0.0000
FV (134,428.5776)	FV (67,000.8937)	FV (33,038.4294)
Step 3: Determine the present value of the annual payments to be received while in retirement.		
PMT_{AD} 134,428.5776	PMT_{AD} 67,000.8937	PMT_{AD} 33,038.4294
n 30.0000 (95 − 65)	n 40.0000 (100 − 60)	n 28.0000 (90 − 62)
i 3.8462 =	i 3.8835 =	i 4.3478 =
$[(1.08 \div 1.04) - 1] \times 100$	$[(1.07 \div 1.03) - 1] \times 100$	$[(1.08 \div 1.035) - 1] \times 100$
FV 0.0000	FV 0.0000	FV 0.0000
PV_{AD} (2,459,687.3784)	PV_{AD} (1,401,844.7317)	PV_{AD} (552,100.7956)
Step 4: Determine the amount of the annual payment required to meet the goal to fund the retirement.		
FV 2,459,687.3784	FV 1,401,844.7317	FV 552,100.7956
n 40.0000 (65 − 25)	n 25.0000 (60 − 35)	n 22.0000 (62 − 40)
i 8.0000	i 7.0000	i 8.0000
PV 0.0000	PV 0.0000	PV 0.0000
PMT_{OA} **(9,494.7905)**	PMT_{OA} **(22,163.8903)**	PMT_{OA} **(9,955.5193)**

Investment Planning Concepts & Calculations

I. INTERNAL RATE OF RETURN (IRR)

	Answer 133.		Answer 134.		Answer 135.
CF_0	(25.0000)	CF_0	(150.0000)	CF_0	(56.0000)
CF_1	1.5000	CF_1	2.0000	CF_1	1.0000
CF_2	1.7500	CF_2	3.0000	CF_2	1.2500
CF_3	44.2500 (2.25 + 42.00)	CF_3	3.5000	CF_3	1.7500
IRR	**24.9580%**	CF_4	228.7500 (225 + 3.75)	CF_4	2.0000
		IRR	**12.3876%**	CF_5	62.0000 (60 + 2)
				IRR	**4.1325%**

II. YIELD TO MATURITY (YTM)

	Answer 136.		Answer 137.		Answer 138.
PV	(838.3900)	PV	(266.7800)	PV	(934.9600)
n	60.0000 (30 × 2)	n	40.0000 (20 × 2)	n	20.0000 (10 × 2)
PMT	25.0000 (50 ÷ 2)	PMT	0.0000	PMT	20.0000 (40 ÷ 2)
FV	1,000.0000	FV	1,000.0000	FV	1,000.0000
i	3.0960%	i	3.3585%	i	2.4138%
2 x	**6.1920%**	2 x	**6.7170%**	2 x	**4.8276%**

III. YIELD TO CALL

	Answer 139.		Answer 140.		Answer 141.
FV	1,050.0000 =	FV	1,030.0000 =	FV	1,060.0000 =
	(1,000 × 1.05)		(1,000 × 1.03)		(1,000 × 1.06)
PV	(1,000.0000)	PV	(950.0000)	PV	(1,100.0000)
PMT	30.0000	PMT	25.0000	PMT	27.5000
n	10.0000 (5 × 2)	n	10.0000 (5 × 2)	n	10.0000 (5 × 2)
i	3.4276%	i	3.3542%	i	2.1705%
x 2	**6.8553%**	x 2	**6.7085%**	x 2	**4.3410%**

IV.   DURATION

<table>
<tr><td colspan="4" align="center">**Answer 142.**</td></tr>
<tr><td>*Year*</td><td>*Cash Flow*</td><td>*PV of CF*</td><td>*PV × Year*</td></tr>
<tr><td>1</td><td>$35.00</td><td>$33.61</td><td>$33.61</td></tr>
<tr><td>2</td><td>$35.00</td><td>$32.27</td><td>$64.54</td></tr>
<tr><td>3</td><td>$35.00</td><td>$30.99</td><td>$92.97</td></tr>
<tr><td>4</td><td>$35.00</td><td>$29.76</td><td>$119.04</td></tr>
<tr><td>5</td><td>$1,035.00</td><td>$844.99</td><td>$4,224.95</td></tr>
<tr><td></td><td></td><td>**$971.62**</td><td>**$4,535.11**</td></tr>
</table>

Duration = $4,535.11 ÷ $971.62 = **4.6676 years**

NOTE: Remember to use the yield to maturity when calculating PV of CF, not the coupon rate.

<table>
<tr><td colspan="4" align="center">**Answer 143.**</td></tr>
<tr><td>*Year*</td><td>*Cash Flow*</td><td>*PV of CF*</td><td>*PV × Year*</td></tr>
<tr><td>1</td><td>$60.00</td><td>$56.42</td><td>$56.42</td></tr>
<tr><td>2</td><td>$60.00</td><td>$53.06</td><td>$106.12</td></tr>
<tr><td>3</td><td>$1,060.00</td><td>$881.49</td><td>$2,644.47</td></tr>
<tr><td></td><td></td><td>**$990.97**</td><td>**$2,807.01**</td></tr>
</table>

Duration = $2,807.01 ÷ $990.97 = **2.8326 years**

Answer 144.

$$\text{Duration} = \frac{1+0.0498}{0.0498} - \frac{(1+0.0498)+25(0.05-0.0498)}{0.05[(1+0.0498)^{25}-1]+0.0498}$$

$$\text{Duration} = 21.0803 - \frac{1.0548}{0.1683}$$

$$\text{Duration} = 21.0803 - 6.2674$$

$$\text{Duration} = \textbf{14.8129 years}$$

Answer 145.

$$\text{Modified Duration} = \frac{\text{Macaulay Duration}}{1+y}$$

$$\text{Modified Duration} = \frac{4.6676}{1+0.0414}$$

Modified Duration = 4.4820

Note: See Problem 142 for calculation of Duration of 4.6676

Answer 146.	Answer 147.
$\dfrac{\Delta P}{P} = -D\left[\dfrac{\Delta y}{1+y}\right]$	$\dfrac{\Delta P}{P} = -D\left[\dfrac{\Delta y}{1+y}\right]$
$\dfrac{\Delta P}{P} = -2.8326 \times$	$\dfrac{\Delta P}{P} = -14.8129 \times$
$\left[\left((1+0.0784)-(1+0.0634)\right) \div (1+0.0634)\right]$	$\left[\left((1+0.0398)-(1+0.0498)\right) \div (1+0.0498)\right]$
$\dfrac{\Delta P}{P} = -2.8326 \times (0.0150 \div 1.0634)$	$\dfrac{\Delta P}{P} = -14.8129 \times (-0.0100 \div 1.0498)$
$\dfrac{\Delta P}{P} = -0.0399 = (4\%)$	$\dfrac{\Delta P}{P} = 0.1411 = \mathbf{14.11\%}$
Note: See problem 143 for calculation of duration of 2.8326	$\$1,002.73 \times 1.1411 = \mathbf{\$1,144.2152}$
	Note: See problem 144 for calculation of duration of 14.8129

V.   PERFORMANCE MEASUREMENTS: HOLDING PERIOD RETURN

Answer 148.	Answer 149.	Answer 150.
$\dfrac{65-50+(5\times 1)}{50} = 40\%$	$\dfrac{75,000-69,000+10,000}{69,000} = 23.1884\%$	$\dfrac{7,000-2,000-1,800}{2,000} = 160\%$

VI.   PERFORMANCE MEASUREMENTS: ARITHMETIC MEAN

Answer 151.	Answer 152.	Answer 153.
$\dfrac{98.5000}{8} = 12.3125\%$	$\dfrac{52.6000}{5} = 10.5200\%$	$\dfrac{79.000}{5} = 15.8000\%$

VII.   PERFORMANCE MEASUREMENTS: GEOMETRIC MEAN

Answer 154.	Answer 155.
$GM = \sqrt[5]{(1.10)\times(1.15)\times(1.39)\times(.88)\times(1.03)} - 1$	$GM = \sqrt[5]{(1.25)\times(1.17)\times(.96)\times(1.00)\times(1.09)} - 1$
$GM = (1.5938)^{1/5} - 1$	$GM = (1.5304)^{1/5} - 1$
$GM = 1.0977 - 1$	$GM = 1.0888 - 1$
$GM = .0977$ or **9.77%**	$GM = .0888$ or **8.88%**
Or	Or
$PV = -\$1$	$PV = -\$1$
$FV = \$1(1.10)(1.15)(1.39)(.88)(1.03) = \$1.5938$	$FV = \$1(1.25)(1.17)(.96)(1.00)(1.09) = \$1.5304$
$n = 5$	$n = 5$
$i = 9.7703\%$	$i = 8.8827\%$

Answer 156.
$GM = \sqrt[4]{(.94)\times(1.02)\times(.96)\times(1.46)} - 1$
$GM = (1.3439)^{1/4} - 1$
$GM = 1.0767 - 1$
$GM = .0767$ or **7.67%**
Or
$PV = -\$1$
$FV = \$1(.94)(1.02)(.96)(1.46) = \$1.3439$
$n = 4$
$i = 7.6683\%$

VIII.   THE SHARPE PERFORMANCE MEASURE

Answer 157.	Answer 158.	Answer 159.
$\dfrac{0.0600 - 0.0200}{0.0900} = 0.4444$	$\dfrac{0.0500 - 0.0150}{0.0700} = 0.5000$	$\dfrac{0.1000 - 0.0300}{0.1500} = 0.4667$

IX.   THE TREYNOR PERFORMANCE MEASURE

Answer 160.	Answer 161.	Answer 162.
$\dfrac{0.0800 - 0.0100}{1.2500} = 0.0560$	$\dfrac{0.0600 - 0.0150}{0.8000} = 0.0563$	$\dfrac{0.1000 - 0.0250}{0.9000} = 0.0833$

X.   THE JENSEN PERFORMANCE MEASURE

Answer 163.	Answer 164.	Answer 165.
$\alpha_p = \overline{r}_p - [\overline{r}_f + (\overline{r}_m - \overline{r}_f)\beta_p]$	$\alpha_p = \overline{r}_p - [\overline{r}_f + (\overline{r}_m - \overline{r}_f)\beta_p]$	$\alpha_p = \overline{r}_p - [\overline{r}_f + (\overline{r}_m - \overline{r}_f)\beta_p]$
$\alpha = .08 - [.02 + (.10 - .02).8]$	$\alpha = .10 - [.015 + (.12 - .015)1.25]$	$\alpha = .05 - [.02 + (.10 - .02)1.1]$
$\alpha = .08 - .084$	$\alpha = .10 - .1463$	$\alpha = .05 - .1080$
$\alpha = -.004 \text{ or } (.4\%)$	$\alpha = -0.0463 \text{ or } (4.63\%)$	$\alpha = -.0580 \text{ or } (5.80\%)$

XI.   TIME-WEIGHTED RETURN VS. DOLLAR-WEIGHTED RETURN

A.   TIME-WEIGHTED RETURN

	Answer 166.		Answer 167.		Answer 168.
CF_0	(25.0000)	PV	(100.0000)	CF_0	(45.0000)
CF_1	0.5000	n	4.0000	CF_1	1.5000
CF_2	0.7500	PMT	0.0000	CF_2	61.5000 = (60 + 1.50)
CF_3	0.5000	FV	130.0000	IRR	**18.5831**
CF_4	50.5000 [50 + 0.50]	IRR	**6.7790**		
IRR	**20.7088**				

B.   DOLLAR-WEIGHTED RETURN

	Answer 169.		Answer 170.		Answer 171.
CF_0	(4,000) [200 × 20]	CF_0	(45)	CF_0	(75)
CF_1	(1,500) [50 × 30]	CF_1	(50.50) [52 – 1.50]	CF_1	(78) [80 – 2]
CF_2	(2,625) [75 × 35]	CF_2	123.00 [120 + 3.0]	CF_2	194 [190 + 4]
CF_3	(1,125) [25 × 45]	IRR	**18.4792**	IRR	**17.0286**
CF_4	19,250 [350 × 55]				
IRR	**27.2275**				

XII.   MARGIN ACCOUNTS – CALCULATING MARGIN CALL

Answer 172.
$\text{Margin call} = \dfrac{\text{debit balance}}{1 - \text{maintenance margin}} = \dfrac{\$100.75 \times 0.40}{1 - 0.35} = \dfrac{\$40.30}{0.65} = \$62$

Answer 173.

$$\text{Margin call} = \frac{\text{debit balance}}{1 - \text{maintenance margin}} = \frac{\$12 \times 0.50}{1 - 0.40} = \frac{\$6}{0.60} = \$10$$

Answer 174.

$$\text{Margin call} = \frac{\text{debit balance}}{1 - \text{maintenance margin}} = \frac{\$325 \times 0.30}{1 - 0.50} = \frac{\$97.50}{0.50} = \$195$$

XIII. MARGIN ACCOUNTS – CALCULATING MARGIN DEPOSIT

Answer 175.	
Required Equity	
Current Value of Stock	$80.00
Equity %	45%
Required Equity	$36.00
Current Equity Position	
Current Value of Stock	$80.00
Loan Amount ($120 × 50%)	(60.00)
Current Equity Position	$20.00

Deposit Amount = Required Equity – Actual Equity = $36 – $20 = **$16 per share**

Answer 176.	
Required Equity	
Current Value of Stock	$25.00
Equity %	35%
Required Equity	$8.75
Current Equity Position	
Current Value of Stock	$25.00
Loan Amount ($50 × 35%)	(17.50)
Current Equity Position	$7.50

Deposit Amount = Required Equity – Actual Equity = $8.75 – $7.50 = **$1.25 per share**

Answer 177.	
Required Equity	
Current Value of Stock	$40
Equity %	35%
Required Equity	$14
Current Equity Position	
Current Value of Stock	$40
Loan Amount ($100 × 30%)	(30)
Current Equity Position	$10

Deposit Amount = Required Equity – Actual Equity = $14 – $10 = $4 per share
$4 per share × 150 shares = **$600**

XIV.   ADJUSTED RETURNS

Answer 178.	Answer 179.	Answer 180.
r = .06 + .02 (1 − .28) = **7.44%**	r = .06 + .01 (1 − .35) = **6.65%**	r = .03 ÷ (1 − .33) = **4.48%**

XV.   WEIGHTED AVERAGE RETURN

Answer 181.

	FMV	E(R)	E(R)$
A	100	.14	14
B	70	.10	7
C	50	.06	3
	220		24

Weighted average return $= \dfrac{24}{220} =$ **10.91%**

Answer 182.

	FMV	E(R)	E(R)$
A	80	.08	6.4
B	95	.10	9.5
C	120	.12	14.4
	295		30.3

Weighted average return $= \dfrac{30.3}{295} =$ **10.27%**

Answer 183.

	FMV	E(R)	E(R)$
A	65	.09	5.85
B	30	.16	4.80
C	45	.14	6.30
	140		16.95

Weighted average return $= \dfrac{16.95}{140} =$ **12.11%**

XVI.   STANDARD DEVIATION: HISTORICAL RETURN

Answer 184.					Answer 185.				
Year	*Return*	*Average*	*Difference*	*Difference Squared*	*Year*	*Return*	*Average*	*Difference*	*Difference Squared*
1	9.3%	14.3%	(5.0%)	0.0025	1	12.6%	10.5%	2.1%	0.0004
2	25.4%	14.3%	11.1%	0.0123	2	(18.0%)	10.5%	(28.5%)	0.0813
3	18.0%	14.3%	3.7%	0.0013	3	10.0%	10.5%	(0.5%)	0.0000
4	7.0%	14.3%	(7.3%)	0.0054	4	32.0%	10.5%	21.5%	0.0462
5	12.0%	14.3%	(2.3%)	0.0005	5	16.0%	10.5%	5.5%	0.0030
Total	71.7%			0.0220	Total	52.6%			0.1309

$$\sigma = \sqrt{\frac{.0220}{4}} = 7.42\%$$

Using the sigma register $(\Sigma +)$

9.3 $[\Sigma +]$

25.4 $[\Sigma +]$

18.0 $\Sigma +$

7 $[\Sigma +]$

12 $[\Sigma +]$

[shift] [Sx,Sy]

7.4241

$$\sigma = \sqrt{\frac{.1309}{4}} = \mathbf{18.09\%}$$

Using the sigma register $(\Sigma +)$

12.6 $[\Sigma +]$

18.0 $[+/-]$ $[\Sigma +]$

10.0 $[\Sigma +]$

32 $[\Sigma +]$

16 $[\Sigma +]$

[shift] [Sx,Sy]

18.0929

Answer 186.

Year	Return	Average	Difference	Difference Squared
1	12.5%	15.8%	(3.3%)	0.0011
2	29.2%	15.8%	13.4%	0.0180
3	(14.0%)	15.8%	(29.8%)	0.0088
4	38.0%	15.8%	22.2%	0.0493
5	13.3%	15.8%	(2.5%)	0.0006
Total	79.0%			0.1578

$$\sigma = \sqrt{\frac{.1578}{4}} = \mathbf{19.86\%}$$

Using the sigma register $(\Sigma +)$

12.5 $[\Sigma +]$

29.2 $[\Sigma +]$

14 $[+/-]$ $[\Sigma +]$

38 $[\Sigma +]$

13.3 $[\Sigma +]$

[shift] [Sx,Sy]

19.8594

XVII. STANDARD DEVIATION: PROJECTED RETURNS

Answer 187.

Expected Return	=	(.20)(−.20) + (.40)(.10) + (.40)(.20)
Expected Return	=	−.04 + .04 + .08
Expected Return	=	.08

Standard Deviation	=	$[(-.20) - (.08)]^2 (.20)$	=	.0158
	=	$(.10 - .08)^2 (.40)$	=	.0001
	=	$(.20 - .08)^2 (.40)$	=	.0058
			σ^2 =	.0217
			σ =	.1473 or **14.73%**

Answer 188.

Expected Return	=	$(.20)(-.05) + (.40)(.05) + (.40)(.10)$
Expected Return	=	$-.01 + .02 + .04$
Expected Return	=	$.05$

Standard Deviation	=	$[(-.05) - (.05)]^2 (.20)$	=	.0020
	=	$[(.05 - .05)]^2 (.40)$	=	.0000
	=	$[(.10 - .05)]^2 (.40)$	=	.0010
		σ^2	=	.0030
		σ	=	.0548 or **5.48%**

Answer 189.

Expected Return	=	$(.20)(-.10) + (.40)(.15) + (.40)(.10)$
Expected Return	=	$-.02 + .06 + .04$
Expected Return	=	$.08$

Standard Deviation	=	$[(-.10) - (.08)]^2 (.20)$	=	.0065
	=	$[(.15 - .08)]^2 (.40)$	=	.0020
	=	$[(.10 - .08)]^2 (.40)$	=	.0002
		σ^2	=	.0087
		σ	=	.0933 or **9.33%**

XVIII. STANDARD DEVIATION OF A TWO-ASSET PORTFOLIO

Answer 190.

$$\sigma = \sqrt{W_A{}^2 \sigma_A{}^2 + W_B{}^2 \sigma_B{}^2 + 2 W_A W_B [\sigma_A \sigma_B r_{AB}]}$$

$$\sigma = \sqrt{(.40)^2 (.18)^2 + (.60)^2 (.24)^2 + 2(.40)(.60)[(.18)(.24)(.40)]}$$

$$\sigma = \sqrt{.0052 + .0207 + .0083}$$

$$\sigma = \sqrt{.0342}$$

$$\sigma = .1849 \text{ or } \mathbf{18.49\%}$$

Answer 191.

$$\sigma = \sqrt{W_A{}^2\sigma_A{}^2 + W_B{}^2\sigma_B{}^2 + 2W_AW_B[\sigma_A\sigma_Br_{AB}]}$$

$$\sigma = \sqrt{(.40)^2(.18)^2 + (.60)^2(.24)^2 + 2(.40)(.60)[(.18)(.24)(.00)]}$$

$$\sigma = \sqrt{.0052 + .0207 + .0000}$$

$$\sigma = \sqrt{.0259}$$

$$\sigma = .1609 \text{ or } \mathbf{16.09\%}$$

Answer 192.

$$\sigma = \sqrt{W_A{}^2\sigma_A{}^2 + W_B{}^2\sigma_B{}^2 + 2W_AW_B[\sigma_A\sigma_Br_{AB}]}$$

$$\sigma = \sqrt{(.40)^2(.18)^2 + (.60)^2(.24)^2 + 2(.40)(.60)[(.18)(.24)(-.80)]}$$

$$\sigma = \sqrt{.0052 + .0207 + (.0166)}$$

$$\sigma = \sqrt{.0093}$$

$$\sigma = .0964 \text{ or } \mathbf{9.64\%}$$

Notice that as the correlation (r_{AB}) decreases, the standard deviation of the portfolio also decreases indicating an offsetting of variability.

XIX.   CONSTANT GROWTH DIVIDEND DISCOUNT MODEL

Answer 193.	Answer 194.	Answer 195.
$V = \dfrac{D_1}{r-g}$	$V = \dfrac{D_1}{r-g}$	$V = \dfrac{D_1}{r-g}$
$V = \dfrac{3.50(1.03)}{.075-.03}$	$V = \dfrac{4.00(1.04)}{.08-.04}$	$V = \dfrac{3.00(1.05)}{.10-.05}$
$V = \mathbf{80.1111}$	$V = \mathbf{104.0000}$	$V = \mathbf{63.0000}$

XX.   PERPETUITIES

Answer 196.	Answer 197.	Answer 198.
$\dfrac{3.000}{0.0800} = 37.5000$	$\dfrac{4.000}{0.050} = 80.0000$	$\dfrac{2.500}{0.075} = 33.3333$

XXI.   CAPITALIZED EARNINGS

Answer 199.	Answer 200.	Answer 201.
$\dfrac{150{,}000.0000}{0.1200} = 1{,}250{,}000$	$\dfrac{2{,}000{,}000.0000}{0.1000} = 20{,}000{,}000$	$\dfrac{750{,}000.0000}{0.0800} = 9{,}375{,}000$

XXII.   REAL ESTATE – CALCULATING MARKET VALUATION

Answer 202.

$$\text{Market Value} = \frac{\text{Annual NOI}}{\text{Market Capitalization Rate}} = \frac{\$200{,}000}{.10} = \mathbf{\$2{,}000{,}000}$$

Answer 203.

Step 1: Calculate NOI

Estimated Gross Income	$500,000
Less Vacancy Loss @ 10%	50,000
Effective Gross Income	$450,000
Less Expenses	45,000
Net Operating Income (NOI)	$405,000

Step 2: Calculate Market Value

$$\text{Market Value} = \frac{\text{Annual NOI}}{\text{Market Capitalization Rate}} = \frac{\$405{,}000}{.12} = \mathbf{\$3{,}375{,}000}$$

Answer 204.

Step 1: Calculate NOI

Estimated Gross Income	$150,000
Less Vacancy Loss @ 9%	13,500
Effective Gross Income	$136,500
Less Expenses	
Real Estate Taxes	999
Insurance Expense	2,142
Maintenance Expense	4,865
Management Fee	7,894
Net Operating Income (NOI)	$120,600

Step 2: Calculate Market Value

$$\text{Market Value} = \frac{\text{Annual NOI}}{\text{Market Capitalization Rate}} = \frac{\$120{,}600}{.11} = \mathbf{\$1{,}096{,}364}$$

Answer 205.

Step 1: Calculate the Return for the Portfolio using the Treynor Performance Measure

$$\text{Treynor ratio} = \frac{\overline{r}_p - \overline{r}_f}{\beta_p}$$

$$\overline{r}_p = (\text{Treynor ratio} \times \beta_p) + \overline{r}_f$$

$$\overline{r}_p = (0.10 \times 1.0) + 0.04$$

$$\overline{r}_p = 0.10 + .04$$

$$\overline{r}_p = 0.14$$

Step 2: Calculate the Sharpe Performance Measure

$$\text{Sharpe ratio} = \frac{\overline{r}_p - \overline{r}_f}{\sigma}$$

$$\text{Sharpe ratio} = \frac{0.14 - 0.04}{0.20}$$

$$\text{Sharpe ratio} = \mathbf{0.50}$$

Answer 206.

$$R_{AB} = \sqrt{0.16} = 0.40 \ (R^2 = 0.16 \therefore R = 0.4)$$

$$\sigma^2 = W^2_A \sigma^2_A + W^2_B \sigma^2_B + 2W_A W_B [\sigma_A \sigma_B R_{AB}]$$

$$\sigma^2 = (0.6)^2 (0.25)^2 + (0.4)^2 (0.10)^2 + 2(0.6)(0.4)[0.25 \times 0.10 \times 0.4]$$

$$\sigma^2 = 0.0225 + 0.0016 + 0.0048$$

$$\sigma^2 = 0.0289$$

$$\sigma = \mathbf{17\%}$$

Answer 207.

$$R_{AB} = \sqrt{0.36} = 0.60 \ (R^2 = 0.36 \therefore R = 0.6)$$

$$\sigma^2 = W^2_A \sigma^2_A + W^2_B \sigma^2_B + 2W_A W_B [\sigma_A \sigma_B R_{AB}]$$

$$\sigma^2 = (0.375)^2 (0.16)^2 + (0.625)^2 (0.12)^2 + 2(0.375)(0.625)[0.16 \times 0.12 \times 0.60]$$

$$\sigma^2 = 0.0036 + 0.0056 + 0.0054$$

$$\sigma^2 = 0.0146$$

$$\sigma = \mathbf{12.08\%}$$

Answer 208.

Multistage Growth Dividend Discount Model

Step 1. Compute the value of each future dividend until the growth rate stabilizes (Years 1–3).

$D_1 = \$1.35 \times 1.015 = \mathbf{\$1.37}$
$D_2 = \$1.37 \times 1.015 = \mathbf{\$1.39}$
$D_3 = \$1.39 \times 1.015 = \mathbf{\$1.41}$

Step 2. Use the constant growth dividend discount model to compute the remaining intrinsic value of the stock at the beginning of the year when the dividend growth rate stabilizes (Year 4).

$D_4 = \$1.41 \times 1.017 = \$1.43$
$V = \$1.43 \div (0.07 - 0.017) = \mathbf{\$26.98}$

Step 3. Use the uneven cash flow method to solve for the net present (intrinsic) value of the stock.

$CF_0 = \$0$
$CF_1 = \$1.37$
$CF_2 = \$1.39$
$CF_3 = \$1.41 + \$26.98 = \$28.39$
$I/YR = 7\%$
Solve for NPV = **$25.67**

Answer 209.

Bond Valuation

Sara			**Kent**		
PV	=	($896.11)	FV	=	$1,000
N	=	5	N	=	10
I	=	6.5	I	=	8.0
FV	=	$1,000	PMT	=	$40 (calculated)
PMT	=	$40 (calculated)	PV	=	**($731.60)**

	Answer 210.		Answer 211.		Answer 212.
Step 1: Determine the present value of the tuition payments as of today.*					
$CF_{15\ to\ 17}$	0.0000 (3 CFs)	$CF_{10\ to\ 17}$	0.0000 (8 CFs)	$CF_{12\ to\ 17}$	0.0000 (6 CFs)
$CF_{18\ to\ 25}$	35,000.0000 (8 CFs)	$CF_{18\ to\ 20}$	15,000.0000 (3 CFs)	$CF_{18\ to\ 19}$	10,000.0000 (2 CFs)
i	2.8571 =	$CF_{21\ to\ 22}$	30,000.0000 (2 CFs)	CF_{20}	20,000.0000 (1 CF)
	$[(1.08 \div 1.05) - 1] \times 100$	$CF_{23\ to\ 25}$	15,000.0000 (3 CFs)	CF_{21}	10,000.0000 (1 CF)
NPV	233,635.2652	CF_{26}	0.0000 (1 CF)	CF_{22}	20,000.0000 (1 CF)
		$CF_{27\ to\ 31}$	15,000.0000 (5 CFs)	$CF_{23\ to\ 27}$	10,000.0000 (5 CFs)
		i	2.8302 =	i	3.8462 =
			$[(1.09 \div 1.06) - 1] \times 100$		$[(1.08 \div 1.04) - 1] \times 100$
		NPV	153,167.0041	NPV	81,928.6136
Step 2: Determine the annual payments needed to fund college tuition costs.					
PV_0	233,635.2652	PV_0	153,167.0041	PV_0	81,928.6136
n	7.0000	n	21.0000	n	10.0000
i	8.0000	i	9.0000	i	8.0000
PMT_{OA}	**(44,874.8864)**	PMT_{OA}	**(16,483.3175)**	PMT_{OA}	**(12,209.7794)**

*The cash flow subscript represents the age of the oldest child. For example, $CF_{15\ to\ 17}$ represents the cash flows for age 15 through 17 of the oldest child.

The following timelines are provided for your assistance. The cash flows reflect the tuition payments in today's dollars. The arrows ($\downarrow$) reflect the beginning and ending of the funding period. For problem 210, the first deposit is made at period 16 and the last payment made at period 22 for a total of seven payments.

Problem 210

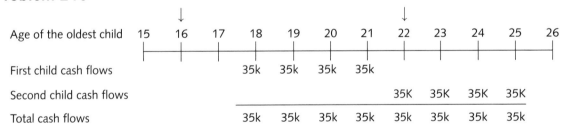

Problem 211

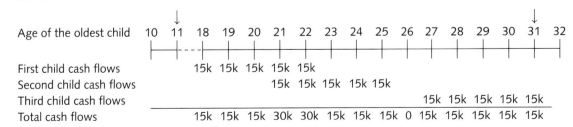

Problem 212

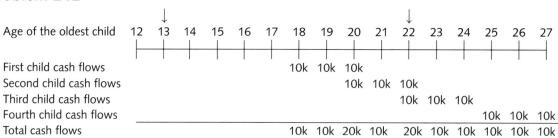

	First child cash flows						10k	10k	10k							
	Second child cash flows							10k	10k	10k						
	Third child cash flows								10k	10k	10k					
	Fourth child cash flows													10k	10k	10k
	Total cash flows						10k	10k	20k	10k	20k	10k	10k	10k	10k	10k

Answer 213.

Step 1: Determine PV of annual income needed in retirement.

Income	78,000
Social Security	−20,400
	57,600

Step 2: Inflate PV of the annual income needed in retirement to a FV at retirement based on the expected inflation rate.

PV	57,600.0000
n	25.0000
i	3.0000
PMT	0.0000
FV	(120,601.6087)

Step 3: Determine the present value of the annual payments to be received while in retirement.

PMT_{AD}	(120,601.6087)
n	30.0000
i	4.8544 $[(1.08 \div 1.03) -1] \times 100$
FV	0.0000
PV_{AD}	1,976,631.2790

Step 4: Determine the amount of the annual payment required to meet the goal to fund the retirement.

FV	1,976,631.2790
n	25.0000
i	8.0000
PV	(15,000.0000)
PMT_{OA}	**(25,632.7208)**

Answer 214.

Step 1: Determine PV of annual income needed in retirement.

Income	96,000
Social Security	−26,400
	69,600

Step 2: Inflate PV of the annual income needed in retirement to a FV at retirement based on the expected inflation rate.

PV	69,600.0000
n	17.0000
i	4.0000
PMT	0.0000
FV	(135,573.8745)

Step 3: Determine the present value of the annual payments to be received while in retirement.

PMT_{AD}	(135,573.8745)
n	32.0000
i	5.7692 $[(1.10 \div 1.04) -1] \times 100$
FV	0.0000
PV_{AD}	2,072,551.1549

Step 4: Determine the amount of the annual payment required to meet the goal to fund the retirement.

FV	2,072,551.1549
n	17.0000
i	10.0000
PV	(40,000.0000)
PMT_{OA}	**(46,131.1148)**

Answer 215.		
Step 1: Determine PV of annual income needed in retirement.		
Income	57,600	
Social Security	−32,400	
	25,200	
Step 2: Inflate PV of the annual income needed in retirement to a FV at retirement based on the expected inflation rate.		
PV	25,200.0000	
n	32.0000	
i	3.0000	
PMT	0.0000	
FV	(64,892.0854)	
Step 3: Determine the present value of the annual payments to be received while in retirement.		
PMT_{AD}	(64,892.0854)	
n	25.0000	
i	3.8835	$[(1.07 \div 1.03) - 1] \times 100$
FV	0.0000	
PV_{AD}	1,066,207.3946	
Step 4: Determine the amount of the annual payment required to meet the goal to fund the retirement.		
FV	1,066,207.3946	
n	128.0000 (32 × 4)	
i	1.7500 (7 ÷ 4)	
PV	(5,000.0000)	
PMT_{OA}	**(2,173.6613)**	

Exam-Focused Multiple-Choice Questions

Problems

1. Determine the yield to maturity of a 15-year bond selling for $1,196.00 that has a coupon rate of 8% (paid semiannually).
   A. 3%.
   B. 4%.
   C. 5%.
   D. 6%.
   E. 7%.

2. Judy is interested in purchasing a bond with an 8% coupon paid semiannually. The bond has a 5-year maturity and is yielding 10.5%. What is the appropriate price for this bond?
   A. $920.66.
   B. $904.64.
   C. $1,000.00.
   D. $1,118.42.
   E. $1,101.39.

3. Henry makes annual year-end deposits of $15,000 into a bank account where he earns an annual rate of interest of 8%. His interest is compounded quarterly. How much money will Henry have at the end of year 6?
   A. $110,039.
   B. $110,716.
   C. $111,435.
   D. $456,328.

4. Rita took out a $180,000 mortgage loan exactly 5 years ago. The interest rate was 7% and the term was 30 years. Rita paid the loan as agreed. What is the amount by which she has reduced the loan?
   A. $10,563.14.
   B. $169,580.37.
   C. $10,419.63.
   D. $169436.86.

5. Ron wants to give his daughter $10,000 per year for 5 years. He plans on starting his gifts in exactly 6 years. How much should he deposit today to meet this obligation? Assume Ron earns an annual rate of interest of 7%.
   A. $27,321.35.
   B. $29,233.84.
   C. $31,280.21.
   D. $43,872.11.

6. If a bond is selling at par and callable at par what is the IRR equal to?
   A. Macaulay Duration.
   B. Market Price.
   C. The adjusted yield to call.
   D. The coupon rate.

7. On July 4th Bill won the lotto! He has a choice between a lump sum payment of $2,000,000 or $200,000 paid as an annuity for 25 years starting today. What is the breakeven discount rate?
   A. 8.54.
   B. 8.78.
   C. 9.27.
   D. 9.98.

8. A bond is selling for $897, interest payments are semiannual and the coupon rate is 8%. What is the yield to maturity if the term is 5 years?
   A. 10.71.
   B. 6.48.
   C. 8.33.
   D. 8.47.

9. Today Jack purchased an investment grade coin for $40,000. He expects the coin to increase at a rate of 12% compounded annually for the next 7 years. How much will the coin be worth at the end of the seventh year if his expectations are correct?
   A. $78,952.91.
   B. $79,939.82.
   C. $86,848.20.
   D. $88,427.26.

10. Joey wants to accumulate $74,000 in 6.5 years to purchase a motorcycle. He expects an annual rate of 8.5% compounded quarterly. How much does Joey need to invest today to meet his goal?
    A. $23,529.87.
    B. $42,834.92.
    C. $56,300.83.
    D. $45,357.94.
    E. $43,508.91.

11. Randy purchased a house for $275,000 with a down payment of 20%. If he finances the balance at 6.125% over 15 years, how much will his monthly payment be?
    A. $2,241.57.
    B. $2,327.34.
    C. $2,339.22.
    D. $1,871.37.

12. Guy, age 65 comes to you to ask which of the following payout methods he should accept from his retirement plan. Assume Guy lives to age 90 and that he can earn 8% after tax.
    Option 1:   Lump-sum payment of $440,000.
    Option 2:   An annuity paid for a term certain of 15 years of $48,000 per year.
    Option 3:   An annuity, second to die payment, paid over the joint life expectancy of Guy and his son. Assume a 27 year joint life expectancy in the amount of $36,750.

    A. Option 1 because it has the highest future value.
    B. Option 1 because it has the highest present value.
    C. Option 2 because it has the highest present value.
    D. Option 3 because it has the highest present value.
    E. Option 3 because it has the highest future value.

Exam-Focused Multiple-Choice Solutions

Solutions

	Answer 1.			Answer 2.			Answer 3.	
Answer	D		Answer	B		Answer	B	
n	30.0000 (15 × 2)		FV	1,000.0000		n	4.0000	
PV	1,196.0000		i	5.2500 (10.5 ÷ 2)		i	2.0000 (8 ÷ 4)	
PMT	(40.0000)		PMT	40.0000		PMT	0.0000	
FV	(1,000.0000)		n	10.0000 (5 × 2)		PV	1.0000	
i	3.0000		PV	**(904.6395)**		FV	1.0824	
3.00 . 2 =	6%					1.0824 − 1	0.0824	
						i	8.2432	
						n	6.0000	
						PMT	15,000.0000	
						PV	0.0000	
						FV	**(110,715.9519)**	

* 1,000 × 4% = 40

	Answer 4.			Answer 5.	
Answer	C		Answer	B	
n	360.0000		n	5.0000	
i	0.5833 (7 ÷ 12)		i	7.0000	
FV	0.0000		PMT_{AD}	10,000.0000	
PV	180,000.0000		FV	0.0000	
PMT	(1,195.5445)		PV	**(43,872.11)**	
PMT	(1,195.54)*		FV	(43,872.11)	
i	0.5833 (7 ÷ 12)		n	6.0000	
n	60.0000 (5 × 12)		i	7.0000	
PV	180,000.00000		PMT	0.0000	
FV	**(169,580.37)**		PV	**29,233.84**	
180,000 − 169,580.37	**10,419.63**				

* Note: To make this calculation work, you will need to put this in whole cents because that is how mortgages are paid.

Answer 6.		Answer 7.		Answer 8.	
The answer is D; the IRR is equal to the coupon rate.		Answer	D	Answer	A
		PV	2,000,000.0000	PV	897.0000
		n	25.0000	n	10.0000
		PMT_{AD}	200,000.0000	PMT	40.0000
		FV	0.0000	FV	1,000.0000
		i	**9.98**	i	5.3571
				5.3571×2	**10.71**

Answer 9.		Answer 10.		Answer 11.	
Answer	D	Answer	B	Answer	D
PV	40,000	FV	74,000.0000	PV	220,0000 (275,000 × 0.80)
n	7.0000	n	26.0000 (6.5 × 4)	n	180.0000
i	12.0000	i	2.1250 (8.5 ÷ 4)	i	0.5104 (6.125 ÷ 12)
PMT	0.0000	PMT	0.0000	FV	0.0000
FV	**88,427.26**	PV	**42,834.92**	PMT	**1,871.37**

Answer 12.
Answer C is the best choice. Option 2 has the highest PV; however, Option 1 may outweigh Option 2 because the PV of Option 1 is guaranteed. Option 2 will only be better if Guy consistently earns 8% or better for the entire 15 years. With the small difference in present value it may be safer to go with the guaranteed value.

Option 1:

PV	440,000

Option 2:

n	15.0000
i	8.0000
PMT_{AD}	48,000.0000
FV	0.0000
PV_{AD}	**(443,723.37)**

Option 3:

n	27.000
i	8.0000
PMT_{AD}	36,750.0000
FV	0.0000
PV_{AD}	**(434,016.69)**

Notes

Notes

Notes

Notes

Notes